He lived to serve God, family, and community—
but the forces of hate conspired to make him a martyr.

NO RANDOM ACT

Behind the Murder of Ricky Byrdsong

Dave and Neta Jackson

WATERBROOK
PRESS

No Random Act
Published by WaterBrook Press
2375 Telstar Drive, Suite 160
Colorado Springs, Colorado 80920
A division of Random House, Inc.

ISBN 1-57856-508-1

Published in association with the literary agency of Alive Communications, Inc.,
7680 Goddard Street, Suite 200, Colorado Springs, CO 80920.

Printed in the United States of America
2002—First Edition

10 9 8 7 6 5 4 3 2 1

Contents

Prologue: July 2, 1999 1

1   Born in Revolution 8

2   God's Fifty Acres 12

3   Too Smart for the Local Yokels 18

4   Life Is a Gift 22

5   Hitler's Promised Revenge 28

6   "Yes, You!" 33

7   The Climber 37

8   Defined by Love 42

9   Idle Hands Are… 49

10 A Long Way from Home 53

11 Searching for an Enemy 58

12 The Decision 65

13 Christianity, the Ultimate Trojan Horse 75

14 Salt and Pepper 80

15 Nature's Eternal Religion: Hate 89

16 Number One Mentor 94

17 Publish or Perish 101

18 Westward, Ho! 106

19 Shoot 'Em Up 113

20   Baby Byrd 118

21   Looking for the "Great Promoter" 123

22   Head Coach and Motivator 128

23   Escape 137

24   A Walk on the Wild Side 146

25   The Chickens Come Home 155

26   Turning Point 160

27   A Hale of a Revival 169

28   Time-Out! 177

29   Finding a Patsy 187

30   Walking on Water 195

31   The Setup 202

32   Going Deeper 209

33   RAHOWA! 217

34   No! No, No, No! 224

35   Shock Waves 230

36   Stronger than Hate 243

37   Is God Really Good? 253

Afterword: Not an End, but a Beginning... 257

A Personal Note from the Authors 261

Acknowledgments 265

Notes 269

You're gonna have to serve somebody,
Well, it may be the devil or it may be the Lord
But you're gonna have to serve somebody.

—BOB DYLAN

The stories in this book are true but dramatized. Much of Ricky Byrdsong's story comes from "oral history"—interviews with family, friends, and colleagues—for which we have created scenes and dialogue to portray the events. On the other hand, while the story about the World Church of the Creator has also been dramatized, it is based on their own documents and writings, tape-recorded interviews, police reports, and newspaper accounts. Much of the actual wording has been documented in the endnotes.

Prologue

July 2, 1999

On the day Ricky Byrdsong was shot, he was in the zone. He'd had hints of being in the zone before—when he landed his first head coaching position at Detroit Mercy, when his Northwestern Wildcats broke five hundred for the first time in twenty years, even the night he took his so-called walk on the wild side into the Minnesota stands.

But compared to now, those were faint previews.

The handsome, six-foot-six black man leaned into the future, beckoned by the cusp of opportunity. His new career as vice president of community affairs at Aon Corporation, the world's second largest insurance holding company, fit like a Campagna suit. He was making a difference for hundreds of kids through his Not-Just-Basketball Camps. His own family thrived. The capital campaign he headed up for his church had shifted into high gear. Best of all, he had just received word that a publisher wanted his book, *Coaching Your Kids in the Game of Life.*

"Hey, Pastor," he grinned at Lyle Foster of The Worship Center in Evanston, Illinois, after hearing the news. "I'm going to take you all over the country with me when I do my book tour!" But it wasn't even that dream that put Ricky Byrdsong in the zone.

Time and again he'd told God, "I want to make a difference. Even if it costs me my life, I'm willing!" Nothing else mattered, and *that's* what put him in the zone!

"We all need to get there," he told his church one Sunday when he had been invited to preach. "Don't you know that I had to come to that point in my own life? Don't you know that they didn't want me talking about God to the basketball team? Don't you know that I had to say, 'But it doesn't matter now'?

"Don't you know that they didn't want me having Bible study in my own office with my own staff? But I said, 'It doesn't matter now.' Don't you know that they'd rather that I not quote any Scriptures to the newspaper? I was a coach of a major institution, and my words were going everywhere. They wanted me to keep that kind of talk in the church. But I had to get to the point where I said, 'It doesn't *matter* now.'

"We've all got to get to that point."

That's an extreme zone! Go there and someone might try to take you out.

Ricky knew this. It made him keyed up about what lay ahead as June turned to July in 1999, the last year of the century. A new millennium was around the corner. Something big was brewing…he could feel it in his bones. He didn't know exactly what—would his book really get published? Would the capital campaign finally take his church out of a warehouse and into a sanctuary? The previous Saturday at a leaders' meeting, Pastor Lyle had said, "You can't expect the people to move up to a new level if you don't lead the way." Most took it as a general encouragement, but Ricky got serious.

On Sunday, Ricky had surprised even himself at the level of commitment he called for from the members…but deep inside he felt God was on the verge of something big. He had to think big for The Worship Center. He had to think big to finish his book. He had to think big if he wanted God to use him to make a difference.

On Tuesday he had felt compelled to go to the church prayer meeting and just lay himself out before God, prostrate on the floor. *Use me. I want to make a difference.*

By the time Friday, July 2, arrived, Ricky's spirit crackled with anticipation. He wasn't sure what all God was doing in his life, but he wanted to be ready.

•　•　•

On July 2, 1999, the Reverend Matt Hale, *Pontifex Maximus* of the World Church of the Creator, pushed his chair back from his desk in the red room, the world headquarters office, an upstairs bedroom in the small, two-story frame house his grandfather built in East Peoria, Illinois, in 1909. At age twenty-seven, Hale still shared the house with his father, a retired police officer who had divorced Hale's mother twenty years before.

"They think they can play with us," he muttered as he frowned deeply and tapped the edge of the certified envelope from the Illinois State Bar Association on his knee. The message inside reported the board's decision to deny his appeal for a law license based on character and fitness deficiencies.

In spite of the organization's humble facilities, Hale boasted a membership approaching ten thousand, with chapters—or contact points, as he called them—in twenty-one states and twenty-two countries. "By the time all of this is over," he swore, "our enemies will regret their decisions dearly." [1]

It was time for Racial Holy War—RAHOWA! After his first denial in February, Hale gained national attention by appearing on sixteen prominent talk shows and news forums, discussing his racial views and his anger over the board's decision. Should he go back to *Today, Montel Williams, The Leeza Gibbons Show, Politically Incorrect, CBS Evening News,* or was there a more powerful response?

There was always Brother Benjamin "August" Smith, his frustrated twenty-one-year-old disciple. Smith was a plain-looking young man whose receding hairline and dark eyebrows accentuated his prominent nose and oval face. He had taken the name August in honor of "the great white ruler," Augustus Caesar. When asked publicly, Smith always responded as taught: "We believe we can legally come to power through nonviolence. But Hale says if they try to restrict our legal means, then we have no recourse but to resort to terrorism and violence." [2]

●　　●　　●

That day, while driving in the Chicago area, Benjamin Smith heard Matt Hale's news release announcing that the Illinois state bar's hearing board had unanimously denied him a law license. Smith understood: Their legal means had been restricted again by what white supremacists considered the Jewish Occupational Government, or JOG.

What other recourse was there?

Before proceeding with his mission, Benjamin Smith had one more detail to clear up. He stopped by the Wilmette post office. This affluent suburb north of Chicago had been home for his family for most of his life. His mother, a high-end real estate agent, had been a member of the village board of trustees. His father had been a physician at Northwestern Memorial Hospital for nineteen years, though now he, too, sold real estate.

Inside the post office, Smith purchased a certified-letter card, filled out the form, and wrote on the back in a rough scrawl:

> Although I have not been a member of the World Church of the
> Creator since April 1999, due to my past public support of that
> legal religious organization run by Matt Hale, I find it necessary to
> formerly [sic] break with the World Church of the Creator because
> I am unable and unwilling to follow a legal Revolution of Values—
> Benjamin N. Smith[3]

He handed the card to the postal clerk. It would provide Matt Hale and the World Church of the Creator a degree of deniability and protection.

Now he was ready. Smith headed south toward the West Rogers Park neighborhood of Chicago, home to thirty-three thousand Jews and twenty synagogues, most of them Orthodox. To August Smith the modest bungalows built in the first half of the century, with their neat lawns and detached garages, must have looked like a shooting gallery.

He turned his light blue Ford Taurus onto quiet, tree-lined West Estes Avenue. On the seat beside him were two loaded pistols and boxes of ammunition he had purchased three days before.

August glanced at his car clock—8:20. Jews would be walking to and from synagogue at this time of the evening. He snorted his disgust and recalled what Matt Hale had taught him about God: *"We Creators reject all this nonsense about angels and devils and gods and all the rest of this silly spook craft.... We do not believe in a world of spirits and spooks, and we most certainly do not believe in the Bible which was written by a gang of lying, Jewish scriptwriters.*"[4]

There. Two of them, probably father and son, walking down the street wearing their yarmulkes.

Smith stopped his car and stepped out, one gun held low to his side as he approached the pair who had turned up the walk to an attractive brick home. They were talking with animated gestures as though this were *their* holiday instead of a white Independence Day. At fifteen feet, Smith raised his .380 and squeezed off several rounds. The blasts were deafening, and the gun kicked far harder than Smith had expected. He saw the father running up the driveway toward the back of the house as the teenage boy bolted through the front door.

Stunned, Smith realized that he hadn't hit either of them. Frustrated, he returned to his car and drove slowly eastward.

On the corner was another one, wearing a long black coat and oversized hat—on such a hot evening—with little curls hanging down his cheeks. This time Smith stuck his .22-caliber Ruger out the window and pulled the trigger again and again and again. The man on the sidewalk ducked and ran, then suddenly stumbled and fell to the ground. The Hasidic Jew rocked back and forth, clutching his left arm and shoulder with his right hand as blood oozed through his fingers.

"Wow! Wow! I got him! Wow!"

Before Smith left the neighborhood fifteen minutes later, he had wounded six Jews and terrorized several others.

• • •

That evening Ricky Byrdsong drove north on Lake Shore Drive toward his beautiful home in Skokie, his cell phone to his ear. "Pastor?"

"Coach! What *are* you doin'? This is the fifth time you've called me today."

"I know. I know, but—"

"You call anyone else today?"

"Oh yeah, all afternoon! But I was just wondering… Sherialyn wants to take the family to Great America tonight, but with the holiday and all, it's going to be a mess. You ever been in a situation where your wife wanted you to do something, and you really wanted to do something for her, but you didn't think it was—"

"Hey, Coach? No comment!" Lyle Foster laughed. "Absolutely no comment on that one."

"Okay, okay. I was just wonderin'." Then he paused for a moment. "Hey, Pastor, about the capital campaign. We're really gonna do it, aren't we? I mean, we're gonna raise all that money and build out the sanctuary like we planned, right?"

"Of course."

"No, I'm serious! We're gonna do it, aren't we?"

"Don't worry about it, Coach. With God's help, we *will* do it."

"Good! See ya, Pastor."

Ricky punched another button and postponed the Great America idea until another day. Thirty minutes later he was driving up his quiet, tree-lined street, past the upscale homes of his neighbors and into his driveway.

Jocelyn, Sherialyn's teenage sister from Atlanta, was spending the summer with them, and after supper, Sherialyn hustled Jocelyn into the family minivan to give her a driving lesson around the neighborhood.

"Sabrina! Kelley! Ricky-J!" called Ricky, appearing in the kitchen in jogging shoes and shorts. "Come on, let's shoot some hoops."

The familiar *thump, thump, thump* of the ball on their neighbor's driveway was punctuated with the rattle of the backboard and the occasional swish of the net. It was a way to spend time together that suited the athletic Byrdsong family just fine.

Tonight was no different. He and the three kids played till the sun met the horizon. Ricky felt so grateful. He had a great family, he was helping to make a difference in the lives of kids through his job, and the writing of his book was progressing smoothly and might influence thousands of families!

"Hey, let's go for a walk before it gets dark."

Sabrina, age twelve, didn't want to go. But Ricky Jr. was already over the shrubs and into his own yard, grabbing his bike so he could keep up with his dad's long strides.

Ricky jogged slowly as they turned the corner and headed west. Kelley was ahead on her bike, Ricky-J just behind him. The remains of a golden sunset shone through the branches of the towering elms.

• • •

Driving north on the four-lane McCormick Boulevard, with all the adrenalin pumping through him, Benjamin Smith had trouble holding his speed to the 40-mph limit. This was no time for a traffic ticket. The canal and park now separated him from the Rogers Park neighborhood he had just ravaged, but there were other concentrations of Jews he might visit—like Skokie just to the west.

Three and a half miles north, Smith turned west off McCormick Boulevard onto Church Street and then north on Central Park. Once into the quiet Skokie neighborhood, he stopped to reload his weapons. It was almost 8:45 P.M. There still ought to be some Jews out on the streets, he reasoned, and he wanted to be ready. But as he cruised slowly north, he didn't see any. Finally, he turned west.

The sunset still shone like brass, silhouetting the overarching trees and everything in front of Smith. There—up ahead, there were some people going the same direction he was but on the other side of the street. He slowed just in case. No, this was a really tall dude—certainly no Jew—and a couple kids.

He was almost up to them before he realized that the tall jogger was a black man with two young ones on bikes. *What were n——s doing here? This wasn't a black neighborhood!*

Smith picked up his Ruger and leaned out the window. Rolling past them at fifteen yards, he couldn't miss.

1

Born in Revolution

The World Church of the Creator, which spawned Benjamin Smith, was founded by another Ben—Ben Klassen, born on February 20, 1918, just as the bloody Russian Revolution rolled over the steppes of the Ukraine where his family lived in the village of Rudnerweide.

Six years later, little Ben Klassen stood on the steps of his house surveying the yard. A few May flowers were blooming, but no one had planted new ones that spring. Instead, nearly everything the Klassens owned was planted in the yard, ready for the great auction. The farm machinery was parked under the trees. The furniture was positioned on the lawn like rooms without walls. Chickens clucked resentfully in cages, and the horses and cows rolled their eyes from where they were tied to the fence.

The remaining villagers moved among the items, reverently fingering each one. Clusters of sturdy, sandy-haired Cossacks from the countryside stood around the edge of the yard with their arms crossed, muttering to each other.

"No!" yelled Ben as he flew down the steps and across the yard. "Not my wagon! You can't have my wagon." He grabbed its handle from Heidi Dyck and began to pull it toward the house.

"It's okay, Ben," said his teenage brother Korni, kneeling down and putting his hands on the boy's shoulders. "We can't take it with us on the ship."

Ben dropped his head and his lower lip protruded. "She's always wanted my wagon."

"Well, maybe now her father will buy it for her. Wouldn't you rather one of your friends have it?"

"No. If I can't have it, I'm going to smash it!"

"You mustn't do that, Ben. We need all the money we can get for our trip. Maybe Father will build you a new one in Mexico." With a down-turned mouth, Ben slowly let go of the toy wagon's handle and returned to the steps to watch the auction.

By evening everything the Klassens had owned had been sold except for a few personal possessions packed in small suitcases, boxes, and an old-fashioned trunk. Even the farm now belonged to someone else. The Friesens from across the road graciously invited them over to dinner. Ben's father, Bernhard, sighed as he picked up his fork. "I hope we got enough money from the sale. But with so many Mennonites leaving Russia, no one seemed willing to pay a fair price."

Mennonites were still "foreigners" in Russia, having come from Germany to colonize the Ukraine near the end of the eighteenth century at the invitation of Catherine II.* The Revolution ravaged the relatively prosperous Mennonites. Some of their villages changed hands between the Red and White Armies twenty-three times, suffering ruin each time the fighting raked through their homes before the Red Army finally secured control.

Then came famine. In two years some six million people starved to death. In fact, as many as twenty million people died in Russia as a result of the Communist Revolution, the vast majority of them civilians. Bernhard Klassen had squirreled away enough grain for his family to survive the famine, but then came the ruthless communist commissars under the leadership of an ambitious party member, Joseph Stalin, to gather everyone's "collective share" of grain for the sake of the revolution. Every bushel was carted away to support the army and feed those in the cities. The farmers were left without food for the winter or seed grain for next year's crop. With little hope that things would improve, the Klassens joined some twenty thousand Mennonites who were fleeing for their lives.

The Klassens, with Henry, eighteen; Korni, sixteen; Sarah, twelve; Katie, ten; and six-year-old Ben, stayed with relatives for the next couple of

---

* For why Mennonites were in Russia, go on the Internet to http://www.daveneta.com/no-random-act/mennonites.

weeks. Then in June 1924—passports, visas, and travel tickets in hand—
the Klassens were ready to go. The new owners of their home let them use
the cleaned-out blacksmith shop for a good-bye party. They decorated the
soot-darkened interior with flowers and ribbons. Friends and relatives from
the whole village and even neighboring villages brought cakes, sandwiches,
and tea. The Mennonite preachers delivered stirring sermons about God's
protection, and then they sang, "God be with you till we meet again."

But everyone knew they would never again meet in beautiful Rudnerweide. *Beautiful* Rudnerweide was nothing but a memory, even for those
who remained.

The next morning, Franz Friesen loaded the Klassens and their few
belongings on his buckboard and headed across the bridge over the Sisikulak
River. Silence gripped the Klassens as they savored their last sight of their war-
torn home. Finally, Ben's father and brothers turned and looked down the
road ahead. What would they face in the uncertain future? His mother and
sisters sobbed quietly as the wagon jostled along, but young Ben, small legs
dangling over the back of the wagon, stared at the village shrinking into the
distance, thinking about all they had lost and the thieves who had taken it.

● ● ●

A year and a half after leaving Russia, and after an abortive attempt to
establish a Mennonite colony in Mexico, the Klassens joined relatives in
Saskatchewan, Canada.

The once proud and chiseled face of Ben's father had morphed into a
gaunt echo with a drooping, untrimmed mustache and eyes that did not
sparkle with enthusiasm but flickered like a flame nearly out of fuel. His
mother's soft doe eyes had become haunted and surrounded by dark circles.
They were just a family of refugees.

Young Ben had seldom seen snow before arriving in Canada that cold,
dreary night in the middle of December. Somewhere in their travels or in
Mexico, he had picked up intestinal worms, and they had left his body thin
and ill-prepared to combat the piercing cold. His uncle, Jacob Wiens,
picked up the family from the railway station with a box sled and skimmed

them across the frozen fields to a two-room, clapboard house that he had recently erected for his family.

Ben was so tired and cold that he hardly noticed the challenge of compressing two families into a two-room house. But the next day—with two crying infant cousins—the space seemed intolerably cramped.

When Christmas morning came, Ben examined the meager gifts he received and realized they were all hand-me-down or makeshift items. There was a hemmed-up jacket from the Canadian Mennonite relief agency and socks he'd seen his mother knitting for days from recycled yarn. His sister Katie got his older sister Sarah's blue dress.

Why hadn't Santa Claus left them anything new?

Slowly, it began to dawn on Ben that Santa Claus wasn't real. In fact, the more he thought about it, the more Santa had been a cruel hoax. There was no benevolent "St. Nicholas" who brought toys to good boys and girls. There was no one to make it up to them for being driven out of Russia. They were on their own.

It may have seemed to Ben that they had left the Garden of Eden in the Ukraine, but in spite of its barren and hostile winters, Saskatchewan was wheat country, and Bernhard Klassen knew how to grow wheat. Within a few weeks he found and arranged to buy a 640-acre farm four miles south of town with a decent two-story house and a large barn, other buildings, and some farm machinery.

By pooling financial resources and borrowing from other Mennonites, each family that came from Russia soon secured a farm and was on the road to restored prosperity. But somehow Ben's father was too busy and his mother too overwhelmed to help him see how many people had reached out to them or to point out that God had inspired all the mutual aid they had received. God had even helped them get out of Russia just in time. As many as forty-five thousand Mennonites who did not leave in the 1920s were later imprisoned in forced labor camps or exiled to the Asiatic Russian interior or Siberia. Whole villages were "removed" and never found again.

God had been gracious to the Klassens, though no one helped Ben to see it that way.

2

God's Fifty Acres

Pausing on the front steps before going inside, Jannie Byrdsong frowned at the newspaper she'd picked up at the store. The war in Europe dominated the news that summer in 1944. D-DAY…PARIS LIBERATED…BATTLE OF THE BULGE. Earl was somewhere over there. Draft notice came; he had to go. Never mind that he had a wife and five young mouths to feed at home *and* a mother to support.

"Jannie? That you?" Earl's mother, a tiny, wizened woman with light skin and graying hair, appeared at the front door of the small house. "You got a letter from Earl?"

"Nothing today, Nanny Byrd. Just the paper."

Wouldn't be so bad if she could get a job. Jannie had worked as a maid before she got married—that was how she met Earl. After high school, she took a job with one of the white folks in Atlanta, where Earl was a chauffeur. He told her she was the prettiest young thing he'd ever seen. Especially liked those freckles dancing across her nose. Goodness, but he was persistent! Tall, light-skinned, and thin-lipped like his mother. Dashing. They courted for several months, sitting on park benches on their way home from work, occasionally taking in a matinee at one of the local movie theaters where blacks were allowed. He asked her to marry him on a Monday; they got married on the following Saturday. Nine months later Earl Jr. was born.

The other babies came as regular as the seasons—Edward, David, Donoval, Curtis. Earl worked as a house painter till he got drafted. Jannie was still young—only twenty-eight—but she couldn't work steady, not now, not with five rambunctious boys and another on the way. They had to make do with the pitiful small check the army sent them and the few odd jobs she could pick up.

Jannie turned to the classified ads in the back of the paper, her eyes running up and down the tiny print. She could hear the boys out back, playing in the dirt of their two-bit property that supported one cow, a mess of chickens, and two hogs. The street in front of their house in south Atlanta was unpaved, and all the houses along it had outhouses in the back. But the city was crowding in. Just a quarter mile away, a low-rent housing project was being proposed that would quintuple the neighborhood's population. She'd been growing increasingly uneasy. How could she raise five—no, six—children in the city by herself? No telling how long the war was going to last, or when—or, God forbid, even *if*—Earl would come home. But if she could plant a garden, raise vegetables, have room for the boys to run off some of that energy…

Jannie's eye caught an ad, and she read it again: *FOR SALE: Fifty-acre farm, located in Lithonia, Georgia, Route #2, Parkway Road.*

Lithonia. Where was *that?* No matter. She would find out.

"Nanny Byrd! Look here at this ad!" Jannie Byrdsong let the screen door bang shut behind her.

• • •

A few days later, Jannie left the five boys with Nanny Byrd, put on her best dress and walking shoes, and caught the streetcar to north Atlanta. From there she transferred to an eastbound Greyhound bus. As the city receded, Jannie could see Stone Mountain rising majestically in the distance to her left. On either side of the road, fields of corn and cotton flashed by. Pine forests and broadleaf trees crawled over the hillsides and tucked into the valleys. A small smile played on her lips. The countryside felt familiar. Just like home, back in Lamar County, where she grew up.

The bus stopped in Lithonia, and Jannie got off. Her smile broadened. Lithonia was a town right out of a storybook. Wagons pulled by mules plodded past rickety old farm trucks parked at the feed store. A train pulled in at the depot, where people were waiting to board. She could hear the familiar ringing of hammer on steel—a blacksmith shop was right down the street. Blacks and whites went about their business on the town's main street.

Jannie snagged an old woman. "Excuse me. Can you tell me how to get to Parkway Road?"

"Parkway? Oh, you mean Baptist Line."

"Baptist Line?"

"Named after the Antioch Baptist Church—you'll see why. Take that road there till you get to the church, turn right on Baptist Line till you pass the Rock House, and then you're there."

The old lady was right. Jannie did see. When she got to the church, the paved road suddenly stopped and the dirt road began. The church sat up on a hill like a beacon, serving as the dividing line between two worlds: white and black. But that didn't worry Jannie. She was used to Georgia towns that offered city services to white folks but somehow ran out of money when it came to the black part of town. Another day, maybe, it would be different. Right now, she had a farm to see.

As she trudged the red dirt road under the hot August sun, she passed small farms with truck gardens out back and a few animals in the pastures. People waved at her from where they sat on their front porches, and children ran out to the road to greet her. Yes, yes, her feet seemed to say. This is where you belong.

The Rock House was aptly named, unlike any other house along that road. Built of granite, the wraparound porch was supported by rock columns and a massive tin roof. Given the many people she saw about the place and the large number of old cars parked along the road and beside the house, she thought several families must live there. A question pricked her mind about "suitable neighbors," but the road turned sharply and she was there.

"Her house" sat on a hill directly in front of her. A narrow dirt driveway climbed the hill about thirty yards then split in two directions around a majestic black walnut tree and met again in front of a large clapboard house. The drive also circled a freshwater well, and three large oak trees acted as sentinels.

Jannie's heart was beating fast as she approached the house. She passed a young girl with a pan full of freshly picked figs. Figs! Jannie's mouth watered. But then she saw the old black woman standing in the doorway of the house, an apron tied around her ample middle, hands on her hips, and her mouth working a wad of snuff.

"Can I he'p you?" said the old woman, eyes narrowed suspiciously.

Jannie held out the newspaper ad. "I came to see the farm. I'm looking to buy it."

The wad of snuff kept working as the woman looked her over. "We just rent here. White folks don't want this old place, and n———s ain't got enough money to buy it! Ain't nothing but a rock pile anyway!"

Jannie's heart soared at the word "rent" and chose to ignore the rest. "May I see the house?"

The old woman spit and reluctantly stepped aside.

• • •

All the way home on the bus, Jannie could hardly contain her excitement. The house was old—antebellum old—and ill-cared for, but a lesson in history. Twenty-four-inch-wide boards ran around the base of all the walls. Two large fireplaces shared a common chimney and provided heat. The rooms were large. The floorboards had cracks between them, supported underneath by huge, hand-hewn beams held together with wooden pegs instead of nails. Pillars made of irregular field rocks supported the whole house.

She had walked about the farm, marveling at the two creeks of fresh, clear water gurgling through the valley beneath muscadine, the wild grapevines hanging above. Several fields showed signs of a recent harvest. Cows grazed lazily in green meadows, surrounded by rocky forests of pines, oaks, and hickories. She had stopped and listened. The sounds of birds and critters in the woods and breezes rustling the grasses and leaves filled her ears.

The farm was just what she'd been looking for. But the next big question was, how was she going to pay for it?

The next day she went to the Realtor. How much? The owner was asking fifteen hundred dollars with five hundred for a down payment. A steal as far as property values went. "Can you do that?" asked the Realtor.

Five hundred dollars? She only had forty dollars saved. Jannie tilted her chin. "I want that farm. I need it for my kids. This is what I've got." She thrust out the forty dollars.

The agent looked at Jannie then looked away and sucked in his breath. Suddenly he began to chuckle. "Jannie Byrdsong, if you have enough spunk to try to purchase a farm with only forty dollars in your pocket, then I'm dumb enough to take a chance on you."

He took out his own checkbook and wrote out a check to cover the rest of the down payment. Then he and Jannie figured out a monthly amount to pay him back.

Jannie floated home. God was good! She was blessed! Miracles did happen.

That night she wrote a long letter to Earl, telling him all about *their* farm. Then reality hit. How was she going to move her household, plus the cow, hogs, and chickens all the way to Lithonia—much less run a farm all by herself? And the baby was due after Christmas. She needed Earl. She needed him now.

She sat down and wrote another letter. "Dear Mr. President…"

• • •

Jannie Byrdsong never knew whether Franklin D. Roosevelt ever received her letter. What she does know is that she got a letter from Earl later that fall saying he was receiving an early discharge and would be home "soon." And he added, if the baby was a boy, could they name him Charles Elliot after his commanding officer?

The baby couldn't wait for daddy. Charles Elliot was born ten days into the New Year. Earl Byrdsong got his discharge twenty days later. Once again the house was full of his voice, which rumbled with so much authority that it compelled the children to listen when he spoke.

Jannie couldn't wait to show him the farm. On a crisp February day, they took the bus to Lithonia and tromped over the fifty acres. She could tell that Earl was pleased. A light shone in his eyes as they drank in the fields and forests. Only a few acres had been tilled. Some of the acres were rocky. But it was land. *Their* land. A good place to raise a growing family. A good place to keep the boys busy and learn the value of honest work. Maybe it would temper Earl's drinking. Someday, someday, the Byrdsong children were going to make something of themselves. She just knew it.

Earl had only one question. "When can we make the move?"

"As soon as the boys finish the school year," Jannie said. "June."

3

Too Smart for the Local Yokels

In the spring Ben Klassen trudged across the still-frozen fields behind his sister Katie to the one-room Oskaloosa school. His secondhand pants ended above his thin ankles, and his lunch pail—an old corn syrup can—carried only a couple of biscuits and a hard-boiled egg. Oskaloosa was an English school. He had been learning English as fast as he could, but the native Canadians weren't quick to receive all these foreign-speaking outsiders. Ben had been pushed headfirst into a snowbank often enough by the local bullies to make school—even with a big sister along—about as appealing as the purgative he had been taking for his intestinal worms.

Nevertheless, after hiking two and a half miles, his dread was overcome by curiosity when he saw four or five black kids among the twenty children playing in the schoolyard. The only other black people he had ever seen were some Africans who worked in the galley on the ship in which Ben's family had crossed the Atlantic.

"What's your name, eh?" said a black boy about Ben's age.

"I be Ben Klassen, and what would be your name?"

"Earl, Earl Lafayette. You play ball, eh?"

"Yah. I play de ball."

"Catch this!"

Ben fumbled the toss and went running to retrieve it.

"Oh yeah. Well, you're not going to be much help on our team."

"Are all those your brothers and sisters?" Ben asked.

Earl looked around the schoolyard as though he were seeing the kids for the first time. "No, not all of them." He laughed with an easy grin. "Just the colored ones."

In the weeks to follow, Ben grew to envy Earl's athletic ability. Ben worked hard to learn baseball, and in the annual field day competitions with other county schools he did his best in the Olympic-style contests. For some reason he felt driven to match the black kids who so often brought Oskaloosa school the county championship.

Over sixty years later, Ben Klassen remembered those early contests and softball games with the intensity of a war veteran, claiming that he was soon able to play ball as well as anyone else. An elderly Earl simply laughs. "Oh, I don't know. We were just kids."[1]

Earl came over to Ben's house to play a couple times, but life on an isolated farm was rather lonely. Apparently, Ben had few if any childhood playmates. But he excelled in solitary accomplishments.

A shallow lake on their property stretched nearly a mile. When the weather got warmer, Ben built a raft of old boards and equipped it with outriggers to keep the narrow vessel from tipping over. Then he attached a wooden box to the raft as a seat and spent day after day lazily rafting back and forth on the lake in the summer sun...alone.

In the winter, Ben hunted rabbits. One day he bagged twenty with his single-shot .22. He also set up a trap line for muskrats, rabbits, weasels, and badgers. He got ten cents apiece for rabbit hides and as much as five dollars for a badger skin. One day Earl Lafayette casually sauntered by on horseback to see what was going on; otherwise trapping was as solitary as rafting.

The harshness of the wind-blown prairie seemed to squeeze the warmth out of the Klassens' family life. After the disappointing Christmas when he concluded Santa was a hoax, Ben didn't record any family Christmas celebrations and few other festivities. In fact, from that time on, he never again mentioned his mother in his autobiography until her death in 1946, except to note once that, when he lived as a young bachelor-teacher two and a half miles down the road from the family farm, she kept him supplied with milk, eggs, bread, and cookies.[2]

• • •

By 1929, Ben skipped a grade to enter the sixth grade as an eleven-year-old, but there was no one else in sixth grade and no one in the seventh, either. His teacher, Miss Berger, had to manage a one-room school for all the students. So she put Ben in with seven other eighth graders, who were mostly sixteen and seventeen years old. One of Earl Lafayette's sisters was also in that class, and this gave Ben additional incentive: If black kids could outplay him, he certainly wouldn't let them outstudy him.

He worked hard and it paid off, but when he got better grades than the others, they would invariably retort, "You think you're smart, don't you?" But by the end of that year, Ben passed his graduation exam along with three other students. The other half of the class, including the Lafayette girl, did not receive diplomas.

Ben was elated and began to feel superior to the average schoolmate. Even though the other kids resented his attitude, he developed it into a principle he later taught others: "The inferior hate the superior. The dumb hate the intelligent. The blacks hate the whites. The ugly hate the beautiful. The poor hate the rich. The unsuccessful hate the successful."[3] But as for his classmates, Ben would get even by hating them all right back. "To hell with them" became his motto. He would face the world alone.

• • •

In spite of the depression that reduced grain prices from $1.33 to $.33 per bushel, Ben's father agreed to spend $150 in 1931 to send him to the German-English Academy at Saskatchewan, a small Mennonite school located 150 miles northeast of Hershel.

Again he couldn't help drawing attention to his brilliance, this time by trying to make his teachers look foolish. Once when a teacher said the total degrees of every triangle always added up to 180, Ben went to the board to prove him "wrong" by drawing a triangle and designating two of the corners as outside angles. Years later, apparently unaware that others may have seen it as a smart-aleck bid for attention, Ben still bragged how his demonstration got a laugh. The year ended with Ben's coming in second in his class to a twenty-three-year-old student. But his reminiscences do not mention one companion or activity to suggest that he was part of a circle of friends.

Of his first year in college, Klassen later reflected that his studies of history had led him to conclude that all religions were "man-made concoctions" and that his perceptions of "heaven and hell, God and the Devil were never the same again."[4] He felt he had made a life-changing discovery.

Having dismissed God, Ben told his cousin Jake Wiens how he had decided to take care of himself. "In this world," Ben said, "money talks. And I am going to talk!"[5]

Klassen next attended normal school where he discovered girls. In the years to follow, he went through quite a few of them. He seemed to measure each girl according to how she served his interests and needs—usually on a rather superficial level—and then he dumped her when she was of no more use to him, adding her to his list of girls he left behind.[6]

When he finished normal school, Klassen landed a teaching job for the next year at Oskaloosa school, the same country school he had attended earlier as a boy. But Klassen quickly developed a distaste for the "country yokels" of the community, considering them unintelligent and uncouth. Nevertheless, he wanted to make a success of his teaching venture, so he read Dale Carnegie's book *How to Win Friends and Influence People*. But Carnegie's philosophy required too much emphasis on the other person, Klassen felt; he had difficulty buying into the others-centered approach of making others feel valued by discussing things of importance to them, of giving to others, of loving your enemies and seeking to turn them into friends. Carnegie's views galled Klassen, especially when local families like the Lafayettes repeatedly invited him over for dinner. The older Lafayette boys with whom he had gone to school—Glenn, Homer, Earl, and Carl—would even stop by the school after class for a friendly chat. But Klassen considered relationships a waste of his valuable time.

He soon became exasperated with teaching and, before the year was over, he lost control of the class and actually became involved in a physical fight with two of his male students.[7]

4

Life Is a Gift

To the Byrdsong children, the farm in Lithonia was like heaven on earth. The three older boys—Earl Jr., Edward, and David—roamed "God's fifty acres" like the first explorers on a new continent, fishing in the creeks, hunting in the woods, swimming where the waters pooled, picking the berries that grew wild along the roadside. The "babies"—Donoval, Curtis, and Charles—were gradually replaced by three more boys and two girls.

The older boys crammed more adventure into the daylight hours than seemed humanly possible. They also soon learned that it took hard work to establish a farm. But Jannie Byrdsong had a philosophy about work: *Take pleasure in it.* Love what you do. Put everything you've got into it. Life is a gift; don't ever take it for granted.

Earl continued painting houses for a living, so there were plenty of farm chores to go around for the boys: milking the cow, feeding the chickens, collecting eggs, slopping the pigs, watering the mule, cutting wood for the cook stove and fireplaces, mending fences, drawing water from the well by the walnut tree. And school. Chores and school put structure and balance into their otherwise freewheeling childhood.

Earl had only a third-grade education, but he was self-educated, reading everything he could get his hands on. Jannie had graduated from David T. Howard High School in Atlanta, one of only two high schools for blacks in Atlanta in the 1930s. Some of the older boys were already talking about dropping out and getting a job. But Jannie hoped she could keep her children in school as long as possible.

Progress for blacks in the South wasn't easy in the 1940s and 1950s, but Jannie Byrdsong had a philosophy for that too. Obstacles were challenges that could be overcome by a sound education, sheer determination, and trust in almighty God.

To their mother's dismay, the three oldest dropped out of school. Why stay in school when they could get a job like Dad's right now? First Earl Jr. then Edward followed in their father's footsteps and took up house painting and renovation, driving into Atlanta from the farm each day. Later, the boys shared a room in a rooming house in town.

The Byrdsong boys were tall and charming, just like their father, and Edward was no exception. At least that's what sixteen-year-old Mary Gunn thought when her girlfriend introduced them. At five feet nine inches, Mary was tall for a girl and liked the fact that she had to look *up* to Edward Byrdsong, who was six-one. She was even more impressed when Edward— who was also a year older—drove up in his own car to the Carver Homes where she lived with her mother, Blanche Hollis. He politely opened the car door for her. *I like a boy with good manners,* she thought.

Edward wooed sweet Mary diligently, taking her to the movies on Friday nights (blacks sat in the balcony) and sometimes to a theater to see B. B. King and other popular musicians. When she graduated from high school in 1955, Mary got a job as a bus girl in a local restaurant. And one day that summer, Mary Gunn and Edward Byrdsong met at the courthouse on their lunch breaks and said "I do."

• • •

Ricky Allen Byrdsong was born the following year on June 24, 1956. With his sweet nature and infectious laugh, the first grandbaby on both sides of the family solidified his place in both grandmothers' hearts. Even though Edward Byrdsong and his young wife settled in south Atlanta in a rented duplex, "the farm" still held its magic for Ricky and his little sister, Marcia, who came along two years later. As the children grew, they could hardly wait for summer. The drive out into the country to Lithonia seemed a long way, so of *course* they had to stay a couple weeks until their parents could pick them up again. Only many years later did they realize the distance was only thirty miles—fifteen from the city limit.

The younger "aunts" and "uncles" at Grandpa Earl and Grandma Jannie's were more like cousins, eager to induct Ricky and Marcia into the mysteries of creek, field, and forest. And the *great fun* of chopping wood and slopping hogs.

The bewitching hour was eight o'clock at night. That was when Grandpa Earl, tired from a long day of physical labor, ordered all the children to their beds with his deep rumbling voice. He didn't want to see one big toe or hear the slightest squeak from any of them. Somebody had to go to the bathroom? Use a chamber pot and empty it in the morning.

Not that he didn't have a jovial side, usually brought on in a public place when he'd had a little too much to drink. The kids and grandkids giggled behind their hands, but Jannie didn't think it was so funny. Unfortunately, it was a weakness that unraveled in the personality of his second son, Edward.

• • •

It was the drink that did it.

Mary Byrdsong loved her man, and she tried to make a good home for Edward and her kids. At first the money he made as a painter was enough to support their modest rented duplex in south Atlanta. But more and more of each paycheck was disappearing before making it home. Edward wasn't abusive when he drank; he just wasn't there. Rather, he was lost in his bottle. When Ricky was ready for third grade, Mary put the kids into private school at St. Paul of the Cross. But because she couldn't count on Edward's paycheck to cover the extra expenses, she started working at the Nabisco Company—the night shift so she could be home when the kids came home from school each afternoon.

But Edward's drinking steadily worsened. In her heart, even Grandma Jannie had to admit her second son had become "a sorry man"—the kind of man her own mama had warned her against. As for sweet Mary, this wasn't the life she wanted for her kids. By the time Ricky was ready for fourth grade, Mary had filed for divorce and moved into a triplex on Gordon Road next to her mother, who said she'd help with the kids.

The divorce just put a name on what had already become reality for young Ricky: life without a father. A more immediate challenge was finding his niche as the new kid in the neighborhood. Most of the children around Gordon Road went to West Haven Elementary, just a shortcut through the woods behind the small housing development. West Haven had only recently been forced to desegregate, and whites were leaving the area in record numbers. This was largely lost on the kids, who were more concerned with exploring the woods, walking the railroad tracks that ran behind the cluster of triplexes, and racing their skate-scooters down the hill that led toward the tracks and the woods.

Not that they weren't reminded from time to time. The first year blacks were allowed to attend West Haven, racist words had been scrawled across some of the textbooks that had been left behind.

The neighborhood was full of kids, but nine-year-old Ricky, already tall for his age, gravitated toward Waymon and Joseph Strickland who were a few years older. The older boys teased him about the bus he had to ride and the blazer he had to wear to St. Paul's, but he shrugged it off good-naturedly. "Go on, Waymon. You just jealous 'cause I look better'n you."

He didn't admit to his own private fears. Walking home after getting off the school bus, with Marcia trudging along beside him, Ricky was tense. They walked quickly past white stores and groups of white kids who stared or muttered things Ricky didn't understand. What if somebody stopped them and demanded their pocket money or took their jackets? Sometimes a carload of white kids would drive by, and the kids would yell, "Hey, n———s!" At first Ricky didn't know they meant him and Marcia. No one had ever used that word in his house.

Just up the street from Gordon Road was The Barrier—a "gate" dividing the "black neighborhood" from homes owned by white folks. That was just the way white folks were. All Ricky knew was that if you were black, you better be somebody's maid or gardener or you weren't getting past that barrier. But once Ricky got home and put on his play clothes, all fears were forgotten. While Marcia and her friends jumped rope, Ricky and the other boys shot marbles for keeps. "Aw, Ricky! You got my best cat eye! C'mon, I'll play you for it back." But Ricky often swaggered home with his pocket full of marbles.

Competition intensified among the boys when it came to building skate-scooters. Who could talk his sister out of her clamp-on shoe skates to provide the wheels? Who could ride his scooter down the hill in the fastest time without killing himself?

To Ricky's relief, his mother didn't send him back to St. Paul's for fifth grade. Now he could walk to school like all the other boys. It didn't matter that he had to shepherd eight-year-old Marcia to and from school. He was the man of the house now, and taking care of his sister came with the job. They could play outside after school, but Mama and Grandma, a united force as unyielding as steel on steel, had set down The Rule: Ricky and Marcia had to be *in* the house when the streetlights came on. If the lights came on while they were still outside, the older boys would crow, "Byrd! Better hightail it home 'fore Grandma Blanche finds out!"

Grandma Blanche was not to be messed with—though she had a soft spot for her firstborn grandson on which he capitalized. "Oh, Grandma Blanche, I *love* your pie. You going to make a pie?" Soon Ricky would be eating a pie fresh out of the oven.

Blanche was a woman who saw what needed to be done and did it. One Sunday, coming home from church, she walked into the Davis and Son Café. As she waited to be served, she noticed the lady behind the counter was falling behind and getting flustered. Laying down her pocketbook, Blanche went behind the counter and began waiting on customers…and worked there for the next twenty-three years.

She expected nothing less from her grandson. So Ricky knew that if she said, "Be home when the streetlights go on," he headed for home *before* the streetlights went on.

But that still left lots of daylight hours for doing what kids do best: playing hard. As the boys got older, some of their play got more daring.

Freight trains moved slowly along the tracks behind the housing development, just begging to be hopped and ridden down the track. But when several of the boys got BB guns for Christmas, the woods on the other side of the tracks took on a new possibility: target shooting.

One day Waymon and Joseph Strickland, their "Uncle" John (only a few years older than they were, as often happens in big families), Ricky, and a kid named Larry Johnson went creeping through the woods with BB guns, pretending they were big-game hunters. A startled bird flew out of a bush; Larry swung his gun, squeezed the trigger, and nailed it. The bird fell at their feet, mortally wounded.

The boys' eyes grew wide. "Man, you actually hit it," someone said.

But Ricky was mad. "What'd you go do that for, Larry?" He knelt down beside the bird and gently stroked its feathers. "Bird never did you no harm."

With sudden determination Ricky gathered the bird in his hand and said, "We're going to bury it, give it a decent funeral."

The other boys looked at each other. Good grief. It was just a bird. But it was no use arguing with Ricky once he decided what needed doing. Dutifully they dug a hole under the pine trees, watched as Ricky laid the bird in its resting place and covered it with soft red dirt. He stuck a stick at one end of the hole, and the boys stood in respectful silence for a few moments till Ricky said "Amen."

5

Hitler's Promised Revenge

After the humiliation of the fisticuffs with two of his students, Klassen returned to the University of Saskatchewan in the summer of 1938 and majored in child psychology, determined to figure out "what made those brats tick." Instead, he became intrigued by the events in Europe and Adolf Hitler's annexation of Austria to Germany.

Klassen's life experience to date had many loose ends. From his beginning as a war refugee, the world had seemed hostile with few, if any, dependable friends. He was the youngest and smallest...in his family, in his school, and even when he went away from home. He obviously envied the acceptance others achieved through sports, and yet there was no one to show him how to excel socially using his most obvious asset, his intelligence. Instead, it earned him scorn. From his people's lost paradise in Russia, to the God who had not cared for his family in the way Klassen thought he should, to a mother from whom he seemed distant, to his scornful peers, Ben Klassen had scores to settle.

And Hitler was about settling scores, for Germany and for anyone who wanted to align with him. Klassen learned this from reading Hitler's *Mein Kampf,* which he credits with influencing his whole worldview. In fact, he later says it was the foundation for his philosophy of "Creativity."

To begin with, Hitler provided Klassen with an explanation for the Communist Revolution that had decimated his people. Communism, Hitler declared, was a Jewish conspiracy. Klassen eagerly embraced the propaganda. Finally, he had someone to blame!

But the claim of a Jewish conspiracy was a Nazi lie. While it is true that

Karl Marx was a Jew by birth (born Moses Mordecai Levy), his collaborator, Friedrich Engels, was the son of a Protestant evangelist in an old German family traceable back to the sixteenth century.[1] Additionally, both men borrowed most of their ideas from Hegel, Feuerbach, Owen, Saint Simon, Proudhon, Blanc, and Fourier—none of whom were Jewish. Leon Trotsky (whose real name was Bronstein) was the son of a middle-class Jewish farmer, but he didn't join the Bolsheviks until 1917.[2] And Vladimir Lenin, whom Klassen called Nikolai Lenin, was not Jewish as Klassen believed him to have been.[3]

Furthermore, while many Russian Jews had welcomed the overthrow of the czarist regime in March 1917, all three Jewish worker organizations declared themselves against the communists by 1918, and the opposition of the Jewish middle class was even more pronounced.[4] This lack of Jewish support was so strong that the commissariat for the administration of Jewish affairs, appointed by Lenin's government, issued a manifesto on March 15, 1918, attacking the Jews for their anti-Bolshevist attitude.[5] And while Nazi propaganda also claimed that twenty-four of twenty-five "quasi-cabinet members" of the Communist Party were Jewish, actually there was only one—Leon Trotsky. As for the rest of the 375,000-member party the Nazis claimed was dominated by Jews, only 5.2 percent were Jewish in 1922.[6]

Clearly, while a few communists happened to be Jews, Jewish participation in the party was insignificant. Klassen, however, chose to believe a lie that would give his rage a focus—a focus that quickly grew into an all-pervasive hatred.

•   •   •

Out of grim determination, Klassen returned to teaching at Oskaloosa in the fall, even though he hated the job and was at odds with the whole community. He withdrew from as many social activities as possible and even canceled the Christmas concert—an unheard-of affront to the parents. "To hell with them," he declared. This was becoming his most convenient phrase for dealing with anyone who did not please him. Besides, he had decided to go to the University of Heidelburg to study engineering. He would soon not have to deal with all the "local yokels."

To make it through the last year of his contract, Klassen spent his time developing his worldview, or *Weltanschauung,* as he liked to call it, preferring the German. Forget Dale Carnegie and any attempt to win friends and influence people. Hitler, Mussolini, and Napoleon taught more direct methods of gaining power, power that could control other people. Klassen's *Weltanschauung* included such principles as

- Speak as if you were deeply convinced that what you are saying is absolutely right and that you take it for granted that the person listening believes you.
- In argument, bluff is valuable.
- Turn the debate onto grounds that your opponent knows little about and then talk as if you were an authority on it, even if you are not. It will make your opponent feel ill informed.[7]

Near the end of Klassen's second year of teaching at Oskaloosa school, King George V and Queen Elizabeth made a political tour through Canada to encourage Canadian support for Britain in the event of war. All school children were strongly urged to go see the king and queen at one of their many whistle stops, but Klassen refused to take his students. The school board and parents were furious with him and ended up arranging the trip on their own. Klassen later contended that he didn't care, and that he considered himself done with teaching.

But before he could escape to Germany in the fall, France and England declared war on Germany for invading Poland on September 1, 1939. Klassen was stuck in Canada. With his plans interrupted, he grudgingly enrolled in the University of Saskatchewan in Saskatoon as an engineering student.

There he found a boarding house run by Mrs. Brower. She and her husband had a mentally disabled son of about ten. It was another occasion for Klassen to try on some of the new attitudes he was learning from Hitler. He concluded that handicapped children were burdens to their families and questioned the point of keeping them alive.[8] Later he wrote, "Not all

people are worth saving. Even among the present white race there are para-
sites, drones, insane, morons, pathological criminals, and genetic cripples
that the world and our white society would be better off without. Nature
gives us a further law in this respect—any organism that fails to excrete its
wastes, soon dies."[9]

On June 22, 1941, when Klassen heard the news that Germany had
declared war on Russia, he was delighted to see that Hitler was tying up
another loose end. Klassen believed Germany would inflict long-overdue
retribution upon the communists for their injustices against his family.[10]

Aligning himself with the dispenser of vengeance and retribution brought
a sense of power to the little boy—now grown—who had felt so alone and
powerless. But now that Britain had officially declared war, Canada required
all male university students to be in the Canadian Officer Training Corps.
Klassen found the lectures and parades boring, and he simply refused to
attend. Instead, in October of 1941 he signed up with the Royal Canadian
Air Force to implement a plan he was developing. "Should the war last longer
than expected, I might join the air force after graduation and somehow drop
in on German soil to help strike a blow for the [Nazi] cause."[11]

By this time, Klassen's social life appeared more conventional. He had a
girlfriend, Phyllis, with whom he conducted one of his most extended relationships—until he broke it off with her. As he attended university and
took summer jobs elsewhere, he stayed in an array of rooming houses and
enjoyed the company of several roommates and school colleagues. However, whenever anyone disagreed with him, he jettisoned that person. If a
relationship didn't serve or support him, why bother?

He and friend Joe Doyle (not his real name) began the next school year
boarding with the Saygol family. However, it wasn't long before the young
men discovered that their hosts were Jews, which prompted them to
quickly move out. Later Klassen found a boarding house run by an older
woman named Peg. When he found out that she was a Christian, he began
arguing with her, contending that she was gullible and superstitious to
believe such hocus-pocus. Klassen upset her so much that she asked him to
leave. He laughed it off by saying he didn't like her cooking anyway.

But as Hitler faced defeat, Klassen became more and more despondent. His dreams of moving to Germany waned, and he began to think of moving to the United States. But Canada would not issue a labor exit permit because he was an engineer, critical to the war industry. Also, his new girlfriend, Beth, wanted him to marry her, and they even agreed on a wedding date: June 15, 1945. But as the date approached, Klassen got cold feet and called it off. He was not ready to be tied down, and soon he was dating someone else.

The idea that Canada wouldn't allow him to emigrate galled Klassen. He accused Canada of being like a Russian slave labor camp. "To hell with them!"[12]

On April 30 reports came that Hitler had committed suicide. With no higher power to answer to, and no promise of a hereafter either blessed or damned, why not end it all when you are backed into a corner? Klassen later concluded that since death is inevitable, there are only two considerations, when and how, and that "death is man's greatest blessing when it cancels a life wracked with suffering and stripped of its meaning."[13]

On August 15, V-J Day (following Japan's surrender), Klassen quit his engineering job and headed for the United States. He still had no labor exit permit, no visa, and no passport, but he was determined that nothing—legal or illegal—would stand in his way.

6

"Yes, You!"

The late-evening television news on April 4, 1968, sent shockwaves through Atlanta. Dr. Martin Luther King Jr., civil rights leader and Atlanta's native son, had been shot and killed by a sniper in Memphis, Tennessee. In the days that followed, parents and the teachers at West Haven Elementary looked grim and talked in terse tones. But rumors of riots exploding in ghettos across the country—in Baltimore, Boston, Chicago, Detroit, Kansas City, Newark, and Washington, D.C.—filtered down to Ricky and his friends.

Eleven-year-old Ricky was curious. "Mama! Take me to see the ghetto."

"Huh. You're living in it, son."

What? His pleasant neighborhood of hard-working families didn't look anything like the broken-down city streets he saw on the television news. Only later did Ricky comprehend what his mother knew: that he grew up segregated from white society.

Dr. King's funeral on Sunday, April 7, saw three hundred thousand mourners marching through Atlanta behind the horse-drawn coffin. Snatches of his speeches played on the air and were talked about in school. "I've been to the mountaintop...[and] seen the Promised Land," he had thundered in Memphis the day before his assassination. And he'd told a crowd of thousands in Washington, D.C., in 1963, "I have a dream..."

In the midst of the tragedy, a stubborn belief pulsated through the halls and along the streets and in the air: Even a bullet can't kill a dream.

• • •

There was no way around it. Mary Byrdsong had to find a new place to live—an apartment with three bedrooms. Ricky was thirteen and getting ready to start eighth grade at Frederick Douglass High School. He was too old to share a bedroom with his little sister.

Gone were romping in the woods, shooting marbles, and riding skate-scooters. In their place at the Allen Temple apartments was a community gym complete with several basketball hoops, and tucked between the three-story apartment units. Now whenever Mary Byrdsong wanted to find either Ricky or Marcia, all she had to do was walk over to the gym where boys and girls alike shot hoops or played Horse, three-on-three, or whatever—depending on how many showed up.

But The Rule was still the same: Be home by the time the streetlights come on.

Ricky still took his role as "man of the house" seriously. Sometimes too seriously. Mary Byrdsong was still an attractive woman and saw no reason to "dress poor" just because she didn't have much money. The year was 1969 and miniskirts were all the rage. But she wasn't quite prepared for Ricky's reaction when she put on her new outfit to go to work one night.

"Mama! You're not going out looking like *that,* are you?" Ricky was genuinely shocked. Mothers weren't supposed to look fashionable. They were supposed to look like…well, *mothers.*

Mary Byrdsong was now working two shifts at Nabisco, which meant Ricky needed to be home each evening before his mom left for work, even on weekends. Marcia was scared to be by herself, even in the daytime. Whenever Mama wasn't home, Marcia haunted Ricky's steps. That's just the way it was, and Ricky knew it. A guy does what he has to do, even if he'd rather be out hanging with his friends.

Now that Ricky was in high school, though, he had to leave the house before Marcia to catch the school bus. Afraid to stay home alone even for half an hour, eleven-year-old Marcia walked down the hill to her friend Yolanda's house until it was time to go to school. The system worked fine until the day Marcia forgot her lunch money.

"Just run back home and get it," said Yolanda. "I'll wait right here."

Marcia left Yolanda at the bottom of the hill and ran to their apartment building, up to the third floor, and let herself in with her house key. But the moment she stepped inside the apartment, she heard an odd noise coming from the back room. To this day she doesn't know what made her do it, but she tiptoed back to Ricky's room and peeked inside.

A dark shape was crunched under the bed. Marcia's screams preceded her all the way to the bottom of the hill. As she fled, a window was thrown up behind her. "Marcia! Cia! It's just me! Wait!"

Ricky's voice. Marcia whirled. Ricky waved frantically from the window, disappeared, then reappeared as he came out the door and ran down the hill.

"Ricky Byrdsong!" Marcia was furious. "Are you playing hooky?"

"Don't tell Mama. You know I wouldn't scare you on purpose. I thought it was Mama! I was hiding 'cause I didn't want her to find me."

Loyalty won out. Marcia agreed not to tell. But Mama found out anyway.

So did the school. And Ricky found out the hard way that Frederick Douglass nipped truancy in the bud.

Mr. Hill, the assistant principal, had a one-size-fits-all punishment for erring students: Saturday work detail. Why waste everybody's time with detention, where teachers had to baby-sit bored students sitting in the library after school, when you could put that valuable time to *work?* And work Ricky did—cleaning up the school grounds and scrubbing walls with a few other souls who had been caught by Mr. Hill.

After work detail, Mr. Hill corralled the miscreants into the school office, where they read and discussed the *Desiderata* (Latin for "things to be desired")—a framed poem that emphasized these principles:

As far as possible…be on good terms with all persons.
Listen to others…they too have their story.
Strive for high ideals.
Take kindly the counsel of the years.
Nurture strength of spirit to shield you in misfortune.
Therefore, be at peace with God.

The *Desiderata* set the tone Dr. Lester W. Butts, founder and principal of Frederick Douglass, wanted for his students. You want an education? You need to have discipline. You want to succeed in life? You need to be able to get along with folks.

And if the students failed to get the message, well, there was always Coach Lester. At six feet four inches, Coach William Lester was a big man with a big voice. He coached junior varsity basketball and backed up Dr. Butts and Mr. Hill as the school disciplinarian. So even though Ricky Byrdsong needed only one or two Saturdays on work detail as he moved up the high school ladder, he still shrank into his shirt collar that day in tenth grade when a voice like a thunderclap rolled down the halls of Frederick Douglass between classes: "Hey, son!"

Dozens of students froze in midstride. Heads timidly turned toward the sound. Tall, gangly Ricky caught Coach Lester's eyes locked on him. Ricky's eyebrows went up, and he pointed a silent finger at his chest: *Who, me?*

"Yes, *you,* son!"

Coach Lester reeled in the six-foot-five-inch Ricky with his piercing gaze until they stood eye to eye. Ricky's brain scrambled frantically, wondering what he'd done to sic Coach Lester on his tail. The coach looked him up and down and frowned. "Son, you are too big to be walking these halls and not playing basketball."

Ricky's mouth dropped. That was *it?* He was so relieved he almost missed Coach Lester's next words. "See you in the gym at 3:30—*today.*"

"But, Coach!" Ricky sputtered. "I've never played on a team before." Sure, he'd played in the community gym, but so far his extracurricular activities at Frederick Douglass had consisted of playing sax in the band and turning out for drama club.

The thunderclap roared again. "Did you hear what I said? See you at 3:30!" Coach Lester started to walk away.

"But, Coach! I don't have the right shoes!"

Coach Lester barely turned his head. "Three-thirty! Be there!"

Ricky showed up, not realizing as he stepped onto that basketball court that this was the day God set his feet on a path that led to his destiny.

7

The Climber

At a later point Ben Klassen would rail against what he claimed were "ten million illegal Mexican aliens, who are invading our borders with impunity by the thousands every day.... Like the Texans of the Alamo, we of the Church of the Creator declare war on the mongrels."[1] But in 1945 he thought nothing of entering the United States illegally himself. He picked up his old friend Joe Doyle in Cleveland (Joe had managed to emigrate legally earlier) and headed to Los Angeles.

They found a hotel in which to stay, jobs (Klassen went to work for Bardwell McAllister, a lighting company), and Klassen bought an old car and began living the California free life. A run-in with a traffic cop, however, convinced him that he'd better get his legal status cleared up. Within a few weeks he was back in Canada. The first thing he did upon confronting the colonel in charge at the War Mobilization Board from which he needed his labor exit permit was to give him a twenty-minute lecture, claiming that denying him a permit would be "illegal repression...in direct contradiction of all the principles of democracy for which we supposedly fought a war for the last six years."[2] Of course, Klassen had deliberately avoided fighting that war on the side of democracy. He scorned democracy as a Jewish trick and embraced totalitarianism as practiced by Adolf Hitler.[3] But feigning outrage in the name of democracy served his purpose and put into practice those principles from Hitler and Mussolini: "Speak as if you were deeply convinced that what you are saying is absolutely right" and "In argument, bluff is valuable."

When Klassen finished his tirade, the colonel calmly responded, "Of course. The war is over. There is no problem."

Before he left Canada, Klassen went to see his family in Herschel. His mother was in the hospital awaiting an operation. It was the last time he saw her. He did not bother to attend her funeral two years later. He did not visit his father again or go to his funeral. In fact, it was twenty-five years before he made the effort to visit any of his Canadian relatives again. Klassen didn't say his little mantra for dismissing people he didn't think he needed, but he might as well have done so the way he ignored his family.

• • •

With all the postwar reports coming out of Europe about the Holocaust, Klassen had to decide what he thought of it. On the one hand, Nazi atrocities and death camps sounded barbaric, but if they had really been eliminating Jews, whom Klassen had grown to hate, what was he to think? He adopted a two-pronged, contradictory response.

On the one hand, he swallowed the Nazi propaganda that the Jewish race had become the most powerful in the world; that it controlled media, money, and governments; and that its goal was to "mongrelize and destroy the white race."[4] But then he contended, "There is not a single shred of evidence to back up the allegations that Hitler, or the German government, or any officials in it, ever advocated a policy of extermination of Jews."[5] He appealed to what has become classic Holocaust-denial rhetoric: "The World Almanac of 1938 lists the number of Jews in the world as 16,588,259. After the war the *New York Times,* owned by Jews, placed the number...[at] approximately 17,100,000. It is therefore impossible by any stretch of the imagination that 6,000,000 Jews could have been exterminated and end up in a net gain in a short period of eight years."[6]

Klassen did not think it was necessary to document *when* the *New York Times* supposedly published these figures. Also, they are completely contradicted by the 1947–1948 volume of the *American Jewish Year Book* that placed the world population of Jews two years after the war at only 11,270,000, still down by 5.3 million from the pre-war figure Klassen quoted.[7]

• • •

Two months after returning to California, Klassen quit his job at Bardwell McAllister and went to work selling oscilloscopes. When this didn't work out, he quit and went to work as a salesman for the W. Bert Knight Company. This working relationship quickly went downhill as Klassen began arguing his worldview at corporate social functions, actions not well-received by his fellow employees or by Bert Knight. Knight's coolness to Klassen's philosophy caused Klassen to question whether his boss was actually a "Jew incognito…. Anyway, I said to hell with him."[8]

Next, Klassen got his real estate license and went to work for Augustine and Pierce. That lasted only a few months before Klassen decided there was more money to be made working for Bill Beacom's United Realty. Soon, however, he quit and went into business for himself with a partner.

From Klassen's perspective, six jobs in twenty months was an excellent climb toward success. He'd bettered himself with each move, and he was making good money in the California postwar boom. From another perspective he had crawled over other people, casting aside everyone who did not benefit him. The golden rule of the World Church of the Creator that Klassen later started is: "That which is good for the white race is the highest virtue; that which is bad for the white race is the ultimate sin."[9] However, because their whole philosophy celebrates our animal instincts as "Nature's Eternal Religion," there is no moderation to love their neighbor as themselves, not even if the neighbor is white. Sooner or later it becomes a raw survival of the fittest. Klassen's life profoundly demonstrates that his first loyalty was to himself. Anyone else—friend, family, colleague, or benefactor—was expendable, even if they were white.

With this method of operation, he was bound to tangle with other sharks and duds. And sure enough, Klassen soon decided that his partner displayed "glaring weaknesses" including occasional drunken binges.[10] Klassen bought him out, rented a larger office, and hired four or five salesmen, including an ex-preacher named Stanley Peek. Peek encouraged Klassen to buy into large land development deals in Nevada. They went into partnership together and bought 18,200 acres of mostly sagebrush, calling it the Silver Springs Land Company. In 1951 they added another 6,000 acres to subdivide into 5-acre desert lots for hapless buyers.

In the meantime, Klassen had met a charming blonde who worked in the First National Bank of Glendale, and he decided it was time to settle down. After a whirlwind courtship of about a month, Ben Klassen married Henrie Etta McWilliams on November 22, 1946. His old friend Joe Doyle and his wife, Molly (not her real name), attended the wedding, as did several of Henrie's family members.

Their marriage lasted forty-two years until Henrie died in 1992, and all indications are that she was devoted to him the whole time. However, according to Klassen's cousin Jake Wiens, Henrie wrote to Klassen's relatives in Canada begging them to "pray for my Benny."[11]

To better manage the Silver Springs development, the Klassens moved up to Fallon, Nevada, while entrusting Stan Peek with the management of the Glendale real estate office. While in Nevada, Klassen received a letter from his brother Korni in Saskatchewan, mentioning that he was tired of the harsh Canadian winters. Klassen responded casually, suggesting that he ought to move to some place warmer. A short time later, Ben found Korni and his wife and four boys at his front door, apparently hoping that Ben and Henrie would take them in. Ben loaned his brother five thousand dollars to get him started on some of the Silver Springs prime acreage, but Korni never repaid the loan. Except to note that Korni ended up in a feud with Stan Peek, Klassen's autobiography never mentions his brother again.

Another casualty seems to have been his old friend Joe Doyle. Joe had gone into manufacturing induction coils and had some extra cash to invest in the Silver Springs enterprise. In fact, Doyle moved a portion of his operation to Nevada and built an assembly building on a piece of Silver Springs land. He had even started to put up a warehouse when a severe desert windstorm came along and blew down the walls. Klassen complained about the resulting eyesore left by the rubble and how it detracted from his development efforts. After Doyle had stuck with him through college, helped him come to the States, and stood up with him at his wedding, this dispute apparently ended their relationship.

Rather than going through life gathering an ever-expanding network of wise friends and loyal relatives for counsel or correction, Klassen used people up and cast them off. He claimed to learn facts from others and lessons from his experiences with them—usually negative lessons of how to control or defend himself against them—but he did not have a teachable stance toward anyone. He solicited no advice, found no cause to say he was sorry, and never recorded an effort to restore a broken or strained relationship. Except for the wife at his side, he had again become the little refugee trudging across the frozen fields of Canada to a one-room schoolhouse he considered hostile, facing the world alone.

After the Klassens' daughter and only child, Kim, was born in 1951, Henrie convinced Klassen to switch places with Peek. Peek and his family would operate the Nevada property while the Klassens returned to California, opened an office, and sent prospective buyers out to the desert.

But Klassen didn't trust Peek, and soon he was looking for a way out of the partnership. Peek agreed to buy out Klassen for $200,000, but the money would necessarily come in installments. Things were so strained by this time, however, that Klassen didn't even trust Peek to do that. So in 1952 he sold his share of the Silver Springs Land Company to another investor, Phillip Hess, and walked away with $150,000—also to be received in installments. Klassen preferred to receive 25 percent less and trust a stranger than have anything more to do with Peek. He would quit land development and live like a retired gentleman.

8

Defined by Love

To say Ricky Byrdsong was tall for his age was an understatement. For all his height—or maybe because he had shot up to over six feet at such a young age—Ricky had never thought about trying out for basketball. When he goofed around at the neighborhood gym, he was all elbows, knees, and big feet. The other kids laughed at his gawkiness, and Ricky laughed with them. So when Coach Lester commanded "Be there!" Ricky obeyed, purely out of fear of what would happen if he didn't.

But when he put on the black-and-gold colors of the Frederick Douglass Astros B team, Ricky fell in love with the game. He was inspired by Coach Lester's confidence in him: "You can do it!" He loved turning the coach's confidence into actual skill through drill, drill, drill. Loved learning the value of the different roles. Loved being part of a team.

And he loved the perks that came along with being an athlete. To be more accurate, perks he *thought* came with the position. Once he purposely left his towel on the floor of the locker room, thinking the team manager could pick it up. Except that Coach Lester saw it.

"*Byrdsong!* You pick up that towel right now!" The thunderclap also flashed lightning. "Whaddya think the manager is—your personal servant? Well, think again! He's got better things to do than pick up after you. Ego and laziness have no place on this team, got that? Each member has his role, and it's to be respected!"

Ricky never "forgot" to pick up his towel again. Ever.

Basketball was all the sweeter because a tall kid named Rollie Lewis, one of the few who could goof around with Ricky at eye level, also turned out for the B team. The two became inseparable. Teachers figured out that if they wanted Ricky, look for Rollie; if they wanted Rollie, look for Ricky. The pair was hard to miss, two skinny totem poles walking heads above everybody else, known generally as "Byrd" and "Chicken Man." With adolescent glee they loved to stand close to Dr. Butts, the principal, making him look up—way up—at them. Good thing he had a sense of humor.

Christmas Day of Ricky's junior year, 1972, was typical at the Byrdsong home: presents happily unwrapped, turkey, greens, and macaroni and cheese, followed by Mama and Grandma Blanche taking a hard-earned nap. When the phone rang, thirteen-year-old Marcia dived to answer it, then rolled her eyes. "Ricky! Guess who?" She dangled the receiver by the cord.

Ricky snatched it. It was Rollie. "Hey, Byrd! Wanna go with Corky over to his girlfriend's house?" James "Corky" Abrams, a mutual friend, was dating a girl named Joni Chandler, who attended nearby Southwest High School. "Corky says his girl has a sister, who has a friend…"

A blind date? That sounded fun. All three boys piled into Ricky's secondhand blue Chevy Super Sport and drove over to the Chandler house. The girls were playing Ping-Pong in the basement family room. "My Girl," by The Temptations, boomed from the record player.

That was the day Ricky Byrdsong laid eyes on the girl who would become his other lifelong passion: Sherialyn Kelley.

Sherialyn was *awesome*. Tall and athletic, she carried herself with a certain self-confidence that Ricky admired. His eyes widened when he learned that she played forward on the Southwest girls' *varsity* basketball team and was the starting pitcher for girls' softball. He also liked her fresh smile and dancing eyes under an impressive Afro. She wasn't flirty, just fun. While Rollie was making eyes at Jan, Joni's sister, Ricky and Sherialyn talked. And laughed. And sang with The Temptations. And talked. He had no idea the impact that girl would have on his life.

•   •   •

Sherialyn Kelley's parents had divorced a couple years earlier, and Sherialyn, her younger sister, Kim, and her mother, Gwen, had moved in temporarily with relatives. Of all Sherialyn's aunts, Aunt Lucille was the ringleader when it came to kids and sports. Even though she had three younger kids of her own, all the cousins—and sometimes their friends—often ended up at Aunt Lucille's on the weekends. While hamburgers sizzled on the grill, Sherialyn and her cousins tried to outmaneuver Aunt Lucille and sink a basket in her backyard hoop. The icing on the cake was piling into Aunt Lucille's car on a summer night with a picnic hamper full of fried chicken to go see a movie at the local drive-in, then "sleeping over."

Aunt Lucille always told the kids, "Life is like a card game. You gotta play with the hand you're dealt." Growing up in Georgia, the adults in Sherialyn's life were well aware of the discrimination blacks lived with every day. But Aunt Lucille had her own philosophy: Give the kids so much love, let them know how special they are, and *that* will define them, not what society says or does.

So it was natural that Sherialyn wanted Aunt Lucille to meet Ricky. "He's not like other guys, Aunt Lucille—you know, full of themselves, thinking they're God's gift to girls." Sherialyn rolled her eyes. "He's…just himself."

Aunt Lucille laughed, deciding to reserve judgment for herself. But when Sherialyn brought Ricky over to one of her backyard barbecues, Lucille took an immediate shine to the tall, lanky boy everyone called Byrd. For one thing, he didn't hang all over Sherialyn as if he owned her. He was polite and related to other members of the family with genuine interest, making them his friends too.

With her parents recently divorced, Sherialyn also found a friend and mentor in her athletic coach at Southwest High School. Anna Wade coached Sherialyn in two sports, softball and basketball, for four years, and they became "like family." Sherialyn babysat for the Wades' young son Warren, but more often she and other members of the girls' team just hung out at their coach's house and talked. And talked…like girls do. Coach Wade discovered that she learned a lot about her charges if she just kept her mouth shut and her ears open—at her house, in the car, in the locker room.

Her fondness for Sherialyn and the other girls didn't stop her from being a tough coach, either. Sherialyn was the softball team's starting pitcher but was pitching badly one day. Coach Wade yelled, "Hey! We're not *bowling!*" And Coach Wade didn't have much patience for Sherialyn's frequent laughing fits. Once Sherialyn couldn't stop laughing in the middle of a game, so the coach pulled her from the field and kept her on the bench for the rest of the game.

But Sherialyn was learning. The rivalry between Atlanta high schools—Southwest, Douglass, Therrell—was intense, and once Sherialyn was hit by a ball thrown by an opposing player. In a flash, Sherialyn started after her rival, but Coach Wade grabbed her. "Cool it! Nothing's going to be served by getting into a fight."

Sherialyn pursed her lips in a pout, her feet dancing impatiently. Gradually her body relaxed and she looked at the coach ruefully. "This will make me a better person, right?"

Coach Wade grinned. "Right."

•   •   •

Romance blossomed after that Christmas Day "blind date." Ricky and Sherialyn started hanging out together, and so did Rollie and Jan. Piling into Ricky's Super Sport, he and Sherialyn often doubled with Rollie and Jan to go hear The Temptations, The Four Tops, Earth Wind and Fire, War, and other popular groups when they came to town. Marcia often tagged along on Ricky and Sherialyn's dates because she still didn't like being left home alone when their mom was at work.

But Ricky took it in stride. Little sisters could even be great allies. Sherialyn's sister, Kim, younger by four years and working at McDonald's, made a bargain with Ricky. "You pick me up and give me a ride home after work, and I'll save you a double-decker with bacon." Fine with Ricky. Will drive for food.

•   •   •

Eleventh grade meant varsity basketball for Ricky and Rollie under Coach Larry Cart. Several years earlier, Dr. Butts had hired Coach Cart, a white man, to coach Frederick Douglass's all black team—not a popular thing to do in the 1960s and early '70s with civil unrest all over the nation. But Dr. Butts believed in diversity, and if he couldn't get it in the student body, he was going to get it with his faculty.

Coach Cart rose to the challenge. He demanded discipline, earned good rapport with his players, and developed a state championship team. He taught Ricky, Rollie, and his other rookie players his zone defense. Most of all, he told them, "You can go to college. There are scholarships out there. I'll help you."

Rollie and Ricky looked at each other. College? Their parents hadn't gone to college; their grandparents hadn't gone to college. Now, Sherialyn... *she* was going to college. Practically a straight-A student. But Ricky hadn't really thought about it. Going to college cost money. Could *he* get a scholarship? Really?

True to his word, Coach Cart contacted several college coaches he knew. "Next time you're in Atlanta, I want you to come look at my boys. I've got some good kids here."

Valerie Lockett, the English teacher at Frederick Douglass, confronted Coach Cart. "These athletes are no more ready to go to college than to the moon! I don't mean grades. I mean ready for *life* in the real world!"

Coach Cart just smiled. "That's your department."

All right. Ms. Lockett rolled up her sleeves, went to the principal, and proposed a new class: College Prep 101. Mandatory for any student hoping to get an athletic scholarship. The first class was full of boys, but soon the girls were clamoring to get in too.

When Ricky and Rollie strolled into Frederick Douglass High School for their senior year, they had a new coach, a black drill sergeant of a man named Coach Donald Dollar. Coach Cart had taught them to play zone defense; Coach Dollar wanted his players to play man-on-man. Coach Cart talked to his players reasonably but firmly; Coach Dollar yelled. A new king reigned in the athletic department. Shape up or ship out.

This didn't sit well with Rollie. The more Coach Dollar screamed, the more Chicken Man simmered. One day the coach yelled and Rollie rebelled. Coach Dollar pushed him. Rollie came right back at him, ready for a fight.

Ricky leaped into the fray and pulled Rollie away. "Hey! Come on, Chicken Man. Keep it cool." Their teammates gaped open-mouthed as he led Rollie away. "What are you guys looking at? Nothing's happening here. We gonna practice or what?"

Ricky probably saved Rollie's skin that year in other ways. If Ricky was going to go to college with a scholarship, he wanted Rollie to go too. Together they enrolled in Ms. Lockett's college prep class.

Ever the English teacher, Ms. Lockett assigned classic books to read and discuss: Shakespeare, *To Kill a Mockingbird,* anything by Mark Twain, Ralph Ellison's *The Invisible Man, Gone with the Wind, A Tale of Two Cities.* Several student athletes showed up in her class who couldn't read. They learned by reading the newspaper and their favorite sports magazines.

But the class also had a practical purpose. "When college coaches come scouting, they often do their interviews by taking you to lunch or dinner." Borrowing several place settings from the home economics department, Ms. Lockett taught all those tall, gangly boys and curious girls what spoon to use for soup, what fork to use for salad. She passed a basket of dinner rolls. "Don't put the whole thing in your mouth. Take just one bite."

The boys studied the dinner rolls. "To me this here roll *is* just one bite," drawled Rollie Lewis. Even Ms. Lockett had to join the laughter.

The "interviewees" were critiqued on their manners, how they stood, how they sat, how they dressed, how they spoke. "No, no, no! No college coach or employer is going to give you a job if you mumble, 'Yeah, I be good at dis job.' In *this* class there's only one way to speak. Not black English, not white English. Just proper English, *period.*"

There were questions. "Why we hafta learn all this stuff, Ms. Lockett? This ain't how we do things in *my* neighborhood."

Ms. Lockett had a ready answer. "I'm not preparing you to spend the rest of your life in your neighborhood. When you get to college, you'll discover people from all sorts of backgrounds. You need to know how to get along with all of them. You have to be able to adjust to any kind of situation.

It's called *life*." And Ms. Lockett let them in on her personal secret. "I never think less of myself just because I might not have all the advantages someone else has. I tell myself, 'If they can do it, I can do it too.' "

Ms. Lockett always offered extra help to any student who wanted to stay after class. Not many of the students took her up on the offer, but Ricky Byrdsong never hesitated. "Ms. Lockett! I read this Shakespeare play, but I don't get it."

"That's good, Ricky," she encouraged. "It doesn't matter what you don't know as long as you're willing to ask questions and keep at it until you find out. Don't ever be afraid to ask questions."

Valerie Lockett looked on proudly at graduation as a parade of her boys walked across the stage of the Frederick Douglass auditorium in caps and gowns to receive their diplomas. Thanks to Coach Cart, both Ricky and Rollie had been offered athletic scholarships to Pratt Community College in Pratt, Kansas, by head coach Jim Lewis. Ricky's big grin widened as he waved his diploma at his mother. Mary Jean Byrdsong beamed. Ricky was the first one in the family to go to college. Marcia was proud of her big brother too—even though, in her opinion, *she* was a better basketball player.

Across town, Sherialyn Kelley delivered a speech at graduation as salutatorian for Southwest's Class of 1974. Afterward, the whole gang of friends from both Frederick Douglass and Southwest had a graduation party at Sherialyn's father's house.

Only one thing put a damper on the celebration. Sherialyn had been accepted into the pre-med program at the University of Pennsylvania—a thousand miles from Kansas.

9

Idle Hands Are...

To launch his life as a retired gentleman, Ben Klassen bought a powder blue Cadillac Coup de Ville and had a beautiful new home built for his family east of San Francisco Bay in what became the city of Fremont. But in truth, he wasn't ready to retire. He invested in a company trying to develop a self-lighting cigarette.

Ultimately he lost twenty-four thousand dollars, but the idea of inventing new products captured his imagination. What did the world need? An automatic electric can opener. After fiddling around in his garage workshop for several weeks, he came up with a device he thought was marketable: Canolectric!

Many young families—all white—with children near the age of the Klassens' Kim moved into this new neighborhood. Neighborhood parties ensued, and to fit in to the image of an up-and-coming, all-American family, the Klassens joined the newly built Presbyterian church. Klassen did not attend regularly, and when he did he found the sermons boring. One day he voiced his skepticism about God to the pastor. Rather than try to bring him to faith, the pastor quipped, "If that's what you believe, stick with it." Klassen got the feeling the preacher didn't really believe either.[1]

At first Klassen tried to have his electric can opener manufactured in Germany—a prospect he gloated over—but he found that the import-export costs would have been prohibitive. Still, desiring to become a rich business magnate, he launched Klassen Enterprises, Inc., issued five hundred thousand shares of stock, filed for a patent, and engaged a machine shop to begin production. After a few weeks, the shop's work didn't satisfy him, so he canceled their contract and went to another company. Next he hired a secretary and a sales manager. Klassen ultimately entered a contract with Robbins and Myers and Hunter Fans to manufacture the device in Tennessee. Interest spread, and Klassen received a couple of offers ($150,000 and $250,000) to buy him out, which he declined.

The company went through several stages of expansion, and things seemed to be going well until Klassen hired another salesman, Jack Hainline. Hainline didn't like the sales manager. After doing a little investigating, Hainline told Klassen that the man was nothing but a drifter who had told him several lies about his past sales and promotional successes. Klassen fired his sales manager and promoted Hainline, but Hainline didn't move the product quickly enough for Klassen. After giving Hainline an ultimatum and seeing no improvement, Klassen fired him.

In addition to internal problems, Klassen's company was beginning to face stiff competition from the big boys—General Electric, Sunbeam, Oster, Nu-Tone, and other companies—that were able to provide similar products at a lower price. Robbins and Myers had made several offers to take over Klassen's enterprise entirely and pay him a royalty per unit, and it was beginning to look like that was his only option.

But what would he do then?

•　•　•

Upon turning his can opener over to Robbins and Myers and closing down his offices, Klassen took his family on a Hawaiian vacation to contemplate what he should do next.

The tropical holiday inspired him. His daughter, Kim, enjoyed the beach, but his wife stayed in the hotel much of the time. "Come on, Henrie, enjoy yourself," he coaxed. "We don't get a chance like this every day."

"Look, Ben, I liked it just fine at home, with my friends. Now it feels like everything is up in the air again."

"It doesn't need to be. I've been thinking. I love the tropics so much. Why don't we move to Florida?"

"Florida? What would we do in Florida?"

Klassen dropped the book on the history of Hawaii he had been read-ing and looked with an open mouth at Henrie. "What would we do? We could do anything we want. We could get a new home on the beach with our own pool. I could get a new boat. We could live like a king and queen."

"But what about my friends? What about Kim's playmates?"

"We don't need to worry about her. She's only six years old. She'll make new friends."

Henrie sighed and turned her head aside. Finally she said, "What would you do in Florida, Ben?"

"Oh, I don't know…maybe go back into real estate. Why?"

"Because…because, if you don't have something constructive to do…Well, you don't go to church anymore, Ben. I'm just worried."

"Church? Whatever does that have to do with anything? I'm talking about Florida and something constructive to do. There's a real estate boom going on down there. Are you with me or not?"

"All right, Ben. If that's what you really want to do, I'll go along with it. But—"

"But what?"

"Oh, nothing." She put her hand over her mouth, hurried into the bathroom, and closed the door.

• • •

Once they returned to California, Klassen flew to Florida. There he located and purchased a couple of promising investment properties totaling 680 acres west of Miami, but he decided the Fort Lauderdale area would be the better place to live. He returned to California, collected his family, and was back in Florida within a month, staying first in a Ft. Lauderdale motel and then an apartment while he looked for a house. Not finding what he wanted—a fine house with a pool, all located on a canal large enough to accommodate any size boat Klassen wanted—they had one built in a new high-class waterfront community in Pompano Beach. In February 1959 they moved in.

But traveling to Mexico and Europe, relaxing by the pool, boating in his new twenty-five-foot Owens cabin cruiser, collecting royalty checks for Canolectric, and—oh yes—occasional real estate deals were not enough to keep Klassen occupied for the years to come. Of course there were bigger and better boats and the need for a larger real estate office, but at forty-two years of age, Klassen was bored.[2] He began pondering the purpose of life and felt depressed over the lack of clear answers. But then he gave up trying to figure out life's meaning. Echoing the words of the rich man in Jesus' parable who said to himself, "You have plenty of good things laid up for many years. Take life easy; eat, drink and be merry" (Luke 12:19), Klassen decided to try to relax and let life work itself out. But he had opened the door to life's most important questions, and those questions kept nagging at him.[3]

That proved to be a major turning point in Klassen's life. He was asking the right questions, but having already rejected the only life-giving Source for answers, he became susceptible to the only other "source." In Jesus' parable, God had said to the rich man, "Fool! This night your soul will be required of you" (verse 20, NKJV).

Ben Klassen did not die in 1963, but his soul was claimed.

10

A Long Way from Home

Pratt, Kansas, was a long way from Atlanta, Georgia, in more ways than just miles. The land was gently rolling, broken only by occasional clumps of trees as the surrounding fields marched unhindered to the horizon. The town of seven thousand and Pratt Community College definitely had a small-town feel. Everybody knew everybody, and "everybody" was mostly white. Some citizens were uneasy about PCC's new head coach, Jim Lewis, recruiting black kids from Georgia to their local college.

But one thing that united Pratt the town and Pratt the school was sports. PCC was proud of being a member of the Kansas Jayhawk Community College Conference, which boasted many fine athletes actively recruited by Division I schools. Many Pratt businesses belonged to the booster club for the PCC Beavers and donated money to support trips, buy uniforms, maintain facilities, and update equipment. The booster club filled the bleachers with town folk to cheer the teams on. And people had to admit that the new talent for men's basketball could play.

Ricky Byrdsong arrived on campus grateful to be there, eager to plunge in, and just a tad nervous. He stood with Rollie Lewis gawking at the main building, which housed the Beaver Dome, home to the PCC Beavers sports teams. "Hey, Rollie! We're in college! Can you believe it?"

"I don't know, Byrd." Rollie twisted his scrawny neck and surveyed the small campus. The only other building was the double-wing dormitory, Novotny Hall. "Not many black folks around here."

That was an understatement. Ricky and Rollie probably made up a third of the black population at the school, most of them athletes.

Ricky nodded. For a moment he remembered the white kids who had driven by yelling racial slurs as he and Marcia walked home from school. Then he shrugged. "Yeah, well, so what? People are people, like anywhere else." Ricky had often heard that phrase from both of his grandmothers. "Just feels strange 'cause we haven't met folks yet. Besides, they got basketball, baseball, track, just like back home."

Rollie jerked his thumb toward a sign. "They also got rodeo."

Ricky gaped at the sign. In big letters it said RODEO ARENA, with an arrow pointing across the road from the main building. "A rodeo." A long pause. "Bucking horses, roping calves, riding bulls—stuff like that?"

"I think so."

"*Really?* Man!"

• • •

Head coach Jim Lewis was new to Pratt too—his first college job—and he and the men's basketball team cut their teeth on each other. Sizing up his team, Lewis had no regrets about his new recruits. Ricky had put on another inch; at six feet six, both he and Rollie played forward. Cordy Glen, another Atlanta recruit, was a wing player or guard. Coach Lewis had to wonder why some of the bigger colleges or universities hadn't snapped up these southern athletes—they had good talent, they had decent grades—but decided to count his blessings.

Jerry McCalla, head manager of Gibson Discount Center in Pratt, was an active member of the Beavers Booster Club and rarely missed a game. "Watch that kid from Atlanta—number thirty-three," he told his wife, Kathy, during a home game in the Beaver Dome.

"You mean the kid with the two-hundred-watt grin?" Kathy, snuggling the youngest of the four McCalla kids, had noticed too. Ricky Byrdsong, wearing his number thirty-three blue jersey, was shooting well that night, racking up thirty points in the first half. But in the second half he kept passing off to other team members, letting them have a chance to score.

As a Beavers Booster, McCalla got acquainted with many of the team players, often hiring one or two at Gibson's. But number thirty-three,

Byrdsong—there was something special about the new recruit. Not just his unusual name. A great team player.

Coach Lewis was watching too. *That young man could make All-Conference,* he told himself. He liked the way Byrdsong seemed to have the welfare of the whole team at heart, not just his own stats. When the other players got upset at a referee or grumbled at the team rules, Ricky was usually the first to say, "There's a reason for the rules. It's not going to kill us." Yep, the kid was a good influence on the team.

• • •

"Congrats on being named All-Conference!" Rollie threw his books on his bunk and looked over Ricky's shoulder. "Oh. Letter from your sister? What's new?"

Ricky's face was thoughtful. "Mama's getting married again—in April."

"Married! That guy at Nabisco she's been dating? Strickland?"

Ricky nodded. "Yeah. Guess it's all right. I want her to be happy. It's been hard for her since she and Daddy divorced."

"What does Cia think about it?"

Ricky's grin popped back on his face. "Not happy! She just got rid of *me!* Now she's supposed to get used to a new man in the house? Uh-uh."

Ricky went back to reading his letter, but Rollie had something on his mind. "Byrd, I decided I'm not coming back next year."

That got Ricky's attention. "Rollie! Whaddya mean you're not coming back?"

"I dunno, Byrd. It's not working out. I just want to be back home."

"What happened to wanting to play professional basketball? You gotta play somewhere recruiters can find you. And Ms. Lockett will have your hide if you drop out of college."

Rollie had to laugh. "I know, I know. Maybe I'll check out DeKalb or something else close to Atlanta."

"Man! I'm going to miss you. The Beavers won't be the same without you."

"Yeah, well, they'll live. Gonna miss you too, Byrd."

• • •

Mary Byrdsong married Simon Strickland in April 1975. When Ricky came home that summer from his first year at Pratt, his mom and Mr. Strickland and Marcia had moved into a pretty brick one-level house on Bonnybrook Way—a nice change, Ricky had to admit, from the old apartment complex. Marcia had resigned herself to the move, especially when Mama got her a dog—a black toy poodle she named Fi-Fi.

But the best thing about the summer of '75 was seeing Sherialyn again on a regular basis. Being away from her had been like trying to get used to living without a body part.

"You could come see me for spring vacation," Sherialyn tempted. She wasn't quick to admit it, but she had missed Ricky terribly. She'd met a lot of guys at the University of Pennsylvania, but there was nobody who could light up a room like Ricky.

They both worked at summer jobs, hanging out together whenever they had a chance, talking and laughing. Sometimes she was the butt of his outrageous sense of humor—like the time Ricky conspired with Sherialyn's sister to smuggle her underwear out of the house. Sherialyn discovered her underpants fluttering casually from the antenna of her orange Volkswagen one morning when she came out to go to work.

Other times their talks were more serious. "Ricky, what do you think about God?"

"God? I like God! Even like to go to church sometimes. Not like St. Paul of the Cross, though." Ricky's memories of Catholic school weren't too hot.

"No, I mean, about having a personal relationship with God—becoming a Christian."

Ricky was slightly bewildered. He already was a Christian, wasn't he? Well, his family didn't go to church too often, but what could you expect, as hard as his mom had to work? Sherialyn was a Christian. Her family believed in God and Jesus.

Ricky's high forehead wrinkled in a comical way. "What do you mean?"

"Remember when I wrote you that a bunch of my friends and I took a train to Princeton to see a friend we knew there—just to have fun?"

"Yeah. I didn't see how you could have any fun without me there." Ricky feigned a wounded puppy look.

"Well, that weekend a couple of my friends asked me if I was a Christian. I said the same thing you did. Kim and I went to church pretty regular with my mom and dad when I was little. But then they showed me this booklet called *The Four Spiritual Laws*. It described how sin separates us from God, but God wants to have a personal relationship with us. So that's why he sent his Son, Jesus—you know, to pay the penalty for our sins, so we can be reconciled to God."

"Sherialyn! You're not a sinner. You're the best person I ever met."

"My friends asked if I wanted to pray and ask Jesus to come into my heart."

Ricky's eyebrows shot up. "What did you say?"

"I said no!" Sherialyn giggled. "They wanted me to 'get saved' right then and there!" She shrugged again. "But I did start going to Campus Crusade meetings. I've been thinking about what they said."

Ricky didn't quite know what to make of what Sherialyn told him. He believed in God and always considered himself a good person. But what was she talking about—a personal relationship?

11

Searching for an Enemy

Ben Klassen could not believe that something as evil as communism—ultimately estimated as responsible for more than eighty million deaths[1]—could be a random act. But because he would not believe in the existence of spiritual forces ("spooks in the sky," he called them), he searched for exclusively human scapegoats, never thinking that the same force behind communism might be at work in him. Through reading Adolf Hitler's *Mein Kampf,* Klassen had become convinced that a Jewish conspiracy invented communism. More personally, he believed that this conspiracy had either murdered, subjected to forced labor in Siberia, or driven from their beautiful garden-like villages and estates in the Ukraine nearly a hundred thousand of his own Mennonite people.

For this reason, Jews had always been the enemy Klassen had loved to hate. But it was not until Senator Joseph McCarthy's anticommunist hearings in 1953–54 that Klassen began to conclude that the "conspiracy" had spread to the United States. As McCarthy looked for Communists around every corner, Klassen theorized that Jews secretly controlled the nation's finance, media, and government and were behind the spread of communism.[2] He also claimed that when McCarthy went to the hospital with a severe cold (elsewhere he says flu[3]), the Jews injected the senator with hepatitis to get him out of their way.[4]

Richard H. Rovere, however, in his definitive work, *Senator Joe McCarthy,* says that as a result of the humiliation McCarthy earned in a Senate censure (voted 67–22), he began drinking heavily. Sometimes he would be drunk for days. He was frequently hospitalized and died from alcohol-induced cirrhosis on May 2, 1957, at the Naval Medical Center in Bethesda.[5]

• • •

Gullible to any supposed evidence of a worldwide Jewish conspiracy, Klassen readily latched on to the paranoid, racist propaganda known as *The Protocols of the Learned Elders of Zion.* "These constitute the secret program of the inner circle of the powerful Jewish insiders that rule the world," he said. "In no event were they ever to be seen by the eyes of the Gentiles."[6]

The booklet, which became the most notorious and vicious political forgery of modern times, was not, however, the secret minutes of some conspiratorial Jewish conclave. In fact, there never was an organization such as The Elders of Zion or The Wise Men of Zion. Originally, Serge Nilus, a non-Jew and little-known czarist official in Moscow, copied forty-two pages from an 1858 French novel, *Dialogues of Hell* by Maurice Joly, an anti-Semite and descendant of an old French Catholic family. Nilus republished the excerpt in 1905 as authentic for the Russian Okhrana—or czarist secret police—to incite animosity *against* Jews. Nilus edited several editions of the Protocols, each with a different account of how he "discovered" the document. In the 1911 edition, he claimed it was stolen from a nonexistent Zionist headquarters in France. In another, the document had supposedly been read at the First Zionist Congress in Basel, Switzerland.[7]

After the Russian Revolution in 1917, frustrated supporters of the ousted czar rescued the document from obscurity to discredit the Bolsheviks, claiming the Protocols proved that the revolution had been part of a Jewish plot to enslave the world through a Judeo-communist conspiracy. But years later Stalin used the same Protocols claiming Russian Jews were *against* the Revolution. Obviously, if the Protocols were true, they couldn't have been both pro- and anticommunist.

Hitler, of course, made much of the document and had it translated into many languages. Even American automotive manufacturer Henry Ford, in his series "The International Jew," included the Protocols, circulating a half million copies. But it was not long before Ford discovered that he had been deceived. He immediately halted distribution and publicly apologized. "I confess that I am deeply mortified that this journal…has been made the medium for resurrecting exploded fictions, for giving currency to the so-called *Protocols of the Wise Men of Zion,* which have been demonstrated, as I learn, to be gross forgeries," he wrote on June 30, 1927. "I deem it to be my duty as an honorable man to make amends for the wrong done to the Jews as fellowmen and brothers by asking their forgiveness for the harm that I have unintentionally committed, by retracting so far as lies within my power the offensive charges laid at their door by these publications, and by giving them the unqualified assurance that henceforth they may look to me for friendship and good will."[8]

Still, Hitler continued to circulate the Protocols under the imprimatur of Ford, and Klassen later appealed to it extensively in writing *The White Man's Bible* without honoring the fact that Ford had repudiated his mistakes.[9]

Since then, actual court cases[10] and many other authorities have declared the Protocols forgeries, including an investigation by the U.S. Senate Judiciary Committee. Nevertheless, to Klassen the Protocols were proof of a conspiracy in which he had already chosen to believe. He had come across "secret plans" that proved his theories! He couldn't let go of the idea, regardless of the evidence.

Klassen felt certain that there had to be someone around who understood the world as he saw it. With Joe McCarthy gone, he turned to Robert Welch. In the early 1960s, no organization in the United States was more outspoken against communists than Welch's John Birch Society.

Klassen sold his Pompano Beach real estate office to devote himself practically full time to the John Birch Society and was named the chairman of their Fact Finders Forum. This was the era of "Barry Goldwater for President" and a little book by John Stormer called *None Dare Call It Treason.* Soon Klassen became the south Florida distributor for this anticommunist broadside; proceeds from the eighty thousand copies that passed through his garage were contributed to the Goldwater campaign.

When Goldwater lost the election to Lyndon Johnson, Klassen explained by contending that Goldwater had deliberately thrown the election in order to discredit the conservative movement. "…although he is only a half Jew," Klassen wrote, "…underneath his phony conservative veneer, his true loyalty lies with the Jewish cause."[11]

But Klassen did not abandon politics. Campaigning against busing and the involvement of the federal government in state matters, he was elected to the Florida state legislature in 1965. However, in 1967 after the U.S. Supreme Court ordered Florida reapportioned to give "one man, one vote," Klassen lost his political base in Broward County. He speculated that Jewish leaders had engineered the reapportionment in order to put forth candidates they could control, thereby strengthening their legislative power base.[12] Later that year Klassen ran unsuccessfully for state senator.

While this ended his personal political career, Klassen's way of dealing with adversity was now ballooning into paranoia: He began to suspect that *anyone* who opposed or disagreed with him must be part of the worldwide Jewish conspiracy.

● ● ●

Klassen's daughter, Kim, who was a teenager at this time, remembers that her father "was an integral part of the Calvary Baptist Church of Pompano."[13] She recalls this as a comforting memory of her father's goodwill. Perhaps she and her mother, Henrie, wished Klassen had a different spiritual outlook and tried to get him to go to church. But Klassen has reflected that he had never wanted to go to Calvary Baptist and that he regarded the entire church scene and the Christian faith as "garbage."[14]

Klassen soon took a harder look at the John Birch Society. No matter how conservative it appeared, its founder, Robert Welch, scrupulously avoided any mention of Jewish "participation" in the communist conspiracy. At first Klassen speculated that maybe Welch had found a better way of exposing communism—a backdoor approach, so to speak.

Then Klassen attended the 1969 Fourth of July John Birch Society "God and Country Rally" in Boston. To his shock, the members of the band Welch had selected to entertain the participants were all black! When Klassen regained his composure, he concluded with disgust that the John

Birch Society was also a phony conspiracy.[15] Klassen had become convinced that the Jewish "conspiracy to destroy the white race" included diluting the white gene pool. Therefore, he was against all race mixing—from slavery (which he claimed Jews had engineered) to social fraternization—because he believed it inevitably led to miscegenation. He wrote that blacks were "absolute poison" to a white society.[16]

When he returned to Florida, Klassen began inviting various leaders of the John Birch Society in south Florida to his small newly-opened bookstore for one-on-one meetings. The first was Jim Cochrane.

"Jim," Klassen asked, "why does the Society protect the Jews?"

According to Klassen, that was the last time he ever saw Cochrane.

Next he grilled the Society's coordinator for all of south Florida. "Why does the Society protect the Jews?"

Sweating profusely, the coordinator lit another cigarette off the butt of his previous one. "Listen," he said, "we all know it's the Jews. Welch knows it's the Jews, and so does just about every member of the Society. If we went against the Jews we would be labeled anti-Semitic, and that would be the end of the Society."

"What about our credo, 'The truth is our only weapon'?" Klassen asked.

When the coordinator failed to give him a satisfactory answer, Klassen concluded, "The Birch Society was running interference for the Jews, all the while pointing the finger at the Communists, while the Birch Society itself was a part of the Jewish conspiracy."[17]

Klassen wrote a scathing resignation letter, charging the Society with being a hoax and a fraud set up by the Jews themselves.

• • •

In 1963, Governor George Wallace had attracted Klassen's attention when he personally blocked the door of the University of Alabama to black students and proclaimed, "Segregation today! Segregation tomorrow! Segregation forever!" When Wallace sought the U.S. presidency in 1968 as the candidate for the American Independent Party, running on "antidesegregation" issues, respect for law and order, and freedom from excessive federal control, Klassen jumped aboard the Wallace train.

As a means of supporting the Wallace campaign, Klassen established a Florida chapter of the racist Citizens Councils of America, which was headquartered in Jackson, Mississippi. He made headlines for himself and the Wallace campaign by being elected vice chairman of the state committee supporting Wallace and by staging a number of pro-Wallace rallies, including one organized jointly with the Ku Klux Klan. But he soon became impatient—and suspicious—of the poor organization in the new party.

By this time Klassen had developed his technique for determining whether an individual or organization was a front for the Jewish "conspiracy." He would raise the subject of Jewish involvement in the rise of communism, and if they didn't immediately agree that the Jews were behind it all, he would conclude that they were part of the conspiracy.

Klassen flew to Montgomery, Alabama, and confronted Wallace's national campaign manager with the question of Jewish involvement in the rise of communism. Thinking Klassen was accusing the American Independent Party of racism and anti-Semitism, the campaign manager quickly volunteered that that couldn't be so, because he was a Jew himself.[18] Bingo!

That encounter went so easily, Klassen decided to see how Dr. Medford Evans, one of the most prominent officials in both the John Birch Society and the Citizens Councils, might respond. The day after Evans spoke at a banquet of two hundred faithful supporters of Wallace, Klassen sat down for coffee with him and zeroed in on "the question."

"So, Dr. Evans, what do you make of the Jewish involvement in the worldwide Communist conspiracy and our current, so-called civil rights movement?"

"Well, it may be that the Jews once had control of the Communist regime in Russia, but they're out now. In my opinion, the Russians control the Communist Party."

That was enough for Klassen. As far as he was concerned, Evans's answer disqualified both organizations.[19]

By this means—no matter how radically right-wing a person or group was—Klassen rejected the John Birch Society, the Citizens Councils, the American Independent Party, and even George Wallace. In addition Klassen researched the Ku Klux Klan, Matt Koehl's Nazi Party, Gerald L. K. Smith's Christian Nationalist Crusade, and the National States Rights Party. Either because of supposed Jewish control or inadequate racism, none of these groups—no matter how radical—met Klassen's requirements.

What could he do but start his own organization? He called it the Nationalist White Party, and it received a charter from the state of Florida in November 1970.

12

The Decision

Ricky Byrdsong hated to say good-bye again to his mother and sister as they milled around Atlanta International Airport, waiting to see him off for his second year at Pratt Community College. He was excited to be going back—after all, he had made All-Conference his first year; his second season ought to be even better—but it meant not seeing Sherialyn until Christmas. And no Rollie to room with this year. Rollie Lewis had enrolled at DeKalb Community College in Decatur, Georgia, closer to home.

It was going to be a long year.

"Mom! Promise you and Cia will try to come for Thanksgiving, all right?"

Other college-bound students were saying good-bye to gum-chewing younger siblings and mothers dabbing their eyes. One lanky young man, though, looked kind of familiar.

"Don't I know you?" Ricky jabbed a friendly finger in his direction, guessing the other boy's height at six feet.

He got a friendly grin. "I know *you*. You're Ricky Byrdsong, forward starter for Frederick Douglass." The young man stuck out his hand. "Carlton Evans, from Macon." He grinned. "We beat you at state two years in a row."

Ricky smacked his forehead. "Man! You really know how to hurt a guy. Wait a minute…Carlton Evans. *Carlton Evans?* You're my new roommate!"

Carlton grinned again. "Yeah. I met Coach Larry Cart at the Boston Shootout last spring. Told me I should go to Pratt. Said you were there. So I applied. Then I got this letter saying my roommate was Ricky Byrdsong."

Ricky threw back his head and laughed. "Shoulda known."

The two new friends talked on the plane all the way to Wichita, where Coach Lewis picked them up. Then they talked all the way to Pratt as the car rolled past miles of harvested fields, family farms, and dairy cows.

"Wait a minute!" Carlton cried at one point. "Did I just see a herd of *buffalo?*"

Coach Lewis chuckled. "Oh yeah. This land right here is a buffalo refuge."

By the time the two high school rivals were choosing beds in their assigned room in Novotny Hall, Carlton knew all about Ricky's mom getting married again; how Ricky scared Marcia to death the one time he tried to cut classes; and that he had a girlfriend named Sherialyn Kelley who was in her second year of pre-med at the University of Pennsylvania and was probably the prettiest girl in the whole world, an awesome basketball player, and smart, too. Carlton noticed that Ricky talked about Sherialyn a *lot.*

It didn't take long for Carlton to realize that Ricky had made a lot of friends at Pratt Community College. Ricky had the habit of stopping and talking to everybody he met, even when he was hurrying to class. But he didn't forget his old friends, either, and they didn't forget him.

"Hey, Ricky," said Cordy Glen just a few weeks into their second fall term. "Want a job at Gibson's Discount Center? Jerry McCalla, the manager, is a Beavers fan—you probably saw him at our games last year. You'll get along great. I recommended you to him."

Cordy was right. Ricky Byrdsong and Jerry McCalla hit it off right away. "Say, Rick," Jerry said soon after Ricky started work as a stock boy at Gibson's, "why don't you come to church with us on Sunday and then come over to the house for dinner?"

A home-cooked meal? No way was Ricky going to turn down that invitation. Going to church was an interesting experience though. The McCallas attended the Church of the Nazarene—not anything like Second Mount Vernon Baptist Church, which Ricky had attended from time to time back in Atlanta. The music was different too. The congregation sang out of the Nazarene hymnal, and Ricky had never heard some of the hymns before. But the McCalla family seemed like people who took their faith seriously. They weren't just "Sunday Christians" who cussed a blue streak on Monday. Ricky liked that.

Not to mention that Kathy McCalla was a great cook.

•   •   •

"Carlton!" Ricky snatched the textbook out of his roommate's hands. "University of Oklahoma is playing Kansas State at Manhattan, Kansas. I gotta go see that game! Come on, I want you to go with me."

Carlton hesitated. "Ricky, you know I'm broke."

Ricky rolled his eyes then pulled a five-dollar bill out of his pocket. "See this, Carlton? Any time I have five dollars, *you* have at least two-fifty. So don't *ever* tell me you're broke."

That weekend, Ricky covered Carlton's expenses—bus fare, food, and overnight accommodations. And when they got back, he went to see Jerry McCalla. "Do you think you could get Carlton a job at Gibson's too?" Soon Jerry was picking up both boys at the campus and taking them into town to Gibson's.

Sunday church and dinner at the McCalla household became a regular habit. *That* was different for Ricky. Sunday had usually been the day he slept in. But it was great having a family so far away from home. Soon he was bringing Carlton with him, along with his dirty clothes to stick in the washer while he whipped Jerry at pool in the basement or horsed around with the four McCalla kids. Randy and Ryan, ages ten and eight, liked to play touch football with the college guys. Andrea, age five, insisted on sitting on "Byrd's" lap during church. (Later that year she announced to her kindergarten teacher, "I have five brothers. My two big brothers are black.")

And then there was Rodney, age three—otherwise known as Moose. Ricky laughed out loud when he heard the nickname. "You're right! That's one big kid!"

•   •   •

November had dressed Kansas in shades of gold when Ricky arrived at the McCalla household one Sunday. "I got a call from Sherialyn. She told me that she got saved—decided to became a Christian." He looked a little anxious. What did that mean, exactly? What would it mean for their relationship?

So Ricky and the McCallas talked about God and salvation and what it meant to live a life of faith. The McCallas were delighted. They hadn't met Sherialyn Kelley yet, but she seemed like a young woman with her priorities straight.

Another letter had Ricky crowing with excitement. "My mom and Marcia are coming Thanksgiving weekend. But I'll be playing in the tournament in Dodge City. Do you think you could—?"

"Tell you what. We'll pick them up and bring them to the game," said Kathy. "You write right back and tell them they're invited to stay at our house after the tournament!"

Thanksgiving weekend was like a family reunion. The McCallas picked up Mary and Marcia at the Wichita airport and drove them to Dodge City to see Ricky play. Eager for his mother to see his college campus, Ricky talked his mother into returning to Pratt with the McCallas to spend a night and enjoy Kathy's hospitality.

The visit from his mom and sister was over all too soon. But the McCallas practically adopted Ricky and Carlton that year, even buying them a used car so they could get to work and to church without needing a ride from Jerry. The boys even began calling Kathy and Jerry "Mom" and "Dad."

But as the months went by and the neighbors noticed the comings and goings at the McCalla household, tongues started wagging. Cheering black athletes on the basketball court was one thing, but bringing them into your home, in this neighborhood…

Jerry McCalla knew there were some things Pratt wasn't ready for. He sat down with Ricky and Carlton for a serious talk. "Don't get me wrong, but take my advice: Don't date the white girls. It could cause a whole lot of trouble for you, for the school, for everybody." Ricky and Carlton looked at each other. "I'm not talking a moral issue here," Jerry added. "Just common sense."

Ricky's answer was quick. "Don't worry about it, Dad. I'm not planning on dating *any* other girl, because I wouldn't want to hurt Sherialyn."

Sherialyn. He got a letter from her several times a week. Ricky often arrived at the McCallas' house waving the latest. "Mom! Mom! Look at the Bible verse Sherialyn sent me. She always knows just what I need to hear." Sherialyn had been steeping herself in Bible study and often shared with Ricky what she was learning. One of her favorite verses was Jeremiah 29:11: " 'For I know the plans I have for you,' declares the LORD, 'plans to prosper you and not to harm you, plans to give you hope and a future.' "

She knew Ricky was anxious about his future. Pratt was only a two-year program and this was his last semester. What was he going to do now?

• • •

Snow was still on the ground, but spring was definitely strewing signs around campus as the Beavers boarded the team bus for a Jayhawks conference game. Coach Lewis counted heads; two team members were missing! A few minutes later the offenders ran up, mumbling something about not being able to find their equipment.

But Coach Lewis was on a short fuse. He let loose all the four-letter words he could cram into a five-minute tirade. Having said his piece, the team meekly rode to the game. As the Beavers were getting suited up in the visitors' locker room, Ricky Byrdsong said, "Could I talk to you, Coach—in private?"

Coach nodded. "What's up, Byrd?"

Ricky was polite, but he had something to say. "With all due respect, Coach, you don't allow us to curse when we're at practice or representing the school in any way. I think you ought to obey your own rule."

Coach Lewis flushed. It took him a minute to sort through the hundred and one things he *could* say. But then he nodded. "You're right, Byrd. I'll apologize to the team. And thank you for speaking to me in private."

True to his word, in his pregame pep talk, Coach Lewis admitted he'd been out of line. "I disobeyed my own rule. I owe you guys an apology."

The apology seemed to energize the team, and spirits were high as they ran out onto the floor. That night they brought home a Beavers win.

As the season wound down, spring break was fast approaching. Ricky was determined to go see Sherialyn. But he had something he wanted to do before Easter.

"Dad," he said to Jerry McCalla, "I've decided to get baptized. I want to make a public commitment to be a Christian."

It was probably a first for that Church of the Nazarene, baptizing not one, but *two* young black men from Georgia. When Carlton heard Ricky was getting baptized, he decided to renew his own Christian commitment. Since the Church of the Nazarene gave candidates for baptism the option, Carlton chose to be sprinkled. But Ricky decided to get baptized the Baptist way, by immersion. All six feet six inches of him—body, soul, and spirit.

●　●　●

Carlton braced himself when Ricky returned from spring break. His roommate had gone to Pennsylvania to see Sherialyn, and Carlton knew he was going to hear "Sherialyn this" and "Sherialyn that" all day, every day, for some time.

But Ricky was given something else to think about when a recruiter from Iowa State University came to Pratt to scout Cordy Glen. That didn't surprise Ricky and Carlton. Cordy was a phenomenal basketball player. But to Ricky and Carlton's astonishment, the recruiter, Coach Dave Harshman, seemed interested in them too. "If you'd like, we'll get our head coach, Lynn Nance, down here to talk to you."

Ricky wanted to whoop. But now he had to do some fast thinking and praying. He'd been hoping for a school closer to Sherialyn. When Sherialyn heard the news, she put in her own two-cents' worth. If Iowa State offered Ricky a scholarship, she thought he should take it. If she and Ricky were supposed to be together, God would work it out.

Ricky was relieved and grateful. Sherialyn always knew the right thing to say.

Cordy turned down Iowa State for Southwestern Louisiana University. But Ricky was awed when he heard that Coach Nance was still coming to talk to him and Carlton. He asked the McCallas if the interview could be at their dining room table; he wanted Mom and Dad McCalla to be present.

The talk with Coach Nance resulted in the offer of athletic scholarships for both Ricky and Carlton—even though Carlton was only finishing his first year at Pratt. To Jerry McCalla, Nance as much as said, "I can get talent; I can teach skills. But I need more players that bring a positive attitude, loyalty to the team, and integrity to the game. That's a rarer gift."

That was how Jerry and Kathy McCalla felt about their two "adopted" sons: a rare gift.

•　•　•

"Put on your suit, Carlton."

"My suit! Why? We're not going to interview for a *job* or anything."

But Ricky was already pulling Carlton's Sunday suit out of the tiny dorm closet. "No, we're going to do something more important—thank our boosters."

Looking their debonair best, the two young men paraded up one side of Pratt's main street and down the other. Into Taylor's Print Shop. "Mr. Taylor? My name is Ricky Byrdsong, this is Carlton Evans. We want to thank you for supporting the men's basketball program at Pratt, and for cheering us on from the bleachers. Your support means a great deal to us." They shook hands warmly with Mr. Taylor, swapped a few favorite highlights from the season, then took their leave.

On to the next store or business. Polite, charming, warm, *grateful*. Members of the Beavers Booster Club couldn't help but return Ricky's big smile.

Long after the two young men had returned home to Atlanta, gone on to Iowa State, married, had careers…Pratt remembered.

• • •

Ricky already thought Sherialyn was the greatest girl in the whole world, even before she got saved. He was alternately amazed and delighted that this beautiful girl loved him. God had given him life, health, a loving family, intelligence, talent, opportunities, a wonderful girl, and a future—even though he didn't know exactly what that future held. He was grateful! He was ready to follow Jesus with Sherialyn, even if it did mean cooling their jets when he and Sherialyn were together.

But he wasn't sure he wanted to become one of those starchy church folks who were so heavenly minded they were no earthly good. All some church people seemed to talk about was not smoking, not drinking, not dancing, and not listening to "devil music." His own father was an alcoholic, so Ricky understood the problem big time. But he didn't personally think a person would go to hell for drinking a beer now and then or listening to the Four Tops.

But he had to admit Sherialyn knew her Bible better than he did. She soaked it up like bread sitting in milk. The more she read, the more excited she got about the promises of God. And memorize! He'd never been very good at memorizing. But she learned verses till they seemed imprinted on her brain. Which he liked. Many times when she shared about the latest Bible verse she'd come across, it was the perfect encouragement Ricky needed that day.

Not that he and Sherialyn had a whole lot of time to talk about their newfound faith that summer. Ricky got a summer job working on an oil rig just off the coast of New Orleans. It paid well, but it meant weeks away from home. He could think of only one solution to this long-distance romance: He had to talk Sherialyn into transferring to Iowa State.

• • •

Becoming a Christian had been an about-face for Sherialyn. Coming back to Atlanta that summer of 1976, she tried to tell people what had happened to her, but a lot of her friends just looked at her like, "Girl! What do you mean 'saved'? What do you think you've been saved *from?*"

It was true. By most people's standards, Sherialyn Kelley already had a lot going for her—looks, talent, brains, friends, and a can-do attitude. Even though her family had suffered their share of discrimination, they had never let other people's prejudices define them. No, Sherialyn Kelley was determined to go far.

The only trouble was, she hadn't figured on God. Hadn't given God any credit. Hadn't factored in what God might want to do with her life.

Last fall when she had prayed the prayer printed in the back of *The Four Spiritual Laws* booklet, she had put God at the center of her life. From that point on everything else—*everything,* even Ricky—revolved around that.

Did he understand that? He said he did. But when she was with him, sometimes it seemed like he was just the same old Ricky—goofy, fun, friendly to a fault, enjoying life. Sometimes she wondered if he had a serious bone in his body. Of course, that was one of the things that attracted her to Ricky. He was *always* laughing! He could cheer up a turkey destined for the Thanksgiving table.

She missed him while he was out on that oil rig. Not that she was bored. All her friends were home from college—Gale Clemons from the University of Georgia, Jan Chandler from Georgia Tech, Darlene King from Tuskegee—and they could always think of stuff to do together. Like running on the high school track to lose those five pounds they'd all picked up in college.

Who could know that Darlene, niece of the famous Dr. King and one of Sherialyn's best friends, would keel over while the girls were running and die right there on the track before medical aid could arrive? The autopsy said she had choked on some food she'd eaten for lunch.

Sherialyn couldn't remember the last time she had cried. But now she did. The tears just wouldn't stop. How could God let this happen? Hadn't the King family suffered enough tragedy already? Dr. King's death from an assassin's bullet had been tragic and evil. But *this!* This made no sense at all. There wasn't even anybody to blame.

But she didn't cry when she stood up to speak at Darlene's funeral. She just said everything she wished she had told Darlene before she died.

Ricky got the news and came back from his job in the Gulf in time to attend Darlene's funeral. Sherialyn didn't blame him that he didn't really know what to say. What could anyone say? But she was glad he was there.

And life had to go on. So once more she packed for college—but this year she was going *with* Ricky to Iowa State.

13

Christianity, the Ultimate Trojan Horse

Klassen's experiment in starting the Nationalist White Party quickly ran into trouble.

It wasn't that there weren't interested participants—a good number of prospects did come forward. The problem was that too many tended to be constrained by their Christian upbringing. While they may have disdained people of other races, someone would invariably object that the Bible deems everyone equal in the sight of God. Others would argue that because Jesus Christ was a Jew, or because God had told Abram "I will bless them that bless thee, and curse him that curseth thee" (Genesis 12:3, KJV), they were not comfortable opposing Jews.

"There was that damn Christianity issue raising its ugly head again!" wrote Klassen to a prospective applicant. "What the white race desperately needs is a new philosophy, in fact a new religion based upon the concepts of preserving the white race."[1]

There, he'd said it! And from there the idea grew within him like crabgrass. Wondering whether he could establish such a religion himself, Klassen decided to read the New Testament to try to determine why Christianity posed so many problems to his cause. He quickly found his answer in the book of Matthew. As he read accounts of Jesus teaching people to love their enemies, sell all they have and give to the poor, and turn the other cheek, Klassen was incredulous. "This is the kind of suicidal advice you would give your worst enemies if you wanted them to destroy themselves," he responded.

"Christianity," Klassen concluded, "was deliberately designed to enslave and destroy the white race! Who had written all this balderdash? Why, the Jews! All the apostles were Jewish. St. Paul, the most prominent writer of all, was really Saul of Tarsus, another Jew. Christ himself was a Jew."[2]

Klassen came across what he supposed was support for this insight in a biting piece of satire by Marcus Eli Ravage titled "A Real Case Against the Jews," which had originally appeared in the January (Klassen wrongly said February) 1928 issue of the *Century Magazine*. However, Klassen didn't realize—or wouldn't admit—that the article was satire. Instead, he took it as the confession of a Jew to the worldwide conspiracy theory.

Ravage was a Jew. In fact, he was the authorized biographer for the famed Rothschild family, but the article Klassen latched on to was indeed a satirical expose of how ludicrous popular anti-Semitic accusations really were. After a tongue-in-cheek overview of the conspiracy theory, Ravage wrote:

Each new [accusation] is more laughable than the last and each new excuse contradicts and annihilates the last.

Not so many years ago I used to hear that we were money-grubbers and commercial materialists; now the complaint is being whispered around that no art and no profession is safe against Jewish invasion.

We are, if you are to be believed, at once clannish and exclusive and unassimilable because we won't intermarry with you, and we are also climbers and pushers and a menace to your racial integrity.

Our standard of living is so low that we create your slums and sweated industries, and so high that we crowd you out of your best residential sections....

We are at once the founders and leading adherents of capitalism and the chief perpetrators of the rebellion against capitalism.

Surely, history has nothing like us for versatility!...

If you really are serious when you talk of Jewish plots, may I not direct your attention to one worth talking about? What use is it wasting words on the alleged control of your public opinion by Jewish financiers, newspaper owners, and movie magnates, when you might as well justly accuse us of the proved control of your whole civilization by the Jewish Gospels?...

Look back a little and see what has happened. Nineteen hundred years ago you were an innocent, care-free, pagan race. You worshipped countless gods and goddesses, the spirits of the air, of the running streams and of the woodland. You took unblushing pride in the glory of your naked bodies. You carved images of your gods and of the tantalizing human figure. You delighted in the combats of the field, the arena and the battle-ground. War and slavery were fixed institutions in your systems....

But we did not leave you alone. We took you in hand and pulled down the beautiful and generous structure you had reared, and changed the whole course of your history. We conquered you...without armies, without bullets, without blood or turmoil, without force of any kind....

This was the beginning of our dominance in your world....

Is it any wonder you resent us? We have put a clog upon your progress. We have imposed upon you an alien book and an alien faith which you cannot swallow or digest, which is at cross-purposes with your native spirit, which keeps you everlastingly ill-at-ease, and which you lack the spirit either to reject or to accept in full.... You Christians have never become Christianized. To that extent we have failed with you. But we have forever spoiled the fun of paganism for you.

So why should you not resent us?[3]

Klassen puzzled over why Ravage would "spill the beans" this way,[4] but, as though he had never taken a high school—let alone a college—literature course and could not recognize satire when he saw it, Klassen said, "This audacious Jew openly bragged how cleverly the cunning Jew...conspired a means to torpedo the great Roman Empire by feeding it a self-destructive new religion, namely Christianity."[5]

No literary devices for Klassen, this was the last piece of proof he needed to complete his paranoid mosaic. First, Hitler had "identified" for him that it was the Jews who had launched communism, destroying his people's beautiful garden in the Ukraine. Then the Protocols had "revealed" that the Jews actually had a much larger plan, a plan to rule the whole world. And now Klassen had "discovered" how they intended to pull it off: by destroying the white race through Christianity!

Klassen also latched on to the Jewish term *goy* (or *goyim*), proclaiming it the Jewish word for cattle. Jews wanted to enslave *goyim* for their own gain, he believed, "but the most treacherous and deadly essence of that program was their obsession for the mongrelization and genocide of the white race.... I felt I had made as much of a major breakthrough as if I had discovered a new world."[6]

Undoubtedly Klassen would have been disappointed if he had asked someone who knew Hebrew what *goy* really meant, or even if he had checked a Hebrew-English lexicon or Bible concordance. He would have discovered several terms for cattle or beasts, none of which are *goy* or *goyim*. *Goy* simply means nation. In common usage *goy* came to mean a Gentile, and *goyim*, the Gentile nations. However, it is also used in both the Talmud and the Torah to refer to the Jewish nation as in Exodus 33:13, "This nation is your people."

Going point by point through the Sermon on the Mount and basic Christian doctrines, Klassen attempted to talk like an authority to reveal Christianity as ridiculous and suicidal. His efforts may persuade the biblically illiterate, but under closer inspection they are full of amateur errors and illogical conclusions.* To drive home his point, he parodied Jesus' instruction to "Love your enemies, do good to those who hate you" (Luke 6:27) by declaring, "Hate your enemies; destroy your enemies."[7]

Before Klassen was finished, he not only blamed the Jews for Chris-

---

* Review Klassen's errors on the Internet at http://www.daveneta.com/no-random-act/christianity.

tianity but also for every war and social tension in the world that involved white people. Everything from bringing African slaves to America (to make money for themselves and to encourage racial intermarriage, thereby destroying the white race), the Civil War (to destroy the white aristocracy and wealth in the South, to force both the North and South to borrow from them, and to kill whites both North and South), and the civil rights movement (to encourage racial intermarriage).[8]

On one hand, Klassen's belief that a sinister plot was afoot in the world could be deemed accurate. Any alert observer might suspect that coordinated forces are hell-bent to confuse personal identity, destroy the family, corrupt children, exploit the powerless, wreck the economy, manipulate governments, divide peoples, and foment wars. But it was not the Jews who were responsible for such a worldwide, history-long conspiracy, and it is not the white race but all humanity, including the Jewish people, that is at risk from those same forces. However, having rejected all possibility of higher powers, both good and evil, Klassen could not see beyond the mortal players. And even concerning them he preferred gross fabrications that fit his theories rather than the truth. In doing so he tended to prove the proverb: "There is a way that seems right to a man, but in the end it leads to death" (Proverbs 14:12).

14

Salt and Pepper

Coach Lynn Nance glanced up at the clock in his new office. Nine o'clock and the secretary *still* hadn't arrived. She better have a good excuse!

The ex-FBI agent and former assistant coach of the high-powered men's basketball team at the University of Kentucky was still settling into his new job as head coach at Iowa State University. There were days when he wondered why he'd taken this job. The team had won only two games the previous season. *Two games!* The players he'd inherited were a sullen lot. One of his players was in jail on a rape charge. Another tough-talking player bragged that the former coach had said, "If I ever have to walk around a big city, I want you for my bodyguard."

Nance was curious. What made this bag of wind so "tough"? A little digging turned up a felony charge for assaulting a Meter Maid. Nance snorted. Yeah, he'd want this turkey for his bodyguard, too, if he planned on fighting *girls*.

Where *was* that secretary?

The young woman finally sauntered in around ten, cracking gum and dumping her purse in the drawer of the desk. "Where have you been?" Nance snapped.

The girl threw him a look. "This is the time I always come in."

"*Used* to come in. I want you here at eight o'clock sharp tomorrow morning."

The gum-chewing stopped, and her jaw went slack, as if she didn't understand "eight o'clock." Coach Nance's blood was nearing the boiling point, but he decided to cut to the chase. "I'd like you to take a letter."

Another blank look. "I don't take shorthand." Her tone of voice was I-don't-do-windows.

By this time Coach Nance wanted to tear his hair out—but he had to be content with stomping back into his office, since he wore a military-style buzz cut, left over from his FBI days. He glared out the door from time to time as the girl hunted and pecked on the typewriter.

Things were going to change around here, *big time.*

Coach Nance clung to the one bright spot in this otherwise dismal excuse for a basketball program. The new recruits. When he took the job, he knew he needed new players badly—fresh blood to turn the team around. Sure, he wanted talent. But even more than talent, he wanted players who weren't always tripping over their own egos. Team players. Players who were teachable. Players who would do whatever it took for the team to win. Players who followed the rules.

Like Ricky Byrdsong and Carlton Evans from Atlanta and Macon, Georgia. The southern black high schools had a good pool of talent largely under-fished by the bigger universities. Carlton was only six feet—not especially tall for a basketball player—but he was a good, solid player. He would make a good starter, even though he was only a sophomore. And Byrdsong. At six-six, his talent was a little more unpolished, but he had good potential. And from what the coach at Pratt had said, Byrdsong was a 100 percent guy, there for the team even when he was on the bench. And that smile! Didn't his face muscles ever get tired?

At one of his daily staff meetings, Nance said, "Evans and Byrdsong. Good recruits. They're going to help turn this team around."

Assistant coach Rick Samuels looked worried. "Last year's players don't like 'em."

Coach Nance threw back his head and laughed. "That sorry lot? Now *that's* a good sign!"

• • •

Ricky thought he'd died and gone to heaven. He had an athletic scholarship to a major university. He was rooming with Carlton Evans again.

And Sherialyn had transferred to Iowa State so they could be near each other.

That was before he turned out for preseason practice with Coach Lynn Nance. By the end of the first day, there was no heaven. He just thought he'd died.

Practice started at 5:30 A.M. The thirty-five wannabes hit the field to run 220-yard dashes until players were dropping like flies. Then they retired to the gym to lift weights until their muscles were screaming for mercy. They finally hit the basketball court to practice basics—dribbling, passing, shooting, rebounding. Back out in the fresh air to run more 220s. Then back to the weight room to pump more iron.

By the time they hit the showers, an undercurrent crackled up and down the locker room. "What's this gotta do with basketball?" "What's Nance think he runnin', boot camp?" "He's tryin' to kill us."

Coach Nance walked in, all six-foot-five of him. The grumbling stopped. The players just stared at the new head coach.

"What's the matter?" Nance raised his eyebrows in surprise. "I thought you guys said you loved this game."

"We do, Coach. We do!" Ricky blurted. Heads nodded; a few more affirmative mumbles.

"Then let's get one thing straight." Nance's steely blue eyes looked at each and every player. "Loving the game is not hearing the fans scream when you score a point. It's not signing autographs. It's not traveling to Hawaii to play a tournament game." The room was void of sound except the *drip, drip* from a leaky shower and Nance's big voice. "Loving the game is being willing to do *whatever it takes* to become a successful team. And right now that means getting in shape. It means doing whatever I say. Because I'm the dictator around here. And I say, if you want to be on this team, you better be here at 5:30 tomorrow morning!"

That night Ricky was too tired to do anything but go to bed. Too tired to see Sherialyn. Too tired to eat.

"Whaddya think, Byrd?" Carlton gingerly lowered his aching body onto his bed. "Gonna stick with it?"

Ricky closed his eyes. It sure would be nice to sleep-in tomorrow, maybe see Sherialyn. But if he did...

What was he *thinking?* If he didn't show up at practice, he'd lose his scholarship. If he lost his scholarship, he'd have to quit school and go back home. What would he say to his mother—who had worked two shifts at the Nabisco factory year after year so he and Marcia could have a decent home and clothes on their backs and food on the table. *"I'm sorry, Mama. It was just too hard."*

Ricky set his alarm for 4:45.

By 5:30 the next morning, he and Carlton were in the locker room. But that morning only seventeen players showed up. Seventeen players willing to do whatever it took.

Coach Nance strode into the locker room and looked around. "Good," he growled. And smiled.

• • •

The Iowa State Cyclones were on the road. Ricky grabbed his duffel from the pile of luggage being dumped from the back of the school van and headed into the airport.

Just then he heard Coach Nance's machine-gun voice spraying the team. "Off with those caps! You know the rule: No caps worn inside."

No caps. In the *airport?* Dutifully, Ricky and most of the other team members snatched off their athletic caps. But a couple of the younger black players with X hats—a salute to Malcolm X—made no effort to remove them.

"Did you hear me? Off!"

Ricky caught the look in the players' eyes. *You made up that stupid rule, Coach, to keep us from wearing our sign of black power. You want to rob us of our identity.* As one of only two juniors on the newly reorganized team (no seniors—they'd all dropped out under the no-nonsense coach), Ricky casually walked over and spoke in an undertone to the rebellion. "Hey! Coach Nance doesn't know an X from a Z. He's not picking on you. That cap could say 'Mickey Mouse,' and he'd still want it off."

Reluctantly the players took off the caps.

On the plane, Ricky lowered himself into a seat beside Steve Burgason, the other junior. White guy, six-six. Local boy from Ames. One of the few left over from Iowa State's pathetic last two years. He was captain of the team and, like Ricky, a new Christian.

"Might fit in these seats if they took out every other row," Ricky groused.

Steve laughed. "Nah, Byrd. They'd also have to cut a hole in the roof to make room for your Afro."

Carlton, sitting across the aisle, guffawed. The good-natured insults and banter bounced all around the plane, and the tension was broken. But after a while Ricky got pensive.

"Say, Burgie, I'm worried about my girl, Sherialyn."

"The Rock? Can't imagine anything shaking her up. That girl knows her own mind."

Ricky half-smiled at Steve's nickname for Sherialyn. Once she'd made the decision to become a Christian, Sherialyn never wavered.

"Yeah, I know. But transferring has been kinda tough on her. Seems really depressed—and that's just not like Sherialyn."

Carlton leaned into the conversation. "Yeah, but didn't her friend Darlene die real sudden last summer?"

Ricky nodded and filled Steve in on the details of Darlene King's death.

"Sherialyn's gonna be all right, Byrd," Carlton cut in. "She's got a strong faith. If she keeps reading the Bible like she does, she's gonna find her way."

Ricky thought about it. "Yeah, you're right." Ricky's grin found its way back between his ears. "Say, you guys wanna come to church with us? Sherialyn and I have been going over to Grand Avenue Baptist. Pastor's name is Tom Nesbitt. White guy, but he can preach!" Ricky's eyes danced. "Even Coach Nance goes to church there."

● ● ●

Sherialyn sat in the library, her third-year biology textbook shoved to one side. The tall windows sent long fingers of sunshine dancing across the table, beckoning students out into the fresh warmth of spring. Sherialyn didn't notice. To the casual observer, she looked like she wasn't doing anything. The tall, slender girl with the neat Afro stared straight ahead. Her hands, resting on an open notebook, were still.

But her mind was alert, sorting through the thoughts that plagued her. Since Darlene's death, she was convinced that the gift of life was not meant to be wasted. She still could make no sense of Darlene's death, but the loss of her friend had brought home a basic truth: God gives each person only a certain amount of time on this earth. He created each person with certain gifts and abilities and a calling.

What was *her* destiny? She was in her third year of pre-med. Everybody oohed and aahed whenever she said pre-med. Her family was certainly proud of her: "Our girl's going to be a *doctor*." So why was she so ambivalent? She was coming to realize that she was studying to be a doctor because she *could*—not because she had any passion for medicine. If she and Ricky got married, how would being a doctor fit with that? What did she want to do and be? She loved sports, she loved working with kids. What she really would like to do was *teach*. But was it too late? What would happen if she switched her major at this point?

Sherialyn reached for a pen, breaking her reverie. At the top of the paper in front of her she wrote PRO on one side and CON on the other. Then she began to list the reasons for and against changing her major to education.

She'd been writing for some time when a shadow fell across her page. A familiar presence dropped into the chair next to her.

"Hey, Ricky. Practice over?" He was grinning ear to ear. Just grinning.

"What?" Sometimes he could be so annoying.

"Guess who the team just elected co-captains for next year?"

She stared at him. *"You?"*

"Yep. Me and Steve Burgason."

Sherialyn was surprised. Steve and Ricky were becoming thick as thieves, even though they'd just met that year. Even made her feel left out at times. The two juniors worked out together, practiced together, went out to Wendy's and stuffed themselves on burgers together. Steve was a nice guy, though—even if he did call her "the Rock." He was a new Christian, like herself and Ricky. He'd been coming to church with them at Grand Avenue. And he *did* have a sense of humor—how would he survive knowing Ricky Byrdsong if he didn't?

She remembered what Ricky had said to Steve after one game. "Man, Burgie! You've got white man's disease!"

"I've got *what?*"

"White man's disease! You're slow, and you can't jump!"

For some reason that had tickled Steve's funny bone. At least both players could admit they were several notches below star quality. But one thing she had to say for both of them: None of the other players measured up when it came to hustle on the court, maybe because they didn't have anything to lose. So why not go all-out?

"Really. Co-captains?" Sherialyn was pleased.

"Yeah. Salt and Pepper—that's us." Ricky laughed, then leaned over and peered at her paper. "What's that?"

She hesitated then slid the paper toward him. "I've been doing some thinking about what I want to do with my life."

•   •   •

As co-captains of the team the next fall, Ricky and Steve did work together like salt and pepper. Roughly half the team was white, half black. The team took its cues from the co-captains and put aside petty rivalries. Steve and Ricky started praying together before games; Carlton often joined them. "Lord, help us to play our best tonight. Protect everyone from serious injuries. Win or lose, we're going to give it everything we've got for the glory of God." Other players started to hang around respectfully during this prayer.

It wasn't clear who had the idea first, but the pregame prayer soon became a Bible study on Sunday nights. Half the men's basketball team—Christian and non-Christian—hunkered into the meeting room at Iowa State's Coliseum on Sunday nights. They tackled the gospel of John. Neither

Ricky nor Steve had had any Bible training. They just let God's Word speak for itself and discussed how what they read applied to their lives on the campus and on the basketball court.

Not that the hijinks ever slowed down. When the Cyclones went to Kansas State for the Christmas tournament their senior year, Ricky and Steve staged a "mock media interview" between games. Dressed in creased slacks, shirt, tie, and sport coat, Burgason could easily pass as an eager-beaver journalist.

Burgason: "Folks, we've got one of the pro scouts for the Seattle Super Sonics here, with his eye on the Big Eight Conference. Coach, what kind of talent do you see at the tournament?" He thrust the hand-held tape recorder he'd gotten as a Christmas present at Ricky's deadpan face.

Byrdsong: "Lots of talent, lots of talent. Some real promising players. Darnell Valentine from University of Kansas, Orlando Blackman from Kansas State…no doubt they'll be hearing from the pros. But there are two players who are standouts, in my opinion. The Cyclones co-captains, Burgason and Byrdsong—now *that's* talent. For superb shooting, ruggedness on the court, rebounding skills—those two are definitely on top of the list in my…whoa! Look at those legs! Hoo, boy. Oh! Where was I? Got distracted by one of the fans…oh, yes! Burgason and Byrdsong…"

Everyone *knew* it was a crackup. Burgason and Byrdsong? Recruited for the pros? Nobody believed *that!* But that didn't stop the local sports columns from carrying stories about that infamous "radio interview" after the tournament.

•   •   •

Graduation was rushing upon them. Coach Nance called his co-captains into his office. "I'd like you two to be my graduate assistant coaches next year. What do you say?"

Steve had a ready answer. "Thanks, Coach, but I've already signed up with the Fellowship of Christian Athletes. I'd like to be involved in some kind of Christian ministry, and this seems to fit."

Nance nodded, spreading his fingers on both hands and tapping them together. "What about you, Byrd?"

For once, Ricky was speechless. Coach with Coach Nance? That was a dream come true! He'd been thinking about his future a lot, and what he wanted to do was becoming crystal clear.

He wanted to marry Sherialyn.

He wanted to have kids.

And he wanted to coach.

15

Nature's Eternal Religion: Hate

To create a new religion that might seduce adherents from an old religion, Ben Klassen, either consciously or unconsciously, included many familiar elements that would help smooth the conversion of quasi-Christians:

- Holy scriptures: *The White Man's Bible*
- A name for the new religion: "Creativity"
- Commandments: sixteen rather than ten
- A golden rule: "What is good for the White Race is the highest virtue; what is bad for the White Race is the ultimate sin."
- An object of worship: the white race, identified not only as "nature's finest" but also as the supreme "Creator"
- A revered prophet or founder: Ben Klassen
- A church: the Church of the Creator (COTC), later called World Church of the Creator (WCOTC)
- "Conversion" and "salvation" articulated in *Nature's Eternal Religion*
- A clergy, including the Pontifex Maximus (the supreme leader), the *Hasta Primus* (Latin for "spearhead," first assistant to the P.M.), and ordained ministers with the title of reverend
- A wedding ceremony with elements and language familiar to Christian ears
- An infant initiation rite reminiscent of baptism or baby dedication: The Creator Child Pledging Ceremony

- A confirmation or membership rite: The Ceremony of Confirmation of Loyalty
- Dietary and lifestyle regulations: Salubrious Living
- A new calendar dated from *Incepto de Creativitat* (the Inception of Creativity, 1973) rather than the birth of Christ. Years after that are *Anno de Creativitat,* hence, for the COTC, the millennium was 27 A.C.
- Special holidays honoring the birth of Klassen, the inception of Creativity, and Martyr's Day
- Reference to members as brother and sister

None of this borrowing was very creative for someone who fancied himself a creator. But in addition to providing a familiar and comfortable context for converts, it served another purpose. It provided a legal buffer for his organization's operations. The First Amendment to the U.S. Constitution provides powerful protections not only for free speech but also for the free exercise of religion—any religion.

Klassen's own statements concerning his motivation for starting Creativity show that it was an entirely utilitarian move. He recognized no personal need for *any* religion, not even the one he started. He was simply looking for a means to energize white people to look to their own interests above those of the rest of the world. Because Christianity taught its followers to love everyone and hate no one, he needed a way to counteract that influence. He believed in Creativity only insofar as it incorporated his personal philosophy and offered a mechanism for combating Christianity. He did not believe in Creativity in the way most prophets or priests of other religions believe in or worship some being, spirit, or entity other than and greater than themselves. But that made no difference. The Supreme Court had made it clear that the U.S. government could not define what is or is not a legitimate religion.

In the years that followed, to help sell the new religion to the white race, Klassen and others in the movement intuitively embraced as many traditionally conservative values as possible—as long as they were compatible with their racial philosophy.

- In conjunction with their suspicion of government intrusion, they became ardent advocates of homeschooling.
- Except in the event of impregnation by someone from a "mud race," they strongly opposed abortion. Lisa Turner, the leader of the Women's Frontier wrote, "The killing of a healthy white child through abortion is the ultimate sin against our race and against nature and any white woman who commits the crime of abortion is a race traitor of the highest order."[1]
- They opposed all sexual deviance—homosexuality, pornography, and promiscuity. "Homosexuality is a disgusting perversion of natural law and leads to the destruction of white civilization."[2]
- They believed in the sanctity of marriage. "Divorce within our church is not a step to be undertaken simply because a marriage is going through difficult times or one partner wants to call it quits in order to 'find themselves.' "[3]
- They honored the husband as the head of the home. "Do we believe white men are the evil oppressors who are responsible for all our woes and problems? Absolutely not. Our men have suffered under the same yoke of Jew tyranny that we, their sisters have."[4]
- They advocated a distinctive-roles partnership in marriage. "We recognize that men and women each have their own roles to play, which are mutually complementary, yet different."[5]
- They honored motherhood. "Do we elevate career over motherhood? Absolutely not. We believe that being a capable nurturing mother to white children is the ultimate holy 'career' for any white woman and is the most natural role for a woman to fulfill, particularly as the white race faces extinction due to suicidally low birth rates."[6]
- While they honored their "fighting white women," they opposed radical feminism. "Feminism, as our enemies well know and as it is espoused by mud-loving Jewesses such as Gloria Steinem, Betty Friedan, Bella Abzug, the National Organization of Women (NOW), and the army of professional agitators worldwide who have pushed the feminist ideology, is an unnatural philosophy which

asserts that men and women are 'equals,' that men are the oppressors of women who must be feared and hated, that primarily white men are responsible for all the injustice in society and for everything that has gone wrong in women's lives, and that women have been 'victimized' by men and must combat them as enemies."[7]

- They advocated fasting, though for health reasons rather than for prayer.
- They fostered clean living, hard work, and self-mastery of life and work.

As these characteristics of the Church of the Creator evolved, the movement became increasingly compelling to some white conservatives from Christian backgrounds. Such people became vulnerable—first of all to the racial message, especially if they had never acknowledged racism as sin—and then to the anti-Christian message, as Klassen argued that Christianity was a Jewish plot.

● ● ●

Before Klassen embarked on writing the "holy books" that his new religion would require, the Province of Saskatchewan named 1971 as the "Year of Homecoming." Klassen's parents were long dead, and even though he had taken extended trips to Europe and elsewhere, he had never taken Henrie to Canada to see the old home farm or meet the relatives—though Henrie had written asking them to pray for Ben. So Klassen decided to make the trip. Besides, it might be a good time and place to test some of his new theories. After all, those relatives had gone through the same war and persecution his family had suffered in being driven from Russia. It shouldn't be too hard to convince them to throw over their Christian beliefs in favor of his racist philosophy. Who knows what he expected? Maybe they would see him as their great white savior come to rescue them from…from what? Perhaps the ever-expanding Lafayette family?

At first his brother Henry couldn't believe his ears when Klassen phoned him to discuss arrangements. After all, Klassen hadn't bothered to call him in twenty-five years. But everyone received Ben and Henrie warmly when they finally arrived, and there were numerous reunions, picnics, and barbecues at which they were guests. One such was held by the Herschel Mennonites in a hall on the hill just south of town. Klassen's niece Ruby Wiens recalls that Klassen dominated the dinner conversation by "running down blacks as animals" to the discomfort of all those around him.[8] No takers among them. The only blacks around there were their neighbors, the Lafayettes. Klassen gave up; perhaps his relatives had become "local yokels" like everyone else in Herschel.

Later Klassen cornered his nephew Peter Klassen. Peter was twenty-two years younger, but he was an attorney, the only other college-educated member of the extended family clan. Certainly *he* would understand Klassen's vision and why he regarded Hitler as the greatest leader the white race had ever produced. But the young attorney wasn't buying it. He knew too much, especially about the consequences of Hitler's racial thinking. Klassen claims that he kept at Peter for three or four hours trying to convince him that his new religion would save the white race, of which he was a part.

Peter Klassen, however, recalls the conversation in far more casual terms. "I rather think he exaggerated both the length and importance of our conversation."[9]

During the next couple of days, the Klassens visited some of Ben's schools in the Saskatoon area, and then they drove on to Calgary where they looked up Ben's childhood classmate George Wiens. This time Klassen avoided hammering him with his beliefs, and the visit proceeded amicably. But before they left, George recalled, "What he did do—and I am still somewhat shocked when I think back to this—was to leave with me a huge pile of paperwork outlining the beliefs and arguments in support of his movement. I did not read it until some time after our meeting, and at that time I developed real doubts about Ben's sanity. I had always considered him one of the most intelligent people I had ever known—I still think that's what he was in those earlier days—but, obviously, something snapped somewhere along the way."[10]

16

Number One Mentor

Because she had added education courses to her science and pre-med major, Sherialyn still had another year to go at Iowa State. Thus Coach Nance's job offer for Ricky to serve as a graduate assistant was a godsend. Not only did it give his "size thirteens" a toehold in coaching on the college level, but Ricky could still be on campus with Sherialyn.

But he had one nagging question. "Coach Nance?" Might as well spit it out. "I know I'm not the most gifted player on this team. Why are you offering *me* a coaching spot?"

Nance leaned back in his chair and laced his fingers behind his closely cropped head. "Two things, Byrd. One, you love the game and you know what it means to work hard. Two, you have the best interest of the team at heart. I know you'll be loyal to me, no matter what your personal opinion might be."

If those were the qualifications Nance was looking for, then he definitely qualified. But just how far did loyalty go? Ricky didn't want to be just a "yes" man.

With a coaching job in hand, graduation seemed like just a formality. "No, don't come, Mama," he told his mother on the phone. "Save your money. I'll be home for a visit, then I gotta get back here for my job… Yeah, Sherialyn's staying here this summer, too. See ya in a few weeks."

But ever since Mama had married Simon Strickland and they'd moved to the house on Bonnybrook Way, going "home" never felt quite the same. Besides, FiFi, Marcia's toy poodle, had *definitely* nudged "big brother" out of the number one spot in his sister's heart, judging by the fuss

Marcia made over that dog. Ricky was eager to get back to Ames and get started.

It felt different, Ricky realized—but it felt *good*—to be on the other side of the equation when the new season's team got together with the staff. By now Ricky had practically memorized Coach Nance's beginning-of-the-year pep talk.

"The rules are simple." Coach Nance, barely into his thirties, commanded fear and respect with his clipped speech and no-nonsense manner. "One! No smoking, no drinking, no drug use while you are on this team. There are no second chances. You break this rule and you're off the team, off your scholarship. Understand?"

Hatless heads nodded soberly around the room.

"Two! Don't do *anything* that would embarrass yourself, embarrass the team, or embarrass this university. Breaking this rule will be dealt with on an individual basis. Same infraction, two different people, might get two different responses. A lot will depend on your attitude. Remember, this basketball team is not a democracy. This is a dictatorship and *I'm* the dictator."

By now, Ricky knew why Coach Nance started off tough. He had to answer for the team's behavior to the university administration, the players' parents, the fans, and the media.

Funny thing, though. Nance didn't run his staff meetings—sometimes two or three a day—like a dictatorship. "I'm thinking about using man-to-man defense against Missouri," he might say. "What do you guys think about that?" Having never been accused of shyness, Ricky ventured some of his opinions along with the other assistant coaches. Coach Nance nodded, considered, sometimes used their ideas, sometimes didn't. But he always listened.

Iowa State's basketball program had undergone a major shift in the past two years and was enjoying some success—including winning two tough games on the road. Ricky and Steve Burgason had been the only graduating seniors from last year, so Ricky was hoping the team would continue to jell with the same positive momentum. But he knew trouble was brewing when some of the black players came to see him with a complaint. "Coach Byrd, this new recruit—Hunter, the kid from Kentucky. Why'd Coach Nance put him in the starting lineup? Coach Nance, he came here from U of K, Hunter's from U of K. Feels like playing favorites to us."

It didn't take a rocket scientist to figure out that the players had come to him because he was a black coach on a mostly white coaching staff. He was sure Coach Nance had his reasons. Tom Hunter (not his real name) had talent, all right—including a forty-inch vertical jump. Ricky didn't think for a moment the issue was racial. But personally? He thought maybe Coach was rushing it. After all, there were some other solid players on the team with a little more experience. And Hunter also seemed to have a talent for rubbing some of his teammates the wrong way.

What did loyalty mean in this situation?

In his gut, Ricky knew. Don't take sides against the coach with disgruntled players or in public. Diverse opinions belonged in the privacy of staff meetings. He chewed thoughtfully on his words before answering. At best, he needed to win the respect of all the players for all the coaches. He needed to do his best not to split the team. At worst, he might be accused of being an Uncle Tom.

"If you have a problem with the starting lineup, you need to speak to Coach Nance personally. I've always experienced Coach to be fair-minded, and I want you to come to feel that way about him too."

It was an honest answer. Coach was tough, but he'd always been fair. Did he make perfect decisions? What coach did? But one thing Ricky knew: Coach Nance had the good of the whole team at heart.

• • •

Coach Nance couldn't resist. After all, at six feet five inches, he was still in great shape and only a smidgen over thirty. He suited up with his players for a preseason pickup game. He'd let Byrdsong or Samuels coach this one.

But something wasn't clicking. There was tension on the floor, and he heard indistinct mutters just out of his reach. He tried to concentrate on the play, but something was going on, tripping the flow.

Then the muttering sharpened. "Outta my way, n———."

Nance whirled and clipped the speaker on the jaw with a fast right. Tom Hunter went sprawling.

To Coach Nance's surprise, Hunter jumped up and lowered his head. "Sorry, Coach. I was out of line. It won't happen again."

Nance glared. "You bet you were out of line. I never want to hear you speak to *any* player like that again."

The next staff meeting was sober. "I know. I shouldn't have hit him," the head coach admitted. But he also knew, given the same instance, he'd do it again.

"Probably just what he needed," chuckled one of the other coaches. "Knock some sense into him."

"If he doesn't sue the university."

The coaches groaned.

Byrdsong spoke up. "Hunter's got more bark than bite. Think I'll invite him to go to church with me and some of the other players. Pastor Nesbitt's got a way of getting through to guys like Hunter."

Coach Nance stifled a laugh. Didn't *that* take the cake. White kid uses a racial slur against a black player. White coach punches the guy out. Black coach takes the guy to church.

•　　•　　•

Ricky knew Coach Nance was pleased with the way the Cyclones were shaping up in his third season as head coach. Why else would the hard-nosed coach loosen the curfew the night before a big game—while they were on the road, no less.

"Curfew is 1 A.M.," Nance growled. "Sharp." The team whooped. An 11 P.M. curfew wasn't unusual on road trips. Coach was all right!

Coach Nance was armed with his wristwatch as the bewitching hour drew near. Ricky was relieved when most of the players appeared at the appointed time. He mentally ticked off names. Wait. Where was Carlton? And Andrew Parker and Charles Harris? Parker and Harris were starters and Harris was the Cyclones' leading scorer.

Coach Nance stuck a note on Carlton's door: *Evans! Knock on my door when you get in.*

Ricky heard the story the next morning. Carlton found the note and went to face the music. Parker and Harris lurked in the background as he knocked on Coach's door. Nance opened the door. He tapped his watch. "You guys are twenty-three minutes late."

"Uh, sorry we're late, Coach. Just lost track of time." All three players looked penitent.

"Uh-huh. You'll sit out the first twenty-three minutes of tonight's game."

When the other team members heard the news, they couldn't believe it. "Coach can't hold Parker and Harris out for the first twenty-three!" "It's not like they came back drunk." "Why can't he just give them a warning or something?"

Privately, Ricky and the rest of the staff wished Coach would bend a little, just this once. They'd won two difficult games on the road. They could do it again. But not with two of their top players sitting out.

But Coach Nance was resolute. Two second stringers started in place of Parker and Harris, who sat out the first twenty-three minutes.

The Cyclones lost by one point in overtime.

When the story hit the papers, other coaches in the league shook their heads. Didn't Nance know there was a time to turn a blind eye? Tex Winter, a veteran coach, got on the phone. "Nance, why'd you catch 'em? Nobody would have blamed you if you'd gone to bed early. I mean, losing the game by one point!"

Nance answered, "It's not about just one game."

Ricky soaked it up. Coach was right. Building a team wasn't about winning or losing one game. It was about building character. No time like the present for kids to learn that the decisions they make have consequences—for themselves and for other people too—and they might as well learn it now when the price was only one game.

● ● ●

Ricky got the phone call on June 24. Simon Strickland, his mother's husband, was dead of lung cancer. "Oh, Mama. I'm so sorry." His mom and Simon had been married only a few years. He hated to think of her going through another loss, more lonely years.

Only later did everyone remember that it was Ricky's twenty-third birthday.

Sherialyn wasn't scheduled to graduate from Iowa State till after the summer session in August. "*Then* can we get married?" Ricky wanted to know. Man! They'd been talking about getting married since high school. Seven years was a long time to wait when he *knew* that no other girl he'd ever met held a candle to Sherialyn Sabrina Kelley.

"I've got to go home and plan a wedding," Sherialyn said. "Maybe October."

"October!" Steve Fisher, recruiter at Western Michigan University, had offered Ricky a position as assistant coach in Kalamazoo, and Ricky was seriously considering it. The job offered more money, and he was about to become a married man. But August...September...October...it shouldn't take *that* long to plan a wedding, should it?

"We *could* go and pick out an engagement ring now," Sherialyn suggested. She was eyeing him with that I-really-shouldn't-have-to-tell-you-this look.

An engagement ring! Of course.

But when it came to the wedding date, there was no moving the bride and her mother. The wedding date was set for October 6, 1979, and Ricky went to Western Michigan to begin his new job without Sherialyn—but not before Fisher agreed to let him off for a week to get married.

The wedding was everything Ricky could have imagined. Pastor Nesbitt from Ames, Iowa, had agreed to marry them. "Pastor!" Ricky teased when he picked up Nesbitt at the airport. "You're likely to be the only white face there!"

Well, that wasn't exactly true. Coach Larry Cart, Ricky's first varsity coach at Frederick Douglass High School (who had also helped Ricky get his Pratt scholarship) had agreed to be one of the groomsmen.

The processional music started, and a nervous Ricky entered from a side door, followed by Rollie Lewis and the other groomsmen, dressed alike in wine-colored tuxedos. His eyes swept the front rows and grinned at his mother. Man! Mama looked good in her royal blue dress, her black hair softly styled to fall around her shoulders. His father, Edward, was sober— thank God!—and cut a dashing figure in his tux. Grandma Jannie Byrd-song beamed at him, sitting alongside Grandpa Earl. And Grandma Blanche Hollis: Ricky knew she wouldn't miss *this* party for the world. Ricky had always been her favorite.

The ring bearer and flower girl made it to the front and capitalized on their cuteness, then the bridesmaids came in, draped in pink. Carmen, Galetha, Jan, his sister Marcia, Sherialyn's sister Kim…

Ricky's heart leaped. There was Sherialyn at the door, on the arm of her father, Joe Kelley. At the rehearsal, she'd been everywhere at once, acting as the wedding coordinator. But now she walked toward him down the aisle, her beautiful, solemn face covered by a sheer white veil that cascaded down her back into a long train. He tried not to show his impatience while Joe Kelley gave her away and shook his hand.

Finally, Sherialyn slipped her hand into the crook of his arm.

His heart was pounding so hard he wondered if the preacher could hear it. He tried to listen to the Reverend Tom Nesbitt. Especially since the congenial pastor was talking to him. "Ricky," he said, "the beautiful bride you have standing beside you has a sparkle in her eye and a spring in her step. Whether or not that stays is going to be largely due to the kind of leadership you give her. You're going to have to let Jesus lead *you* in order for you to lead her and keep that sparkle in her eye."

Ricky's heart squeezed. He loved Sherialyn so much. *O God, help me do that. Help me keep that sparkle in her eye.*

17

Publish or Perish

Claiming that it somehow called into question the historicity of Jesus Christ, Ben Klassen wrote, "Christ himself, who had supposedly the greatest message to deliver to posterity that the world has ever known, left not the slightest scrap of paper on which he had written a single word."[1] In contrast, Klassen hailed the Greek and Roman philosophers whose writings can still be read today.

Rather than wasting time documenting himself, Jesus Christ had been speaking to crowds of thousands, healing and responding personally to the needs of people all around him, and mentoring a team of twelve disciples to carry on after his departure from this earth. As early as the second century, Justin Martyr contrasted the results: "No one trusted in Socrates so as to die for [his] doctrine, but in Christ…not only philosophers and scholars believed, but also artisans and people entirely uneducated, despising both glory, and fear, and death."[2]

Jesus also knew that the Spirit of God transformed—for the better—the lives of those who believed in him. In gratitude they would become his most ardent evangelists. And many others, who could not help but see this new joy and purpose in their old friends, first would become curious, then eager, and finally converts. Two thousand years later, Christianity is the most widespread of the world's religions with more than 1.8 billion adherents on every continent.[3]

On the other hand, though Klassen was able to stir an occasional newspaper headline with his racist statements, he was not attracting crowds of potential followers. He was not healing anyone physically or relieving their emotional pain or setting relationships right between people. He was not feeding the hungry or inspiring others to do so. (In fact, his approach to needy people was "let them wither on the vine."[4]) He did not have a cadre around him who might later record his life. He was not organizing people into a church. History was likely to forget him completely.

So Klassen set out to promote himself—recording his philosophy, organizing a church (on paper), and documenting his personal existence. He produced and self-published more than eight hundred pages of autobiography in two volumes (*Against the Evil Tide* and *Trials, Tribulations, and Triumphs*) as well as another five hundred pages of his letters in two additional volumes. In these he compulsively recorded the names and addresses of people he encountered, dates and times (to the minute), conversations large and small, and hundreds of other trivial facts about himself.

By the summer of 1972, Klassen was far enough along in writing his first book, *Nature's Eternal Religion,* to need a printer. Of course, he had to avoid all Jewish printers, so he struck a deal with the Universal Printing Company in Hialeah, Florida, warning them that the book was controversial and took a dim view of Christianity. Two weeks later Ron Bechtel, the son of the owner with whom Klassen had entered a contract, returned Klassen's manuscript and uncashed check. It turned out the Bechtels were Christians and were not willing to do the job. Now he had to look out for Christians as well. But Klassen actually relished what he took for persecution, saying, "So much for broad-minded Christian tolerance."[5] It didn't take him long to find another printer, however. And he had his first book.

Trips to the Caribbean and Europe followed while Klassen worked on additional publications. Ultimately, he produced fourteen books promoting himself and his ideas.

As a result of his first book, Klassen received occasional speaking invitations. In October 1976, Max Bentley (not his real name), an enthusiastic supporter and former bank robber, organized a meeting in downtown Houston, but Klassen had to share the roster with Andrew Vance (not his real name), also an ex-con and the founder of San Francisco's neo-Nazi group called the National Socialist Movement. Less than a dozen people showed up, and Klassen had no more than fifteen minutes to talk about Creativity—a rather disappointing attempt to spread the word. The next year, Bob DePugh, who had spent four years in prison on a weapons charge connected with his group, the Minute Men, invited Klassen to speak at the Patriots Inter-Organizational Communications Center. It was to be held at the Continental Hotel in Kansas City, Missouri, where DePugh billed it as a conference of all the right-wing radical organizations in the country. DePugh warned Klassen that he was not likely to change anyone's mind, but Klassen thought it might be a good place to promote his book anyway.

Robert Shelton, the Imperial Wizard of the United Klans of America, set up security using five "stress-analyzers" as lie detectors to screen out government spies. Of the 160 people in attendance, only 120 submitted to the test, and 6 of those failed it. Everyone was admitted anyway, but the concern about "security" lent an air of importance to the conference.

Klassen was allowed to be one of three speakers at the main banquet. The theme of the speaker before him was "God and Country, Flag and Constitution." Klassen got up to tell everyone that Christianity hadn't done anything for the white race. They needed to dump God and find a new racial religion, namely Creativity. Even Klassen admitted that the reception to his message was less than enthusiastic.

After this event, Klassen decided it was hopeless to try to cooperate with other groups, no matter how right-wing or racist they might be. He referenced Hitler's *Mein Kampf* as saying "that you do not unite and thereby water down, two (or more) different movements without destroying the main force which built the movement in the first place." Again, he would go it alone. "It is the only way to go. RAHOWA [Racial Holy War]!" he concluded.[6]

•   •   •

During this period of his life, Klassen pursued various real estate ventures near Franklin, North Carolina. Ultimately, he and Henrie sold their home in Lighthouse Point, Florida, in 1983 and moved to North Carolina. There Klassen built the World Center of his new church—an office with an apartment upstairs and various other outbuildings. The Klassens lived on another portion of the property in a cabin that they later expanded into a more spacious home.

Meanwhile, Klassen needed an assistant to help him put out his monthly newspaper, *Racial Loyalty,* typeset additional books, and otherwise get the word out. An efficient secretary could have done the typing, typesetting, mailing, and other office duties, but Klassen thought it would be better to add a little prestige, so he gave the position the title Hasta Primus. In October 1982, Klassen offered the position to an eager young applicant. But that was only the beginning of his search.

1. Timothy Gaffney was named Hasta Primus, but he left after two months because his wife refused to join him.
2. Ron Baxter (not his real name) backed out at the last minute with no explanation.
3. Duke McCoy moved in with wife and dog. Klassen hated dogs and also suspected McCoy was a "Jewish Occupational Government" agent. So Klassen fired him.
4. Tyler Thompson was down on his luck, so Klassen loaned him two hundred dollars for clothes and moving expenses. Thompson got drunk and never showed up.
5. Bill Tucker had what Klassen decided was a domineering wife who ruined the arrangement.
6. Ron Baxter, the second candidate, reconsidered and agreed to give the job a try. But after a few weeks Klassen discovered that Baxter's father had once had him confined to an insane asylum, and one night he became so panicky that he couldn't walk down the lane in the dark between Klassen's home and the headquarters. He was not Hasta Primus material. Klassen let him go.
7. Kenny Wells (not his real name), the "Dude," a radio announcer and disc jockey who wanted to help the cause, proved to be what Klassen described as "a big, fat slob in his early fifties" who had failed at a dozen other jobs and was willing to take this one on

any terms. Six months later the Secret Service showed up to question the Dude about some threats he had allegedly made on the lives of Jimmy Carter and Gary Hart. Klassen let him go.

8. Carles C. Messick III was in debt and needed a seven hundred dollar advance before he could accept the position. Klassen agreed to five hundred, and finally got a reliable assistant.

But why did he loan another down-on-his-luck, wannabe Hasta Primus five hundred dollars? After eighteen months of searching and trying first one and then another, "the simple answer is," said Klassen, "I had…few volunteers to choose from."[7] Other questions also suggest themselves: Had Klassen followed his to-hell-with-them policy for so long—never taking time to understand other people, never sacrificing anything to work out difficult relationships—that he was simply unable to judge human character? Was his movement already proving whom it was for: the dregs of society, losers who could not compete so resorted to blaming other people? What he was attracting certainly could not be called "nature's finest" of any color or by any measure!

18

Westward, Ho!

The honeymoon would have to wait.

Western Michigan University was already into its preseason games, and Ricky Byrdsong couldn't pull vacation time after only a few months on the job. He knew he'd probably get teased, but he couldn't wipe the grin off his face. He and Sherialyn had tied the knot at last. He kept busting out singing, "My love is for only you in my heart!"

Ricky was proud to be an assistant coach for the black-and-gold Broncos. ("Black and gold!" he crowed to Sherialyn. "My old high school colors!") His first full-time job as an assistant coach was for a Divison I team, and Ricky was determined to learn from head coach Les Wothke. Sherialyn, meantime, armed with a bachelor's degree and a teaching certificate, found a temporary job as a science technician at the community college in Kalamazoo, then switched to teaching junior high math for the spring semester.

But the shoe pinched. "Were we outrageous when *we* were in junior high?" she asked Ricky as they went jogging one weekend, working off some stress.

"What's the problem?" Ricky's eyes were laughing. "I thought you wanted to teach."

"Uh-huh. I do. But teaching pubescent thirteen-year-olds is *definitely* not it. Uh-uh. No way."

"You don't have to." Ricky grinned. "Just tell the principal that your husband took a job out of state, so you won't be back next year."

Sherialyn pulled up short. "Took a job out of—Ricky! What are you talking about?"

"Rick Samuels called me." Ricky was still grinning.

"Aha." A light went on in Sherialyn's head. Rick Samuels had been Coach Nance's graduate assistant when Ricky first played for Iowa State, then full-time assistant when Ricky took the graduate assistant position. He and his wife, Jan, had provided a home away from home for both Ricky and Sherialyn while they were at Iowa State. Samuels had often said, "Byrd, when I get a job as head coach, I'm coming for you."

"Samuels got the nod as head coach at Eastern Illinois University in Charleston. He wants me to come assist."

"Uh-*huh*." Sherialyn pursed her lips thoughtfully. That was Ricky, spurred by loyalty to a former coach and colleague. She didn't blame him for jumping at the chance. Rick Samuels was a great coach and a serious Christian. And if the job paid better and got her out of teaching junior high as well, that was icing on the cake!

• • •

Ricky and Sherialyn finally managed to take their honeymoon to Las Vegas in July, in-between Kalamazoo and Charleston. Walking hand in hand down the glittering streets, they probably didn't notice when heads turned. But they made a striking couple. Ricky was a sharp dresser and at six-foot-six was hard to miss in a crowd. Sherialyn wore self-confidence and joy like a bright summer sarong. The honeymooners soaked up the hot, dry desert air during the day and took in some of the stage shows and music concerts at night. "Just having fun" felt almost like their carefree dating days back in high school—with a luxury hotel and a marriage license thrown in! Not to mention that Sherialyn had Ricky's undivided attention for a few days.

As newlyweds it wasn't that big a deal to pack up and go to Illinois. But it helped to already have friends in their new town. Rick Samuels helped Ricky build a screened-in porch on the "lease-purchase" house they found in Charleston, while Sherialyn bounced nine-month-old Tiffany Samuels on her hip and asked Jan if they'd found a good church. The Byrdsongs tried out the Southern Baptist church Jan and Rick were attending and stayed.

Coach Rick Samuels had a mission: to raise the level of competition for the Eastern Illinois Panthers to Division I. "We gotta have a big guy, Byrd." Ricky hit the recruiting trail, picking up a Chicago newspaper in Rantoule at noon, hanging out at the Public League high school games in the afternoon and the Catholic League games in the evening. And he found his big guy: Kevin Duckworth—seven feet, 325 pounds, who would later spend twelve years in the NBA. Coach Samuels just smiled and sent Ricky back out on the recruiting trail.

Sherialyn got a job coaching girls' junior varsity basketball and teaching science at the local high school. This was definitely more to her liking! And when Jan Samuels, pregnant with her second child, had to go into the hospital to treat an infection, Sherialyn said blithely, "Sure, we'll take care of Tiffany. Don't worry about a thing."

But at the end of the weekend babysitting stint—being startled awake in the night by a screaming toddler, sweeping up endless trails of cracker crumbs, changing poopy diapers, and being on duty every minute—Ricky and Sherialyn eyed one another with mutual agreement: Maybe they'd wait on having kids.

At times Ricky's being on the road so much was tough on the young marriage. But Ricky enjoyed the fraternity of coaches he ran into on the recruiting trail, at tournaments, and on the road during basketball season. On the court, he studied their coaching styles, forgave their personality quirks, and sifted what he liked from what he didn't like. Off the court, he reeled them in as friends, followed their careers, asked their advice, and traded ideas.

Like any other young assistant, he dreamed about landing a job as head coach at a major university one day. But he knew he had to earn the right to stand in those shoes.

● ● ●

Carlton Evans trotted into his house in Chandler, Arizona, and got the phone on its fourth ring. "Evans here."

"Carlton! Have you heard? I'm coming to the University of Arizona!"

Carlton wagged his head. Wasn't that just like Byrd. He hadn't heard from Ricky in months, and now he was calling as if they'd talked only last week.

"Whaddya mean you're coming to Arizona? All by yourself? Where'd you dump Sherialyn?"

"Okay, funnyman. *We're* coming to Arizona. A guy named Ben Lindsey just got the head job at UA and offered me a job as assistant. Sherialyn too! I mean, UA also needs an assistant coach in the women's basketball program."

"Two Coach Byrdsongs at one school? Watch out—Sherialyn will have your job!" Carlton laughed. "Seriously, that's *great,* Byrd. But UA's program hasn't been doing too good lately."

"Yeah, I know. Still, it'll broaden my experience. And to be honest, we're looking forward to a bigger city. Even if you *are* close by."

Phone charges piled up as the two college friends caught up on all the latest news. Carlton had been working with delinquent boys and coaching at the Arizona Boys Ranch outside Phoenix since he graduated a year behind Ricky at Iowa State and married his college sweetheart. "Karen will be so excited to see Sherialyn," Carlton said. Sherialyn and Karen had met at Iowa State, and the two couples had hung out together while still in school.

"Hey," Ricky said, "my mama's getting married again. Great guy, name's Bob Jasper—an ex-Marine. Bob says my mom wooed him with a pan of lasagna."

Carlton guffawed. He liked the guy already.

"Yeah, Bob's good for Mama," Ricky said. "She's got that sparkle in her eye again. Only problem is, they set the date for September 15, her birthday. But there's no way Sherialyn and I can make it back to Atlanta in September. By then we'll be camping on *your* doorstep!"

• • •

Early that summer of 1982, Ricky and Sherialyn loaded up a moving van and headed west to Tucson. The Santa Catalina Mountains could be seen to the northeast, hemming the horizon with a jagged edge.

But there was no turnaround in the basketball program at the University of Arizona. The situation went from bad to worse. The season ended 4-24 and Coach Lindsey was fired. Ricky knew that put both his and Sherialyn's jobs on the line too. He felt badly. He knew it would be hard on her to move again so soon. But an incoming head coach often gets rid of the old staff and brings in his own.

Sherialyn was surprisingly calm. "I've got my promise," she said simply. She opened her Bible to Jeremiah 29:11 (NLT). " 'I know the plans I have for you,' says the LORD. 'They are plans for good and not for disaster, to give you a future and a hope.' See, Ricky? We can trust God to take care of us."

Ricky was amazed. Where did this woman get that kind of faith?

The best happened. Arizona hired Lute Olson, former head coach at the University of Iowa, whom Ricky had met as a college player when Iowa State played UI. The guy stood out in any crowd—snowy white hair crowning a tan, youthful face. Ricky was excited. He knew Lute Olson brought a coaching agenda that fit with his own growing ideals: developing players as whole persons, not just winning games.

Ricky let it be known that he would like to stay with Arizona's program. But he heard that if he wanted the job, the person he *really* had to impress was Olson's wife, Bobbi. No coaching wife was more involved in her husband's program than Bobbi Olson. She took a keen interest in the players and staff.

Ricky and Sherialyn took a big breath and invited the Olsons to their apartment for a get-acquainted evening. Sherialyn was impressed. The slender, dark-haired lady dressed first-class and carried herself with dignity, but she was warm and friendly. As the two couples laughed and shared stories, Sherialyn thought, *I could learn a lot from her about being a coach's wife.*

The feeling must have been mutual, because before the evening was out, Ricky knew he had the job.

Olson and his team of assistants—Ricky Byrdsong, Ken Burmeister, and Scott Thompson—hit the ground running in the summer of 1983 to put Arizona's basketball program back on the map. When Burmeister left and was replaced by Kevin O'Neill, Olson teamed Byrdsong and O'Neill as recruiters and got his money's worth. Ricky's upbeat personality put potential players and their parents at ease. He was enthusiastic about the program's potential. He worked with players' families to answer their questions, give them a great tour of the school, and overcome any hurdles they were facing.

He also wasn't above throwing in a little craziness now and then just to make it interesting.

• • •

"A *gorilla* suit?" Steve Burgason pushed his big frame away from the restaurant table and roared with laughter. "You got O'Neill to dress up in a gorilla suit to meet one of your recruits at the *airport?*"

Other patrons looked their way. They made an odd couple—big men, both well over six feet, black and white. Salt and pepper.

Man! It was great seeing Byrd again. Ricky had been his best man when Steve got married the summer after graduation in '78. Steve had spent a couple years with the Fellowship of Christian Athletes, and soon he and his wife, Ann, would be heading overseas with Athletes in Action, a Christian ministry team. But when Steve heard that the Arizona Wildcats were coming to Ames, Iowa, to play at his and Ricky's alma mater—and that Ricky was assistant coach for the Wildcats—he just had to see the game.

The final buzzer had sounded: Iowa State Cyclones 75; Arizona Wildcats 63. Steve Burgason had found Ricky and clapped him on the back. "Great game, Byrd!"

"Yeah. I saw you cheering for the Cyclones," Ricky grumbled.

Steve laughed. "Come on, I'll take you out to dinner."

The former co-captains polished off an amazing amount of food as they recalled old times. "How's it going, Byrd? How's Sherialyn? She still the Rock?"

Ricky grinned big. "Oh yeah. Sherialyn's great. Looks good. Loves her job. Can't cook, though." He laughed then he looked more serious.

"What?"

Ricky sighed. "Tell you the truth, Steve, it gets rough some times. On the road, women throw themselves at you all the time—you remember how it was. They don't care if you're married or not. I'm holding on, but there's a lot of pressure."

"You guys got a church? A good pastor?"

Ricky stirred his iced tea absently. "Yeah, yeah. We're going to Mount Calvary Missionary Baptist. Sherialyn sings in the choir. But I'm on the road a lot, you know. Don't always make it to church. Sherialyn's usually a good sport—she knows I have to travel. But sometimes…I don't know. I can't figure women out."

Steve snorted. "When you do, you better write a book so the rest of us can read it."

"Now get this." Ricky jabbed his finger at Steve. "This ever happen to you with Ann? Sherialyn's mad at me for something—can't even remember what. So on the way home from work I pick up some roses for her. A dozen red beauties! She takes the roses, says, 'Thanks,' plonks them in a vase, and that's that. Me, I'm completely bewildered. I thought she'd throw her arms around me and everything would be bliss. Don't women adore flowers? So I push her on it. 'Hey, Baby, don't you like the flowers?' 'Sure,' she says. 'But I'd like it even better if you did the dishes.' " Ricky threw up his hands. "See? Can't seem to get it right."

Steve chuckled. But later, as he paid the check and said good-bye to one of the best friends he'd ever had, he felt disquieted. He wished he and Ricky could stay in touch to encourage one another—like in their college days. But it might be years before he saw his old friend again. And something bothered him. Ricky was still his funny, upbeat self. But somehow, he didn't seem quite as connected to his Source.

19

Shoot 'Em Up

With Carles C. Messick III installed as Hasta Primus of the Church of the Creator, the Klassens could finally get away from headquarters. Earlier, in February 1984, the Klassens had taken a quick trip to Egypt, where Klassen speculated on the white origins of ancient Egypt, claiming the civilization's demise came as a result of race mixing with the Arabs and black Africans. They had also helped their now-married daughter, Kim, and her family move from Colorado to Virginia.

But now it was time for more relaxed travel—to the Florida Keys, to the Southwest, and finally another trip to Hawaii. During this latter trip, Klassen was reassured that Hasta Primus Messick was keeping things under control and getting the *Racial Loyalty* newspaper published on time.

Things were going so well—with Klassen writing articles for the paper and sending them to Messick to typeset—that the Klassens took another car trip west, and then in August 1985 another trip to Europe.

But there was an additional reason behind all this travel. In 1981 Klassen had stopped paying his federal income tax. He had written the IRS a letter stating that "the Federal Reserve was an illegal gang of Jewish counterfeiters, and that our Jew-controlled government was taxing us white people and using our own money to exterminate and destroy the white race, and I would be damned if I would contribute any further to the destruction of my own people."[1] Being away from home, out of state, even out of the country made it more difficult for the IRS to catch up with him.

Over the years since having built the headquarters, vandals had attacked from time to time. Once a contractor and his crew working on the building were threatened with gunfire. A Molotov cocktail was thrown at the building, though the structure suffered little damage before the fire was extinguished, and someone had fired a shotgun at their eight-foot-diameter plastic sign, leaving a few holes in it.

Although Klassen had notified the sheriff's department with each occurrence, no one was ever charged, even though Klassen believed the police knew who was responsible.

Then at 3:10 A.M. on June 14, 1986, he received a call from Messick saying that there was a car full of people outside the headquarters building talking loudly about shooting out the yard light and blowing up the church. Messick even claimed that they had threatened to shoot him if he came running out. Klassen called the sheriff—busy line. He threw on some clothes, grabbed his gun, and phoned again, finally getting through to Deputy Jim Barker at 3:20. Then Klassen jumped into his car and headed down the lane. Sure enough, he could see a car coming up the road. It stopped at the intersection, turned around, and headed back past the head-quarters. Klassen heard faint gunfire as he chased after the car.

In the meantime, Messick had sneaked out of the headquarters building with his gun and come up near the property entrance with its signs, *Private Road, Property Owners Only,* and *No Trespassing.* What should he do? Local law enforcement had failed to protect them in the past. Maybe it was up to him. The prowlers had turned off their headlights, and he could not see them. But apparently they saw him. They started their car and headed up the road toward Klassen's house. Pretty soon Messick saw Klassen's car leave from his house and head toward the intruders. The intruders turned on their lights, turned around, and headed back toward the entrance. This was Messick's chance to show his courage. He would make a citizen's arrest.

The car was coming faster as Messick stepped into the road. When the car kept coming, he fired a warning shot. The headlights swerved momen-tarily, then aimed right toward him. Messick took a stance and aimed at the lower half of the vehicle as he squeezed off more than a dozen shots, trying to shoot out the tires. He leapt aside as the car roared past, missing him by no more than two feet, and headed south on the highway.

When Klassen arrived, Messick jumped in beside him. "I think I hit the car," he said as they followed the fleeing vehicle. They gave up after a short distance and returned to await the sheriff.

Two sheriff's deputies finally arrived at 4:05 A.M., having taken forty-five minutes to travel thirteen miles in response to Klassen's emergency call. They heard Messick and Klassen's story and went looking for the car. They found it not far away with some thirty bullet holes in it. Two of the tires had been shot out, and there was a hole in the radiator. The car belonged to William and Patricia Trusty. The Trustys told deputies that they had been driving to visit some old friends, the Lents, to have a drink and ask them to cosign a note for a truck loan. They realized that they had turned down a wrong road; they stopped and turned out their lights, and some-one suddenly started shooting at them.

The next evening six men in three squad cars turned into the COTC headquarters and arrested Messick. After many delays and maneuvers, his trial finally took place in December. He was found guilty of discharging a firearm into an occupied vehicle and assault with a deadly weapon. He was sentenced to seven years and ended up serving twenty months.

Klassen considered the whole trial a kangaroo court. First of all, the Lents had moved from the area nine months before. If the Trustys were such close friends as to be potential cosigners on a loan, why didn't they know about that? Also, the Lents were in their seventies and did not drink, so why were the Trustys stopping by at 3:10 A.M. for a drink? And finally, if the Trustys weren't sure where they were going, why did they enter posted property and then stop and turn off their lights?

Klassen suspected that it was somehow the "omnipresent" Jewish Anti-Defamation League that "set up the whole caper in the first place...to entrap us in a position where we had to use firearms to defend ourselves, to take Carles's guns and ammo away from him, and to get detailed pictures of the interior and layout of our church."[2]

But rather than engage a criminal defense attorney on the case, Klassen and Messick agreed to use the volunteer services of Don Johnson, a para-legal sympathetic to their cause. Johnson had called from Houston offering to come and develop a legal training program for Creativity members to help them deal with legal harassment, and he was willing to represent Messick.

In the process, Don Johnson moved with his wife, Bobbi, into the apartment above the headquarters, taking over Messick's position as Hasta Primus. Klassen agreed to pay $2,000 in moving expenses. The bill actually came to $3,845, and Johnson never paid back the difference. Nevertheless, the movement now had a paralegal on staff, and within a month, Johnson promised, he would write a course accompanied by videotapes for the members.

His wife, Bobbi, promised to pick up the responsibilities of typesetting *Racial Loyalty* and other clerical tasks, enabling the operation to return to normal. But with Messick's trial and all the other troubles, the paper, which had been published for thirty-six straight months, missed six months then two months then three months. Then it virtually died.

• • •

Still concerned about the IRS, Klassen distributed his money among five different Florida banks, hoping that if the government raided one account for his back taxes he would be alerted in time to withdraw his money from the other banks. But the Messick shooting affair had raised the profile of the COTC, and Klassen anticipated increased government attention.

Sure enough, one day while traveling to Phoenix, Arizona, he called the headquarters to discover that the IRS had sent a certified letter demanding a meeting on January 6, 1986. He told Johnson to answer it saying that he was out of state and couldn't possibly make the meeting, something Johnson never bothered to do.

Upon his return home, and believing by this time that Johnson was "an accomplished con-man," Klassen took up with him the problem of the IRS.

"Well," said Johnson, "I've heard through the grapevine that there is a small unincorporated bank in the little town of Chilton, Texas, that has been privately owned since 1914. It still operates under a grandfather clause that exempts it from certain federal controls. In fact, the IRS has to secure a search warrant before it can inspect accounts. That gives any investor enough time to withdraw money before the IRS can seize it."

"But is it safe?" asked Klassen.

"Oh yes. All the money is invested in government bonds, but you still have the convenience of a checking account."

It sounded exactly like what Klassen needed, so he immediately scheduled a trip to Texas. There he found the bank as Johnson had described it and talked to the manager, James T. Davis, who confirmed Johnson's report with remarkably similar details. It didn't take Klassen long to have his personal money and the COTC money—all totaling nearly a half-million dollars—transferred to Chilton Private Bank in Texas.

A grin spread across Klassen's usually sober face.

Back at headquarters, six months went by, but Johnson still hadn't written a word of the paralegal course nor begun filming the videotapes. "But I've been thinking about them," Johnson said. "I expect to start shooting next month." While Johnson's wife, Bobbi, had been mediocre at the office work, Klassen couldn't think of one thing Johnson himself had done except talk. Klassen was further disgusted when, without consulting him, the Johnsons brought in a dog and cat and parked a large doghouse and a cathouse on the landing beside the door to the second floor. This was against Klassen's explicit prohibition against any animals on the church grounds.

With a declining membership in the summer of 1987, this was almost the last straw.

One day he received an envelope from the Republic Bank of Waco. In it was his deposit slip and check for thirty-five thousand dollars that he had sent to Chilton Private Bank. The money had come from his sale of the last piece of Florida development property. But why was it being returned? There was no explanation. He tried to phone Chilton Private Bank only to receive a recorded message that the number was no longer in service. Finally, he learned from the Republic Bank of Waco that the Chilton Private Bank had gone belly up.

In a panic, this nearly seventy-year-old man and his wife took off in their car for Texas to try and find out what had become of their half-million dollars.

20

Baby Byrd

"Isn't Tucson great?" Ricky teased, reaching around Sherialyn and snitching a handful of chips from the basket in her hands. "We can have picnics all year round!"

Coach Olson and Coach O'Neill were manning the grills, and members of the Arizona Wildcat team—Steve Kerr, Sean Elliott, Kenny Lofton, and a host of other huge appetites—were putting away amazing amounts of food at one of Olson's "family picnics" that he often hosted for players and staff. Carlton, Karen, and little DeWayne Evans—Ricky and Sherialyn's godson—had come down from Phoenix for the weekend and added to the fun.

Everyone was in good spirits because the Arizona Wildcats had gotten their groove back: 11-17 in the 1983–84 basketball season; 21-10 in 1984–85; and a satisfying European tour in the spring of '85. Except for a vacation cruise with Ricky to the Bahamas their second summer in Arizona, that had been Sherialyn's first trip overseas. Yugoslavia…France…Spain… the Netherlands…Italy…hey! She was a world traveler now.

Sherialyn plopped a handful of chips onto her paper plate alongside her grilled chicken and sank into a lawn chair to watch the fun. She was proud of Ricky. Things were going well for him at UA, and she knew Lute Olson valued his skills as a recruiter. Even the outrageous gorilla suit. Ricky seemed happy, soaking up the coaching skills he was honing under Lute Olson. But…

Being a coach's wife was tough. The job never ended! When Ricky came home—late—he wanted to look at tapes of the most recent game to see what he and the other coaches may have missed. Or he would be on the phone with a player who was having family problems. Or following up on a player whose grades were marginal. All good stuff, but she and Ricky wanted to start a family soon. What would life be like with a baby? She didn't want to end up parenting by herself.

On one Saturday night when the Wildcats lost, Ricky had gotten so down that he didn't even want to go to church the next morning. What was *that* all about? She had joined the choir at Mount Calvary Missionary Baptist Church and loved it, never missing a Sunday. She didn't have a solo voice, but she sang a good strong tenor. She watched the choir director, Ann Malloy, with admiration and a growing yearning. She'd like to do that some day...direct a choir. Worshiping God in song touched something deep inside her.

Somehow, she and Ricky were missing each other at the soul level. He was so busy they rarely had time to read the Bible or pray together. But a person made time for what was important, didn't he? To her, if it was in God's Word, she wanted to know it. If God said it, she wanted to do it. Reading the Bible, going to Bible study—that was just as important as eating and breathing. But Ricky seemed satisfied to go to church on Sunday and leave it at that.

Sometimes she had nagged Ricky to read the Bible more. But he just looked frustrated, like she didn't think he was good enough. That was when she sensed God reassuring her, "Leave Ricky to me." *Okay, God, no more nagging.*

Laughter erupted from a crowd around Ricky. Karen Evans and Bobbie Olson were wiping their eyes and shaking their heads. Uh-huh, Sherialyn smiled fondly. Never a dull moment with Ricky around. She had a lot to be grateful for. Ricky loved her. She loved him. God would sort it all out.

In the meantime, was she going to accept that job offer from Amphi High School to teach science and coach girls' basketball? Assisting for the women's Wildcat basketball team the last three years had been great, but maybe it was time for a change. She'd talk to Ricky about it tonight.

• • •

Sherialyn strode purposefully into her classroom at Amphi High—no way was she going to resort to shuffling, even if she was eight months pregnant—then stopped in midstride. Pink and blue balloons hung from the ceiling, and pink, yellow, and blue streamers framed the words THERE IS NO JOY GREATER THAN MOTHERHOOD in foot-high letters on the board.

"Surprise!" yelled her students.

So much for her lesson plans. Sherialyn's smile widened as the students presented her with a cake and an appreciation award, followed by baby presents, as they consumed potato chips and liters of soda.

It was springtime, 1987, and Baby Byrd was almost due.

Ricky was so excited about the coming baby. Sherialyn had to laugh at how he threw himself into Lamaze training. It was made for Ricky. He got to be the birth *coach!* "Come on, Sherialyn, breathe! Breathe!" Sherialyn practiced huffing and puffing, secretly wondering whether she was going to remember all this when the time actually came. All the women in her family were prone to say, "Just go ahead and scream, honey. It's all right."

At least the ranch-style house they'd bought—gray stucco with a two-car garage and a great view of the mountains—had plenty of room for the baby crib, baby carrier, stroller, baby bath, changing table, and the growing piles of big blue packages of disposable diapers.

She had wanted to keep working as long as she could. Waiting was the hardest. Their lives would really change once Baby Byrd was here. Playing the organ that Ricky had bought for her had a soothing effect, though. She was teaching herself to play so that maybe she could help out with the choir at church. The music and the words poured deep into her soul. She played and prayed.

• • •

"Congratulations, Coach! You've got a healthy baby girl!" The doctor snipped the umbilical cord, wrapped the baby in a warm blanket, and gently placed her in Ricky's outstretched hands.

Ricky stared, awestruck at the squirming bundle. A balled-up fist poked out of the blanket as if testing the air. He saw the nurses smirking and realized he was holding his firstborn like a football in drop-kick position. He pulled her close to his heart.

"Sabrina," Sherialyn murmured from the gurney. "Sabrina Triniece. Is she beautiful?"

Ricky grinned foolishly. Was she beautiful? He looked at Sherialyn, lying spent and exhausted after twelve hours of labor, yet she had never seemed so lovely. Sabrina was Sherialyn's middle name. How could she help but be anything but beautiful?

He was torn between pride and panic. He was a father!

It was the greatest, most terrifying feeling in the world.

•   •   •

Carlton Evans nudged his wife. Five-year-old DeWayne Evans had crawled into Sherialyn's lap and stayed there during the entire basketball game in UA's stadium. Was DeWayne feeling some "sibling rivalry" since Sabrina had arrived on the scene? After all, he was already sharing his own mommy and daddy with a younger sister and baby brother.

Since the Byrdsongs had moved to Arizona, the two families had gotten together regularly at Thanksgiving to celebrate the holiday and their friendship. But this Saturday was special, getting to see both Coach Byrdsongs in action. The Wildcats played at one o'clock in the afternoon, pulling off a win against the University of Illinois, 78-70. Then Sherialyn's high school varsity team had a game that evening—too late for the Evanses to go back home that night. They decided to stay over and go to church with Ricky and Sherialyn the next day. The new stucco house had plenty of room.

Carlton got a kick out of watching giant Ricky with little Sabrina draped over his shoulder while Sherialyn filed in with the choir at Mount Calvary Baptist. Good choir—no wonder Sherialyn was so gung ho. After the service, Ricky introduced them to the pastor, Rev. Theodus Gantt. "What? You backing out on our Sunday dinner date?" Rev. Gantt teased.

"That's right, Pastor." Ricky looked remorseful for about two seconds.

"Gotta go fire up the grill to feed these two vagabonds." He looked at Carlton and Karen. "You two *are* staying, right?"

Laughter filled the afternoon as the two couples passed their two babies back and forth and chased the older Evans children around the yard. "You really should have seen Ricky playing Santa Claus at Papa Lute's last Christmas," Sherialyn tattled.

Carlton eyed Ricky's long arms and legs. "Tell me it ain't true."

"Hey, why not?" Ricky protested.

"Yeah," Sherialyn said wryly, "but when he walked in the Olson's front door, with the Santa suit hanging off him like a potato sack and going 'Ho, Ho, Ho!' one of Papa Lute's grandkids ran over and said, '*You're* not Santa Claus! You're Ricky Byrdsong!' "

Carlton rolled his eyes. "Byrd impersonating Santa Claus. Have you no shame?" Then, "Hey, Byrd, we really gotta go. It's a two-hour drive, you know."

"Carlton! You can't go yet." Ricky grabbed Carlton's arm and steered him down the hall to the master bedroom. He slid back the closet door. "Pick any three suits you want out of there."

Carlton blinked. "What are you talking about? I can't do that."

"Who says you can't? They're my suits. I say you can. Go on."

Carlton snorted. Ricky was nuts. Those were expensive suits in there.

As he hesitated, Ricky pulled out five suits from the closet and laid them on the bed, then rifled through his shoes on the floor of the closet and set out three pairs. "Look, Carlton. I have more than I need. I want you to have them."

Helpless, Carlton watched as Ricky piled the suits and shoes in the trunk of the Evans' car as Karen loaded the kids into the backseat. Sherialyn and Ricky stood arm in arm, waving as they drove off. Carlton watched in the rear-view mirror until they turned a corner. He couldn't help remembering the time Ricky had waved a five-dollar bill in his face back in college. "See this, Carlton? That means you got at least two-fifty."

21

Looking for the "Great Promoter"

In Texas, after persistent investigation, Klassen discovered that his bank had recently been purchased by John Landon, a key associate of Peter Galanis, arrested as the alleged mastermind behind the nationwide, multimillion-dollar investment scam. At one point, Chilton Private Bank allegedly allowed Galanis's wife, Chandra, to overdraw her account by about $1.4 million. Landon himself was facing an indictment on federal tax fraud and racketeering charges. James T. Davis, the manager with whom Klassen had dealt, was facing a possible five-year jail sentence and $250,000 on each of three charges related to the bank's insolvency.

By the time Klassen arrived, the Texas Banking Commission didn't know of any "government bonds" in which customers' money was supposedly invested…and protected. The $700,000 in cash that the commissioner said was found on the premises ultimately dwindled to $413,000.

After six months of desperate effort, Klassen finally recouped twenty-eight cents on the dollar for the half-million he had squirreled away in Chilton Private Bank.

Never stopping to face the fact that he had lost his money because he deliberately put it in an unregulated bank hoping to cheat the IRS, Klassen began casting about for someone else to blame. He began thinking back on how he had heard of the bank in the first place: Don Johnson had suggested it. He hadn't done a lick of work for the COTC—no paralegal course, no videos—and he had known more details about that remote

Texas bank than one might expect if he had only heard about it through the grapevine, as he had claimed.

"I couldn't help but come to the only conclusion that made sense," wrote Klassen. "Don Johnson had moved into the church for no other reason than to help [the] JOG wreck our movement, and had he ever done a number on us!"[1]

• • •

Less than three months after returning from his frantic trip to Texas to investigate the failed bank, Klassen's phone awoke him at 12:30 A.M. on November 3, 1987. Bobbi Johnson screamed, "Somebody get an ambulance! Don has stopped breathing!"

Klassen called an ambulance, and then he and his wife hurried over to the Johnsons' apartment above the organization's headquarters.

Johnson was lying on his bed, his lips turning blue. Henrie tried mouth-to-mouth resuscitation while Klassen pumped on his chest, but there was no response. When the ambulance got there, the paramedics worked on him a few minutes and then whisked him off to the hospital. But by the time they arrived at the emergency room, Don Johnson, age fifty-two and in seemingly good health, had died of a sudden heart attack.

It caused Klassen to start speculating. He wasn't even sure Don and Bobbi were married. After all, he had never actually *seen* their marriage certificate, and they'd had some bitter fights. With no end to his spreading paranoia, Klassen recalled that Bobbie's mother's husband had also died from a completely unexpected heart attack. Was it coincidence or conspiracy? he wondered.[2]

After Don's funeral, Bobbi took a few weeks off to attend her daughter's wedding. When she returned, Klassen cut her hours and pay in half. She hadn't been producing that much anyway, he reasoned. From that day on their relationship deteriorated, until Klassen gave Bobbi thirty days' notice that she must leave the premises by May 1, 1988. She quit two weeks before the deadline.

•   •   •

After Bobbi Johnson left, Klassen engaged a self-proclaimed con man, Will Williams, as his new Hasta Primus. He came with his girlfriend, Lucinda, whom Klassen required him to marry if they were to live together. Once again the *Racial Loyalty* paper was published regularly for a time, and the group's membership expanded even in such northern cities as Milwaukee, Detroit, Baltimore, and Toronto. But the Williamses brought a dog onto the premises, and Will ended up physically abusing Lucinda. Separately, they left.

When the Williamses departed, the Reverend Victor Wolf joined Klassen as Hasta Primus and editor of *Racial Loyalty*. But at seventy years of age with his energy flagging, Klassen knew he needed more than a new Hasta Primus; he also needed to groom someone to replace himself. While he had been the founder of his movement, he hoped his successor would become the "Great Promoter." Also, having suffered such a financial set-back in the bank fiasco, Klassen hoped his successor might be a "white angel" with money enough to continue financing the movement. However, his efforts to find a replacement threatened to replicate his never-ending search for a reliable Hasta Primus.

Tom Metzger, founder of the White Aryan Resistance (WAR), seemed interested only in absorbing the COTC into WAR, Klassen felt. He quickly dismissed Metzger from consideration.

Prescott Rathborne was heir to a large New Orleans fortune and intensely interested in the movement, but Klassen didn't like him. When Rathborne pushed Klassen to change his racial language to speak of species instead of race, Klassen exploded: "The creed and program as laid down in our books is inviolable at any price. Whether you offered me ten million dollars or one hundred million, I wouldn't change one word of it. I don't need your money." [3] And that was the end of their conversation.

DeWest Hooker may have been too old to succeed Klassen since they were both seventy, but he was a wealthy businessman who owned a villa in

Italy, where his wife and family resided, and a flat in Washington, D.C., where Klassen found him relaxing with someone Klassen assumed was his girlfriend. Hooker promised Klassen ample funding if his big oil deal between Arabs and Israelis went through—a deal Hooker projected would net him twenty-five thousand dollars per day. After Klassen left, he decided Hooker's girlfriend was Jewish and began speculating on who controlled whom. Hooker never paid off.[4]

Rudy Stanko was in prison for selling tainted meat to school lunch programs when Klassen went looking for him. Stanko was an effective racial activist who quickly organized white inmates wherever he went, forcing the prison system to "diesel" him from institution to institution. He was said to have once had fifty white men in the yard shouting, *"Sieg Heil!"* Before, as he put it, the Jews targeted and framed him for cutting into their markets, he had built a two-hundred million dollar meat packing business. Klassen claims to have driven seventy-five hundred miles from prison to prison (eight in all) trying to catch up with Stanko. When he did, Klassen was impressed and ordained Stanko as a "reverend" on the spot. Klassen also asked Stanko whether he would accept the position of Pontifex Maximus when he was released, and Stanko agreed. Subsequently, Klassen began promoting Stanko in every issue of *Racial Loyalty.* Better still, Stanko claimed to have a hoard of gold coins buried somewhere and that he would donate one million dollars to the COTC.[5]

Rudy Stanko was the man!

• • •

It was time to gear up for the next stage of the movement. In *Racial Loyalty* Klassen wrote, "While leadership in the first stage of our development by its very nature belonged to philosophers/ideologues, the second stage...calls for a new type of leadership—activists/organizers."[6] He wanted every Creator to organize a "Primary Group" or join an existing one. He said the Primary Group was the basic organizational cell of the COTC, with two persons minimum, five optimum, and ten maximum so that enemy agents would find it harder to penetrate. Five Primary Groups would organize into

Secondary Groups. Five Secondary Groups would create a COTC Unit. Five COTC Units would constitute a Section. And five Sections would be a Legion with its leader appointed by the Pontifex Maximus.

The task of Creativity in this stage was "to propagandize, proselytize, and organize." Special defense units, variously called White Guard, White Tigers, and White Berets, would protect the COTC. "Above all," he wrote, "we must appeal to the mighty army of our youth!—This advice of Adolf Hitler is still valid today."[7]

Eighteen-year-old Brian Kozel of Milwaukee, Wisconsin, was one of those prize youths recruited into Klassen's army. But Klassen reported to his followers that, on September 15, 1990, Kozel had been walking with several other Creator White Berets to a friend's house when a group of Mexicans drove up alongside, piled out of their car, and attacked them. The White Berets "bravely fought off" their attackers, and when the fight was over, Brian and his companions continued walking down the street. But, according to Klassen, the Mexicans then pulled guns and started shooting. "Brian was shot in the back, through the heart, and died almost instantly."[8]

The COTC had its first martyr!

Milwaukee police offer a slightly different version to the story, reporting that Kozel had been shot shortly after leaving a bar. "He and a couple of buddies were kicking in the sides of passing cars [when] somebody pulled over and shot him."[9]

In *The White Man's Bible,* Klassen had anticipated this day: "Should [they] use assassination against our members, or our leaders, then the white race must meet fire with fire, and retribution and vengeance will be our answer. For every one of ours they kill we will extract ten times their number."[10] But now that it had happened and his movement had its first martyr, there were more strategic concerns: "The best way to avenge Brian Kozel's death is to make sure that the entire anti-white JOG system, which allows sp——s to come into this country and terrorize whites, is totally, completely, and irrevocably destroyed through a Racial Holy War."[11]

22

Head Coach and Motivator

The door to the athletic office at the University of Detroit opened, and Ricky walked out with Dr. McKinnon, former chief of police and member of the Titans interview committee. The solid black man shook hands with Ricky. "How do you think you did in that interview, Byrdsong?"

Ricky thought about the question. Brad Kinsman was an outstanding athletic director—no doubt about that. The University of Detroit historically had a strong program, but it had been decimated in recent years. The city had a reputation for being a rough town. It would be tough, very tough to get strong recruits, but a possible job as head coach was something to take very seriously.

"Dr. McKinnon, I've learned you have only one chance to make a first impression. I think I did well."

McKinnon flashed a smile. "I know Lute Olson, Steve Kerr, and Sean Elliott are holding their breath—hoping we're not going to take you away from Arizona."

"I might be a fool to leave," Ricky grinned. "The Wildcats are hot! Won the Pac-Ten championship two years ago, and this year we're headed for the Final Four." He waved as McKinnon hurried off, then hunted up a pay phone. He'd promised to call Sherialyn as soon as the interview was over.

Sherialyn picked up the phone on the first ring. Ricky could hear Sabrina fussing in the background. "That's great, Ricky," Sherialyn said when he told her how the interview had gone. "I wanted to wait till the interview was over, but Marcia called. Your dad died while he was at work. They're saying it was a heart attack."

• • •

Ricky sat next to his sister, Marcia, at the funeral of Edward Byrdsong. The entire Byrdsong clan was there—Grandma Jannie and Grandpa Earl, all the brothers and sisters. Ricky had such mixed feelings. Edward had been working on his brother's house-painting crew when he'd collapsed. Maybe it was a heart attack. But bottom line, Ricky knew his dad had drunk himself to death. Marcia was tight-lipped, dry-eyed. She was probably relieved. Edward had always been around at extended family gatherings, but never there for them as a father. Bob Jasper had been more of a father in the last six years than Edward had ever been. What difference would his death make? None, really.

That's what made Ricky sad...sad for all the missed years.

But he also felt hope. By God's grace, he would be a different father. He was going to be there for his kids.

• • •

The sportswriters were making a big deal of the fact that, at thirty-two, Ricky Byrdsong was the youngest head coach of a Division I school in the nation. They were also quick to point out that Detroit had won just seven games in each of the last two seasons. Byrdsong was going to have an uphill battle.

Ricky ignored the naysayers and tackled his first major task: putting together his coaching staff. A hundred applications sat on his desk. He pulled in Paul Swanson, who had been assisting at Northwestern University. Out of the pile of applications, one seemed unlikely—a young man named Scott Perry who had coached only on the high school level. He was currently working in a bank. But during the interview, Perry was impressive. So Ricky put it to him. "What do you think you can bring to the program?"

"I love the game," Perry said, "and no one will be more loyal than I will."

Ricky almost laughed. Those were the exact qualifications Coach Nance had said he was looking for when he offered Ricky his first coaching job. "Scott, I'd like to meet your family." As he visited with Scott's parents and wife, Kim, Ricky's certainty grew. Perry had character; he had the qualities Ricky wanted to instill in his players. "Scott's hired," he announced, right in the middle of the family conversation.

After putting together his staff, he concentrated on recruiting talent. Detroit high schools had a wide talent pool if he could just keep the fish from swimming away. But recruiting was something he *knew* he could do. While visiting one promising high school senior, Ricky found himself competing with the television, which had been left on. During the conversation, the eyes of both mother and son kept drifting to the action on the screen. Finally Ricky got up and pushed the off button. There was a startled silence. "Son," Ricky said, "I want your full attention. We're talking about your future."

Even with the uphill battle facing him as head coach, Ricky was excited. This was his chance to build a program from the ground up. He knew the kind of coaching that had motivated him, but would this team respond? Maybe. First, he had to get a few things straight.

He strode into the room for his first meeting with the Titans basketball team and ran into a sea of caps. Marching around the room, he snatched caps off—first one, then another, and another. That done, he faced his new team, who stared at him open-mouthed.

He smiled. "Hi! I'm Coach Byrdsong. You may think you're here to play basketball, and that's true. But you will also attend all your classes, abstain from drugs and alcohol, and participate in this community's Big Brother program. We're here to change Detroit's image, and it's going to begin with you."

●   ●   ●

The Byrdsongs settled into their new home—white brick with black trim—in Lathrup Village and began hunting for a church. The first Sunday, they visited Rosedale Park Baptist. Ricky locked his keys in the car, and the pastor, Haman Cross, had to call AAA. While they waited for the service truck, the two couples—Ricky and Sherialyn and Haman and Roberta—leaned against the Byrdsongs' car and got acquainted. It was the beginning of a strong relationship that would follow the Byrdsongs into the future.

Even though Ricky's job put stress on his church attendance, he found a friend and ally in Pastor Cross. Whenever he was feeling under pressure, whether at work or at home, Ricky would call Haman Cross. "Pastor! I need a time-out." The two men would meet for lunch and talk about church, marriage, job politics, marriage, basketball, marriage...

Ricky was upfront; Pastor Cross liked that. Ricky never hesitated to call and ask for advice, either, whether it was from former coaches or spiritual mentors. Then he'd chew on the meat and spit out the bones.

Sherialyn had signed up for a three-year discipleship course that Roberta Cross had developed for a small group of women. Her dedication sometimes made Ricky feel inadequate. "Sherialyn's a good Bible student," Pastor Cross acknowledged.

"You got that right," Ricky deadpanned. "She can whip out a Bible verse faster than Annie Oakley can draw her six-shooter. Shoot me just as dead too." They laughed. But Pastor Cross had some wisdom to share with Ricky. "When you put together your coaching staff, what are you looking for?"

That wasn't hard. "Staff who share my coaching values but have strengths that I don't."

Haman Cross raised an eyebrow. "Marriage is like that. Our wives have strengths that we don't—and that we men need. We 'staff to our weakness'—which means we learn from the differences our wives bring. What keeps us going is the shared values."

That gave Ricky something to chew on. He was crazy as ever about Sherialyn, even though they both had strong personalities. But the bottom line? They were tight when it came to being committed to their marriage and family. And he couldn't ask for more loyalty from her when it came to supporting his profession.

Pastor Cross gave him something else to think about. "You and Sherialyn are powerful stuff. When the two of you *do* work as a team, you can be invincible." He pointed to the time when Ricky and Sherialyn had reached out to a young single mom at the church, taking her under their wing and providing an "extended family" for her and her children.

Maybe it was teamwork Ricky had in mind when he called Haman Cross, laughing with glee. "Pastor! We're going to have another baby!"

• • •

Ricky drove as fast as he dared. The hospital was twenty minutes away and Sherialyn was lying on the backseat of the car, screaming her head off. *Why* did that stupid hospital nurse keep telling them to wait? When they finally decided to come anyway, Sherialyn's water broke before they even got to the car.

"Ricky!" Sherialyn screamed. "I can feel the head! Can you see the head?"

Ricky stopped for a light and twisted in his seat. A dark head was crowning between Sherialyn's legs. "Hold on, baby! Hold on!"

He stepped on the gas and moments later squealed into the emergency entrance of the hospital. Leaping out of the car, Ricky went running into the lobby. "Help! Somebody help us! My wife is having a baby—outside! Outside! In the car!"

People came running with a gurney. Passersby stopped and stared. Sherialyn was still screaming. "It's coming! It's coming!" They got as far as the lobby, and a doctor made a quick assessment. "Push."

Sherialyn gulped for air and bore down. With one push, the baby was out. Then the procession started up again, making double-time to the maternity floor as patients, hospital staff, and visitors stared.

When the excitement died down, Sherialyn cradled their new little girl. They'd already decided on the name: Kelley, Sherialyn's maiden name, meaning "warrior maid." And Marcia, after Ricky's sister, meaning, "warlike."

"She's going to need to do battle in the world we've brought her into," Sherialyn murmured. Ricky agreed. With an entrance like that, this one was off to a screaming start.

• • •

Baby Byrd number three followed the next year—a boy. His name had been picked out since day one: Ricky Allen Byrdsong Jr. "Powerful ruler." "Cheerful." Scott Perry nearly burst all his buttons when Ricky asked him to be Ricky Jr.'s godfather.

The Titans were slowly coming out of their slump. For a school with a reputation for putting academics above athletics, skillful recruiting was the key. Ricky's own philosophy meshed with that of the school administration: "I rank character and skill one and two, and academics third when I'm recruiting a kid," he told a reporter. "Because if he's got good character, he'll try to do the things you ask him to do."

But at the end of his second season he faced a major personal challenge: The University of Arkansas at Little Rock offered him their head coach job at double his current salary. *Double!* The Byrdsongs made a trip to Little Rock to discuss the job, while newly recruited players, sportswriters, the athletic department, even the larger Detroit community, held their collective breath. Who could blame him for seriously considering it? But what about all his talk about laying a solid foundation and building on it?

Back at home, while they lay awake in the darkness, Ricky turned to Sherialyn. "What do you think?" For a few seconds, there was only silence. And he knew.

"She paused too long," he quipped to a reporter the next day. He already had his own doubts about the wisdom of a move. Sherialyn helped him make up his mind. He felt like he'd be deserting the players he had promised to coach, and he'd made a commitment to the University of Detroit when he signed his contract. What was he if not a man of his word? He turned down the UALR offer.

•   •   •

"Sherialyn! Did you listen to those tapes yet?" Ricky was excited about a certain popular speaker's motivational tapes he had purchased, always on the lookout for ways to motivate his players toward success.

Sherialyn was dividing Sabrina's soft, thick hair into sections and capturing it with colorful hair bands. "I listened to a couple of them."

Ricky caught the flat tone in Sherialyn's voice. "What? He's great!"

"I don't know, Ricky. It's all pull-yourself-up-by-your-bootstraps stuff. Doesn't make any room for the work of the Holy Spirit in our lives. And you know as well as I do that's where the real power is."

Ricky sighed and held out his hand to Sabrina. "Come on, 'Brina. Want to take a walk with Daddy?"

Sherialyn watched them go. Why didn't Ricky seem to understand that you had to go deep with God? But she had made up her mind a long time ago that nagging was not the way to change him. God had to do it. Her job was to pray for Ricky. They'd been married going on twelve years. It was a journey, this growing in love for each other.

Sherialyn filled the house with tapes of a different nature: praise and worship music. She felt like her soul had been waiting for this music all her life. The music was flat-out worship of God; it drew you in and made you sing. Most of the words were straight from Scripture. Not performance music; *praise* music.

So her ears had really pricked up when she heard that Rosedale Park Baptist was having a meeting to discuss forming a praise and worship team. Her organ practice paid off—she became their new organist. And when the worship team leader left a couple of years later, Sherialyn stepped forward to volunteer. Something in her body, soul, and spirit came together in a way that seemed to fulfill what God had created her to do: She was a *worshiping warrior!*

• • •

Ricky Byrdsong snatched his ringing office phone with one hand still juggling stat sheets with the other. But the voice he heard on the other end got his full attention.

"Coach Nance! Great to hear from you! How are the Huskies doing?" Ricky had followed Lynn Nance's career from Iowa State to the University of Washington.

Nance cut to the chase. "Don't know if you've heard, Byrd, but I'm in a tight spot. The father of one of my players—a former player, that is, since

I sacked him this year—wrote the Seattle papers and accused me of racism."

Ricky could hardly believe his ears. "Racism!"

The two men talked a long time as the story unfolded. The kid in question had a brother on the team who was doing just fine. But this kid transferred to UW against Nance's advice, even though Nance said he didn't have a scholarship for him. Nance gave him a chance on the team, even got a Christmas card from the parents thanking Nance for what he was doing for their boys. But the kid was a hothead, goading the other players with black-power slogans, dumping CDs belonging to white players on the floor, and substituting his own music in the team locker room. Nance cut him from the team. The Huskies didn't need that kind of division.

Ricky understood sacking a player at personal cost. He himself had dismissed the Titans' seven-foot junior center and a senior guard after a locker-room blowup. Then he'd suspended his leading rebounder because of a campus altercation—"conduct detrimental to the team." Discipline. Team unity. It paid off in the long run, even if it meant losing a game or two.

But the consequences in Nance's case opened a Pandora's box. The papers were all over it, and the University of Washington had set up a special committee to look into it.

"My job's on the line, Byrd. I'm wondering…what do you think of getting some of my former players to speak on my behalf?"

Ricky not only thought it was a good idea, he called Carlton Evans, Andrew Parker, and some other African Americans who had played for Nance. They flew to Seattle, and Nance called a press conference. The reporters came expecting Nance's resignation, but Lynn Nance wasn't even in the hotel ballroom. Ricky was the first to speak: "Coach Lynn Nance is one of the most fair-minded coaches I know. If Coach Nance has a problem, it's because he demands discipline. Why, he wouldn't let us wear our caps in the building or play our ghetto blasters while we were walking through airports." Everyone, even the reporters, laughed.

Andrew Parker was more graphic. "I might call Coach Nance a —— [the epithet was unprintable] but he's no racist." More laughter.

To the reporters' surprise, the last speaker was a lovely young African American woman who was bouncing a creamy-skinned child with dark eyes on her hip. "My daughter is going to be very surprised when she's older to discover that her grandfather is a racist."

The story—and eventually the committee looking into the allegations—died on the vine. But the coaches association took Ricky to task. "You took a big risk going out on a limb like that," he was told.

Ricky didn't flinch. "I wouldn't have it any other way. Coach Nance helped me get where I am today. He was a father figure to me. No way was I going to stand by and see him shot down."

Escape

In the early spring of 1991, Ben Klassen's wife, Henrie, began having mild pains in her lower abdomen. When the pains didn't go away, they visited their daughter and son-in-law's home in Martinsville, Virginia, which had medical facilities nearby. After several tests, the initial conclusion was a relief: no cancer.

However, Henrie continued to not feel well, so while she stayed for more tests, Klassen returned to North Carolina. The results of the second round of tests were more ominous, and finally the doctors confirmed that she had cancer.

Ten years before, Klassen had denounced the American Cancer Society and the National Cancer Institute in *The White Man's Bible* as Jewish scams bilking the gullible public out of millions of dollars while trying to kill the white race with its poisonous drugs. Surgery, radiation, and chemotherapy were a "horrible piece of sadism" in a "phony battle." Cancer, he declared, was nothing more than the last stages of toxemia, and the solution was simple: Stop poisoning the multitudes! "Is there an answer to cancer? Yes there is and we have spelled it out any number of times before—*Salubrious Living*."[1] Later he incorporated these ideas into Article VII as part of the COTC's creed: "We will not be dictated to by the Jew-dominated American Medical Association, or any other closed shop union, or any group of any nature, including the government itself, that seeks to impose their 'orthodox' medical treatments upon us, whether it be for the treatment of cancer or any other ailment."[2]

However, when it was clear that Klassen's beloved Henrie was desperately ill, and the doctors from this same "evil complex" diagnosed her as having cancer, he submitted to their judgment and did not oppose surgery. Why not treat the cancer according to Salubrious Living? The fact was, Klassen had never followed the Salubrious Living diet consistently himself. He preached it to others, adding a "whole life" mystique to his religion, but he didn't put enough faith in its diet of raw fruits and vegetables to deny his personal craving for steak or lobster when he wanted a good meal or the convenience of Shoney's when he was on the road.[3]

Henrie recovered slowly from her May 10, 1991, surgery, remaining at their daughter's house in Martinsville while Klassen drove back and forth some 270 miles from the headquarters in North Carolina. In mid-June Henrie returned to the hospital for a couple of weeks. Finally, she came home in July and slowly improved until she was able to take a trip to Colorado with her daughter in October.

She survived the trip and enjoyed it, but by mid-October the pain had returned. The doctors found more cancer. At this point there didn't seem to be anything that could be done other than to allow her to return home and help her manage the pain. Her family attended to her until she died on January 24, 1992.

Though there had been nine months of warning, Klassen was devastated by the loss of his wife. There is no question that he was genuinely devoted to her even though she may have grieved over him. In the end she arranged one last gentle plea. Henrie, who had asked her Canadian in-laws to pray for her Benny, requested that two songs be sung at her memorial service: "Springtime in the Rockies" and "Whispering Hope," the last verse of which reads,

Hope, as an anchor so steadfast,
Rends the dark veil for the soul.
Whither the Master had entered,
Robbing the grave of its goal.

Come then, O come, glad fruition,
Come to my sad, weary heart!
Come, O Thou blest hope of glory,
Never, O never depart.

Whispering hope,
O how welcome thy voice!
Making my heart in its sorrow rejoice.[4]

• • •

Six weeks after Klassen lost his wife, the parole restrictions that had held Rudy Stanko in South Dakota were lifted, and he made the trip to COTC headquarters. He rolled in with his Chevrolet Suburban pulling a home-made trailer (an old car body without an engine) filled "with a ton of legal papers, a residue of his legal manipulations during his five and a half years in prison."[5]

Klassen gave him a royal tour and then took him out to dinner. It looked like Stanko was ready to take up the mantle immediately. Earlier, Stanko had written for an issue of *Racial Loyalty,*

It is my avowed purpose to provide the necessary leadership, organizational and promotional talents to…smash the tyrannical Jewish network once and for all time. It is my hope and dedicated goal to bring this about in the next decade, the last decade history has allowed us for the final showdown.[6]

So the long-awaited Great Promoter, the new Pontifex Maximus designate had finally arrived! That night Klassen slept easy for the first time in many months.

Next morning after breakfast, Stanko came over to Klassen's house, and they sat down to discuss plans. "Well, where should we begin?" said Klassen.

"Probably by telling you that I'm heading back to South Dakota today," said Stanko.

Klassen frowned. With the recent loss of his wife, Klassen needed a break. Certainly with a van and trailer full of stuff, Stanko had brought all he needed, at least for the time being. "When will you be back?"

"I don't think I'll be coming back. I don't see the need for it. I can cover everything from home. It won't take me long to incorporate your mailing list into mine and be up and running. I don't see anything else I need to do here."

"My mailing list into yours? Your what? You're not thinking of reviving that thing you started before you went to prison—that Church of the New Order business—are you? Look here, Stanko, I offered you the greatest opportunity of your life. This is the one and only white man's religion." Klassen stopped, his face graying and his breath catching in his throat. After a moment, he shook his head as though to clear the threatening nightmare. "What about the headquarters?"

"You mean these little buildings?" Stanko waved his hand. "No problem. They're just real estate. Sell 'em. They don't mean anything to me or anybody else as far as I can see."

"You damned liar. You…you told me you were enthusiastically looking forward to taking on the most important and challenging mission in your life. I followed you around to eight different prisons helping you gain release. I loaned you five hundred dollars. I've been promoting you to our membership for months."

"Sorry, buddy. That's how it goes sometimes."

"You mean you never even intended…"

"Hey, what can I say?"

"Well, I know what *I* can say. Get out of here!"

Stanko shrugged and walked out. And to Klassen's surprise, he got in his van and drove away. Later, Klassen discovered that Stanko had stolen the COTC's mailing list of about thirty pages.[7]

Since then Stanko has dusted off his COTC ministerial credentials whenever it suits him, as it did in 1999 when he tried to gain access to

Montana's women's prisons as an ordained minister. He also sells COTC literature when he needs a little extra money.[8]

Klassen admitted, "I was back to square one. To whom could I entrust this great responsibility? I went over my membership list. I wracked my brain. There was not a single willing, qualified volunteer."[9] Finally he recalled Charles Altvater, a COTC member from Baltimore. He was completely dedicated and, when Klassen asked, willing to take on the responsibility.

But in May 1992, after Altvater had spent less than a month at the headquarters, Klassen decided he was unqualified for the role of Pontifex Maximus. Altvater accepted the demotion without rancor and returned to Baltimore to continue waging RAHOWA. On December 14, 1992, he was indicted in Baltimore on sixteen criminal counts, including attempted murder, reckless endangerment, possession and manufacture of explosives, and destruction of property. According to the indictment, Altvater allegedly placed a bomb on the porch of a Baltimore County police officer's home; he was also alleged to have bombed a state police car on the same day. A search of Altvater's home revealed ninety-two quarter sticks of dynamite. He was convicted and given a five-year term for reckless endangerment and a twenty-year sentence (seven years of which were suspended) relating to the bombing charges.[10]

Left without a replacement, Klassen looked north again. Milwaukee had a strong white supremacist movement represented in the Wisconsin skinhead gang SHAM—Skinhead Army of Milwaukee—also referred to as the Northern Hammerskins. They had been distributing Klassen's publications energetically, and Milwaukee had been the home of Brian Kozel, whom the COTC claimed as its martyr. Klassen approached Mark Wilson, the leader of the Milwaukee group. Maybe he would be willing to take over, and maybe, Klassen reasoned, it was time to move the COTC from its rural southern base to a major population center. Such a concession exceeded his intuition about maintaining a guiding hand over the movement, but he was seventy-four and determined to hand over the overt leadership.

The upshot of their discussions was Klassen's announcement that he was resigning and transferring the title of Pontifex Maximus to Wilson, and that he would sell the movement's property and library and donate the proceeds to the new Milwaukee headquarters. Klassen also arranged to transfer his quarter-million-dollar inventory of Creativity books to Milwaukee for the cost of shipping alone. But since the Milwaukee group had no money, Klassen advanced even that money to them.[11]

Klassen sold the North Carolina headquarters for one hundred thousand dollars to William Pierce, a white supremacist and former publisher of the *National Vanguard,* who once had given Klassen a six-inch by forty-eight-inch plastic tube for burying guns and other valuables.

Relocating the COTC headquarters reenergized the Milwaukee skinheads. And Mark Wilson's new prestige enabled him to establish a close relationship with the growing COTC presence in Canada, particularly in the Toronto area. But in the next six months, the Milwaukee crew managed to publish only two rather weakly written issues of *Racial Loyalty*—a definite disappointment to Klassen. He began to worry that the Milwaukee skinheads' propensity for reckless behavior might spin out of control. Also, he complained, "Everybody looked to me to fund everything, as if I had a bottomless gold mine at my disposal."[12]

Nevertheless, Klassen sent a ninety-five-thousand-dollar check to the Milwaukee COTC (the sale price of the property minus expenses and the shipping costs for the books). But Wilson never thanked Klassen or even acknowledged the proffered position of Pontifex Maximus. Whether or not formal acceptance had been a previously articulated condition, Klassen began telling Wilson that it required his written acceptance before it was valid. This was undoubtedly a precaution to clarify legal responsibility should any liability arise from activities over which Klassen had no control.

Wilson kept promising such a letter, but it never arrived, further piquing Klassen. Similarly, Wilson kept promising that he would soon publish *Racial Loyalty* on schedule, but it never happened. Klassen also discovered that the Milwaukee people were spending "his" money on new salaries for themselves and on the purchase of unnecessary real estate.

Then, against Klassen's advice, Wilson hired Steve Thomas as his office manager. Thomas had spent four years in Leavenworth for the 1966 rape and murder of Phan Thi Mao, a woman in Vietnam. (This crime formed the basis for Brian De Palma's 1989 film *Casualties of War.*) Thomas was still on parole and, as Klassen described it, "had to report to his JOG [Jewish Occupational Government] superiors regularly, a perfect inside pipeline for the Jews to get every scrap of information as to what was going on at our COTC headquarters."[13] Such recklessness against his advice was the last straw as far as Klassen was concerned.

In the meantime, Klassen met Rick McCarty, a psychologist from Niceville, Florida, who had been involved with the Klan and various racial issues. Klassen considered it a good sign when McCarty actually paid for COTC books and promised to read them. As things worsened with Milwaukee, Klassen called McCarty and suggested he come up to North Carolina to talk about how he might get involved. (Klassen still lived in his home, even though he had sold off the headquarters.)

When McCarty volunteered to lead the organization, Klassen saw his chance. He called Wilson on January 20, 1993, and abruptly dismissed him as COTC chief. But unlike Stanko or Altvater, Wilson did not go quietly.

Ever believing in the omniscient Jewish conspiracy, Klassen claimed, "Through telephone tapping and the Jewish spy system, they were already well aware of what we were doing even before I called, and all hell broke loose."[14] When McCarty flew up to Milwaukee to work out a settlement, Wilson loyalists attempted a last minute "coup" against him in his hotel. The alleged plan to intimidate McCarty into abandoning his appointment was accidentally thwarted when police arrested three members of the Wilson faction on concealed weapons charges in the hotel parking lot.[15]

Armed with a written power of attorney from Klassen, McCarty proceeded to meet with Wilson and worked out a deal in which the Milwaukee people returned fifty thousand dollars, the COTC mailing list, and all but 5 percent of the remaining books.

With a "Transfer of Leadership Certificate" in hand, the Reverend Rick McCarty returned to Florida as the new, duly recognized Pontifex Maximus.

• • •

Nearly a year before, Klassen had sat down at the breakfast table while visiting with his daughter. With his elbows on the table and his head in his hand, he said, "Kim, I'm bored with life."

She reached to pour him another cup of coffee. "Dad, you're just weary."

He pulled his cup away. "No. Just listen to me. I'm trying to tell you something." He waited while she slowly sat down. "I'm bored with life as such. Sometime within the next year or so, after I complete publishing the two books I'm working on now and put the church organization in the hands of someone responsible, I think I'll quit—escape all this." He moved his hand from his forehead in one dismissive wave.

Kim touched his arm. "Dad, I love you deeply, and you know there's nothing that would make me happier—or Mom, either, if she were still here—than if you set aside the COTC." She blinked back tears.

The muscles at the sides of Klassen's jaws throbbed. When he spoke, his voice rose as though launching from a ski jump. "That's not what I'm talking about, Kim. I'm thinking of voluntarily making a terminal exit from this corrupt and degenerating world."

"You're...what?"

"Just like I explained in chapter fifty-nine of *The White Man's Bible,* suicide is an honorable and dignified way to die—"

"Stop! STOP!" cried Kim. "Don't quote that stuff to me." Tears were streaming down her face. "There are many good things you could live for."

She got up and fled from the room.

Later, Klassen thought he had perhaps been cruel in telling her of his intentions.[16] But he hadn't wanted it to come as a shock when, on August 6, 1993, while alone at his home in North Carolina, he consumed four bottles of sleeping pills.

Two days later, Kim found his body along with a handwritten note justifying his suicide.

At his request, Kim and her family buried him on his property in what he had designated the Ben Klassen Memorial Park, under a stone inscribed,

He gave the white people of the world a powerful racial religion of their own. He had asked that a small urn of Henrie's ashes be buried next to his heart.

Kim would like her father to be remembered as an honest and courageous man who was a wonderful father and faithful husband. "We certainly had different viewpoints," she admitted in a recent phone interview. In 1979 Kim had abandoned her father's ideas to join the Mormon Church. And after his death, within the context of that faith, she felt comforted. "There has been a very big change in my father's views," she said. "I'm confident that he has come to a great awareness."[17]

But what of the destruction still emanating from the movement he started?

24

A Walk on the Wild Side

At the final buzzer the Titans' score lit up the board. Another win! After roughhousing with the team and tap-dancing with the press, Paul Swanson and Ricky Byrdsong headed for the closest pizzeria. Paul pulled open the passenger door of Coach Byrd's Chrysler Concorde but had to make room first by sweeping a couple of burger bags and several music tapes off the seat. Ricky shrugged good-naturedly. "Hey! You know how messy kids are."

"Uh-huh." Paul held up a twenty-four-ounce Big Slurp and waggled it at Byrd before tossing it in the back. Sabrina was barely six. He was about to toss a Hallmark card envelope after the paper cup when Ricky pointed to the visor. "Hey! Stick that up there where I won't forget it. Mother's Day is coming up."

Paul knew Ricky was happy with the win. After five years of hard work, the Titans were finally having a winning season! But Paul recognized another gleam in Coach's eye. Something was up.

"Okay, Byrd. Let's have it."

Ricky drummed his fingers on the booth table. "Felt bad about luring you away from Northwestern when I asked you to come on board with the Titans. I'm thinking about sending you back."

Like coins rattling through a change sorter, the possibilities sorted themselves in Paul's mind. His eyes widened. "Northwestern? Byrd! They offered you the head job?"

It was no secret that the Wildcats' basketball coach, Bill Foster, was retiring and that Northwestern was on the prowl for his replacement.

Ricky's wide grin confirmed it. "I want you to come with me as my assistant, Swani."

Paul laughed big. "I always did like Evanston." The northern Chicago suburb, home to Northwestern University, hugged Lake Michigan's western shore with distinctive charm. "But you sure about leaving UD right now? You got Detroit eating out of your hand this season." Even the grudging Detroit Public School League coaches who had been passed over for an outsider in 1988 had become Byrdsong fans.

"Yeah. I'm happy with what we've done here." Ricky laughed. "But might as well leave while I'm ahead. Steve Fisher has a slot for Scott Perry at the University of Michigan—they'll get along great." The nonstop grin widened even further. "Besides, it's not every day I get offered a job as head coach for a Big 10 school."

Paul couldn't argue with him there. It was a great career move. And he wasn't surprised, either, when a few days later his phone rang. "Swani! Do you remember where I put that Mother's Day card I had in the car? I can't find it anywhere!"

•   •   •

In the summer of 1993 the five Byrdsongs moved into a two-story house on a tree-lined street straddling the borders of Evanston and Skokie, Illinois. They'd barely gotten the pictures hung when the Fast Break Club—Northwestern's boosters—sponsored a tour to play in several European tournaments. This time Ricky also bought tickets so his sister and mother could travel with him and Sherialyn and the new basketball team. Ricky and Sherialyn's kids, the "three busy Bs," got to run their Grandma Gwen and Aunt Kim ragged in Atlanta.

The team had only been in Europe a few days when Coach Byrd handed out postcards to each team member. "Don't ever take the people who help you for granted. This team is first of all *grateful.*" The thank-you postcards, handwritten by each team member, were mailed to individual boosters who had raised money for the trip.

It also gave Ricky an idea. Corporations had mission statements. Why not a basketball team? Back in his new Northwestern University office, he drafted a mission statement for his players. It began: "A Northwestern basketball player is first of all grateful…"

• • •

Christmas Day in the Byrdsong household had been lively, what with three wide-eyed Byrdsong children diving into the pile of mysterious packages under the tree and hanging all over Aunt Marcia. Now the artificial Christmas tree, grandly dressed in gold and pink, stood alone in the front room. Ricky had gone jogging—it was cold, but no snow yet. Sabrina and Kelley were in the basement playing with their new toys. Ricky Jr. was down for a nap; at last Sherialyn could turn off those annoying musical lights that he insisted on playing ad infinitum. She flopped on the couch in the family room just off the kitchen and idly clicked on the television to channel 38, Chicago's religious station.

A middle-aged white woman was teaching the Bible. Sherialyn listened for a while to the woman's no-nonsense style. But she had a sense of humor, too. Talked about herself, her own weaknesses and failings, what God was teaching *her*. Without even realizing it, Sherialyn's feet gradually slid off the arms of the couch and she hunched forward, watching intently. Who was this person? She really knew the Word! And she didn't pull any punches either. *This is what the Word says…this means you.*

"Cia!" Sherialyn yelled. "Cia! Come see this Bible teacher! Who is she?"

Ricky's sister, Marcia, wandered into the family room and watched a moment. "I've seen her on TV down in Atlanta—I think she's national."

The sisters-in-law watched till the end of the program when the credits began to roll. *Joyce Meyer Ministries.* "Cia! Give me that pad of paper and a pen!" Sherialyn scribbled down the address and phone number to get put on a mailing list. She wanted some of Joyce's teaching tapes.

It was a Christmas gift to herself that kept on giving. Sherialyn listened to the Joyce Meyer tapes in the car and during her regular walks. Ricky would pick up the mail on his way into the house and wag his head. "Here's another one of your blue-and-white tapes!" But Sherialyn found the Bible teachings so practical, so down to earth—exactly what she needed for deepening her trust in God while juggling potty training, ringing telephones, the job pressures Ricky brought home, loneliness when he was on the road, even homesickness for Atlanta and "home."

• • •

Northwestern's team that year had a promising cast: five seniors and two juniors. The players responded to Coach Byrd's motivational tactics by winning nine straight preseason games, making them undefeated as they headed into the Big 10 season. But when the Wildcats lost their first two conference games at the buzzer, the honeymoon was over. The next five games were downhill losses. Ricky knew he had a problem on his hands. The players were distracted by comments yelled from the stands during the games—the negative legacy of being a losing school: "You've never won here!" "If you win this one, it'll be the first!" "What makes you think you can do what no other Wildcats team has done in twenty years?"

"You have a defeatist attitude!" Ricky railed at his players. "You're afraid that what the media are saying is true, that a team from an academic school can't win. You've got to focus! Focus! I don't care what the distraction is!"

But his pep talks seemed to backfire, causing the players to dwell on the distractions all the more. "Feels like we're telling a bunch of teenagers to concentrate on *not* thinking about sex," Ricky grumbled to his assistants.

After losing to Penn State on January 29, Ricky decided his players needed a wake-up call—one they wouldn't forget. The Wildcats were scheduled to play the Minnesota Gophers in Minneapolis on February 5. With a full week between the Penn State loss and their game with Minnesota, Byrdsong closed practices to all outsiders and kicked his unconventional program into gear. What did they have to lose? In one session he told the players to get into their defensive stances and shuffle around the court until they dropped. After eighty minutes, only three players were still standing—starting senior guard Todd Leslie and two seldom-used subs. Ricky rewarded them by letting those three start at Minnesota.

Every exercise that week focused on teaching the players how to block out all distractions. Ricky would give them five things to do and then inject pressure by doing something disruptive, like yelling at one of his assistant coaches, to see if the team could stay on task.

But Ricky had one more ace up his sleeve. On the way to Minnesota's Williams Arena, he forbade all talking. "You guys stay in your seats and study for your hardest class!" Then he warned them: "Tonight *I* am going to be the chaos you guys will have to overcome. Don't lose your focus—no matter what happens." And he gave a heads-up to Paul Swanson: "You're coaching tonight, Swani."

The players didn't know what to expect—but they soon found out. Twice during the first half, Coach Byrd came out on the floor arguing with the referees. He sat on the end of the bench with his arms folded, leaving the coaching to Swanson. Suddenly he got up and began roaming the stands, shaking hands with Minnesota fans. The Minnesota pep band heckled him; Byrdsong just laughed and waved. The big Gopher mascot gave him a high-five.

The media turned their cameras from the play to the stands. Sportswriters were agog. Was Byrdsong crazy? Throwing a temper tantrum? Write-ups the next day called it "Byrdsong's walk on the wild side."

The Gophers won 79-65, but Ricky was pleased. The Wildcats had held steady in spite of all the commotion he had caused.

But the Northwestern hierarchy was *not* pleased; they suspended their first-year coach. Sherialyn was scared. She had been listening to the game on the radio and gotten worried when she heard all the hoopla. Was the pressure getting to Ricky?

Ricky's behavior thoroughly rattled her. To Sherialyn, Ricky seemed wound up and depressed. She disagreed with many of the motivational tactics he had picked up from the popular speaker he often listened to. Phone calls flew back and forth to Pastor Cross in Detroit. Haman Cross encouraged Sherialyn to see the goals Ricky was trying to reach, even if she didn't agree with the means.

The players didn't seem confused. Senior guard Kip Kirkpatrick told a reporter, "I thought all along the guy is a genius. We needed something drastic. He did something drastic." They won two of their next four games with assistant coach Paul Swanson in the driver's seat.

After four games the Northwestern hierarchy called off the suspension. Ricky refused to criticize the university president and the athletic director. The best thing to do was to put the incident behind him and go forward. Later, Ricky admitted to friends, "It was a one-time thing. Wouldn't do it again."

But Ricky's players got the message. If their coach could go for broke, so could they. The rest of the season the Wildcats played inspired ball, even earning themselves a berth at the National Invitation Tournament, where they defeated DePaul then lost to Xavier in overtime. They finished the season 15-14—Northwestern's first winning season in eleven years.

•   •   •

Sherialyn was relieved. With a successful season behind him, Ricky seemed more relaxed. She noticed that Ricky's motivational tapes quietly disappeared. He had been making a special effort to round up the three kids after work and take them to the park to play. He often brought his players and assistant coaches to the house to grill steaks or burgers—his "family-style" approach to coaching. Sabrina, Kelley, and Ricky Jr. were all over the players—they liked having fourteen big brothers.

Maybe *now* the Byrdsongs could settle down and find a church home. Sherialyn and Ricky had tried several churches in the area, but nothing had clicked. They had been in Evanston about a year when she attended a praise and worship conference at the Midwest Christian Center in Tinley Park, Illinois. Worship teams from many different churches shared their music, learned from each other, and worshiped God together. In one of the workshops, Sherialyn wrestled with God. "God, you created me to be a worshiping warrior for you! But I don't have any place to live out my destiny!"

At the close of the workshop, she left her Bible and notebook on her seat and headed for the bathroom. Halfway there she halted midstride and looked around, noticing a man in his thirties whom she hadn't seen before. His name tag read *Lyle Foster, The Worship Center, Evanston, Illinois.*

The Worship Center? In Evanston? Why hadn't she heard about it before?

She grilled the couple, Lyle and Lona Foster. "What's The Worship Center?" The church was nondenominational, only five years old, renting space from local schools until they could buy a building. But the part that caught her attention was how the Fosters talked about worship: "We believe God is calling his people to a lifestyle of worship. When God's people put worship at the center of our lives, others will be drawn to him. Through worship we want to promote unity and reconciliation in the body of Christ."

As they talked, the Fosters learned that Sherialyn's husband was the head basketball coach at Northwestern University, practically in their backyard. "What about you?" Lona Foster asked.

"I'm a worship leader."

"Oh! You sing?"

"Not really."

"Play the keyboard?"

"Not really. The organ some."

The Fosters looked puzzled. But they encouraged her to visit. "We can use all the worshipers we can get."

Sherialyn was intrigued. "Who's the pastor?"

Lyle Foster cheerfully spread his hands. "In the flesh."

"Can you preach?"

Now Pastor Lyle was laughing. "Tell you what, Sister Sherialyn. You come and visit us next Sunday, and then you tell me."

● ● ●

The next Sunday Sherialyn and the three kids showed up at the nursery school in Evanston where The Worship Center was meeting. The Sunday after that, Ricky was with them. He agreed that they needed to find a church, but he'd been a little dubious when he heard that this fledgling church met in a preschool basement. He had to duck his head just to get in the door, and on one side of the room the ceiling was so low he could barely stand up straight.

And the service! Not your average sing-three-hymns, A-and-B-choir-selections, eye-on-the-clock service. A lot of the music was contemporary, and the little congregation really threw themselves into worship. Some of the songs went on for fifteen minutes! Each Sunday was different. Sometimes praise and worship were followed by a ministry time when the pastor laid hands on people and prayed for them about all sorts of things such as breaking the bondage of rejection, needing a job, healing of sickness.

The first few Sundays, Ricky slipped out as soon as he could without seeming rude and waited in the car for Sherialyn and the kids to come out. For a newcomer, the services were a little intense. Besides, he had a lot on his mind. His main project during the summer of 1994 had been a father-son basketball camp involving as many of his players and coaches as possible. Now the Wildcats faced some big challenges in his second season. Attitude was no problem; the team was still charged from last year's success. And he had a fine staff. Jamal Meeks had joined Paul Swanson and Shawn Parrish as assistants. But five seniors on the team had graduated; sophomore center Evan Eschmeyer struggled with a foot injury; a promising recruit from Peoria had suffered a heart attack during the summer that sidelined him for the year; and Geno Carlisle, another star recruit, had undergone knee surgery.

Then there was Kenneth Dion Lee, a promising scorer whose ego needed to be taken down a peg or two. Lee liked his flashy middle name, Dion, but Ricky called him Kenneth just to keep him in line.

A movement caught Ricky's eye. Lyle Foster was making a beeline across the street for the Byrdsong car. Ricky had to give him credit. Pastor Lyle was nothing if not persistent.

Ricky rolled the window down an inch or two. "Hey, Pastor!"

"Coach! Good to see you. How'd the basketball camp go? I was so excited when I heard what you were doing. We need more men like you encouraging fathers to be involved with their sons."

The window moved down a few more inches. "Really? Really? You think so?" The pastor had triggered one of his favorite buttons. "It was great! I want people to understand we're coaching something bigger than just basketball." Ricky opened the door and unfolded himself from the car. Standing together, the six-foot-six Byrdsong and the five-foot-eight pastor looked like the proverbial Mutt and Jeff. But the parking lot conversations soon became a habit with Ricky and the pastor talking basketball and parenting and the game of life.

Yes, The Worship Center was different…but there was something that drew Ricky and his family back.

25

The Chickens Come Home

Thirty-nine-year-old Rick McCarty had his hands full when he took over the Church of the Creator in the spring of 1993. Rumors being spread by the Milwaukee skinheads that Klassen had become senile before his death didn't help secure McCarty's position. Though court records indicate that McCarty had been arrested in 1985 on charges (later dropped) that he operated a telemarketing scam selling soft drink distributorships in Birmingham, Alabama, he was relatively unknown in hate-group circles. Klassen had claimed that McCarty had earned a Ph.D. with a background in business and psychology, but the new Pontifex Maximus would have to use *Racial Loyalty* to give himself a voice from the new headquarters in Niceville, Florida, a tiny community near the Gulf Coast resort town of Pensacola.

McCarty also set about making his mark by appearing on the nationally syndicated *Sally Jessy Raphael Show* with three other white supremacists pitted against some black separatists.

Whether or not McCarty's television debut made much of a national impact, Florida newspapers began taking note of the white supremacist in their midst. On July 17, 1993, a *NW Florida Daily News* article reported that Niceville police had cited the new Pontifex Maximus for driving under the influence of alcohol. On August 2 the *Palm Beach Post* quoted McCarty as claiming that even though the COTC had no church building in Niceville, they had "a warehouse that holds $500,000 in white supremacist pamphlets, newspapers, and books. They are distributed in all 50 states, and 37 foreign countries."[1]

But the events that really drew attention to him were the arrests of far-flung COTC members for various violent crimes.[2]

- Charles Altvater's case stemming from his December arrest for allegedly placing a bomb on the porch of a Baltimore County police officer's home and bombing a state police car was making its way through the courts, with all the accompanying publicity. He had not been named Pontifex Maximus, but he still was a reverend in the church.

- On June 9, 1993, Toronto police arrested the COTC's Canadian security chief, Eric Fischer, along with his brother, Elkar Fischer, and Drew Maynard, charging the three with kidnapping, forcible confinement, and assault for their alleged abduction and beating of someone they suspected of having stolen the local COTC computer. Eric Fischer was a hardcase. As a former member of the elite Canadian Forces Airborne Regiment, he had led such a grueling paramilitary training session in 1992 that one COTC recruit had collapsed and died.

- On July 15, 1993, Los Angeles FBI agents and local police arrested eight individuals, some of whom had ties to the COTC. They were accused of plotting to instigate a race war by bombing the First African Methodist Episcopal Church in south central Los Angeles and trying to assassinate Rodney King. Police stated that the alleged conspirators also had planned to target leaders of the NAACP and the National Urban League; Nation of Islam leader Louis Farrakhan; the Reverend Al Sharpton; rap music stars Eazy-E; and members of the group Public Enemy; as well as unspecified Jewish leaders.

- On July 26, 1993, police arrested two nineteen-year-old Washington state residents, Jeremiah Gordon Knesal, a reported leader of the COTC, and Wayne Paul Wooten for shoplifting at a mall in Salinas, California. During a search of Knesal's car, the officers uncovered three pipe bombs, four loaded long-barrel weapons, military apparel, ammunition, wigs, climbing gear, white supremacist literature, and a page from a Portland, Oregon, telephone book listing Jewish agencies and synagogues. Under subsequent questioning by the FBI, Knesal confessed to his involvement in the July 20 bombing of an NAACP office in Tacoma, Washington. Authorities stated that the Tacoma firebombing was part of a larger plot to attack Jewish and African American institutions, military installations (particularly those housing submarines), and radio and television stations. The three also reportedly planned to assassinate two rap music performers, Ice Cube and Ice-T. In connection with this alleged plot, police also arrested Mark Frank Kowaalski, a twenty-four-year-old ex-convict who was supposedly the state director of the COTC.

• Jurgen Matthews White and Johannes Jurgens Grobbelaar, two COTC activists in South Africa, were stopped by police suspicious that their vehicle had been stolen. Reportedly the two had been attempting to smuggle weapons and explosives into an alleged "survivalist" compound in Namibia. But while being escorted to a nearby police station, the two detonated a smoke bomb and tried to escape. After coming across their abandoned vehicle five miles away, police came under fire from the two suspects. Two officers were shot, one fatally, before law enforcement agents returned fire, killing both COTC members.

It was as though Klassen had handed McCarty a string of exploding firecrackers. McCarty began issuing press releases attempting to distance himself, saying he disavowed violence. Maybe the old man hadn't been going senile after all. Maybe his demand that the new Pontifex Maximus sign papers accepting formal leadership of the organization was a shrewd evasion of trouble he saw coming.

But as a supposed psychologist, McCarty should have seen it too. With all these arrests taking place, McCarty lamented, "This would kind of ruin an organization. I'm hoping [the bad publicity] is going to be one of these things that's here today, gone tomorrow."[3]

The sleeper was a case stemming from May 17, 1991, when thirty-six-year-old George Loeb, another reverend for the COTC, shot and killed

Harold Mansfield, an African American Persian Gulf War veteran, in a Neptune Beach, Florida, parking lot.

The COTC hailed Loeb as a hero and a martyr, claiming in the August 1991 issue of *Racial Loyalty* that the shooting was self-defense and that "Self-defense is our right." But this was not Loeb's first arrest for racial violence. In November 1990 he had been arrested after an African American woman told police that Loeb had followed her and her daughter, calling the woman a racist name and threatening to shoot her. The following January he reportedly started a fistfight with a black neighbor the morning after he had been arrested on charges of disorderly intoxication and resisting arrest. Also, in preparation for the trial on the Mansfield shooting, police seized sixteen hundred pages of personal correspondence and racist propaganda from Loeb's apartment. According to news accounts, the most significant of these documents was a handwritten note to a member of the Ku Klux Klan, in which Loeb wrote on behalf of the COTC, "The frequent use of the word 'n——' should lead to a widespread and violent black uprising that should give whites (and possibly police) the opportunity to kill large numbers of them with impunity. It is our feeling as Creators that shrinking the numbers of blacks worldwide is one of the highest priorities."[4]

On July 29, 1992, after only three hours of deliberation, the jury found Loeb guilty of first-degree murder. The following month he received a life sentence with no chance of parole for twenty-five years.

By the time McCarty took over the COTC, he thought the incident was over until the Southern Poverty Law Center helped Mansfield's family file a one-million-dollar lawsuit "seeking damages and dissolution of the organization for vicarious liability in the murder." It was back in McCarty's face. The COTC was being charged in court with significant responsibility for the murder.

In reflecting on people like George Loeb, Klassen's daughter, Kim, later said, "Well, you know, there are a lot of disturbed people in the world, and I think many had a predisposition to violence before reading any of my dad's teachings."[5] That may be true, but in addition to being a willing magnet for these kinds of people, Klassen had justified and encouraged their "predispositions." There is no other way to read his writings. He continually maintained that the white race was in jeopardy, and then he wrote things like, "If your survival is at stake, is so-called 'illegal' terrorism justified? And the answer overwhelmingly is—hell yes!"[6]

These alleged bombers, arsonists, and murders weren't rare, out-of-control renegades going against the letter or the spirit of Creativity. They were members in good standing, some even "reverends" who were often justified and honored by the church for their actions.

In fact, they were merely doing what Klassen had told them to do. They were launching RAHOWA!

In the face of this evidence, it would be hard for Rick McCarty or any other Pontifex Maximus to convincingly show that the COTC "neither condones violence or unlawful activities nor do we promote or incite them."[7]

In March 1994 the Florida court agreed that the COTC bore liability for murder, and the Mansfield family won their one-million-dollar lawsuit. By then McCarty had disbursed the warehoused books and other assets, closed up shop, terminated his leadership, and dropped off the public radar screen.

26

Turning Point

Ricky walked into Welsh-Ryan Arena on the western edge of Northwestern's campus and ducked a flying ball. It was the first day of the annual Ricky Byrdsong Basketball Camp. A herd of young boys were running up and down the court and enthusiastically lofting balls into the air, a few of which actually made it into the baskets.

The Wildcats had come out on the downside at the end of the second season, but Ricky wasn't discouraged. They'd had a lot of injuries to overcome and were building up a young team. That took time, and he had time. He was only two years into a five-year contract. Besides, these summer basketball camps for kids were always good for a shot in the arm. For one week he had a slew of great kids, all of whom had fantasies of becoming the next Michael Jordan or Steve Kerr for the Chicago Bulls. One week to encourage character qualities such as hard work, integrity, keeping your word, teamwork, valuing every player; one week to underscore the importance of staying in school and that the only real failure is being afraid to try for fear of failing—qualities that would take them a lot further than mere basketball skills alone.

Clad in his purple-and-white Wildcat sweats, Ricky noticed one young basketball wannabe dressed in a dirty T-shirt and shorts, old muddy shoes, and a yarmulke on his head. Ricky caught the boy's ball and said, "Hey, son! You got any other shoes to play in?"

The boy reddened and shook his head. "My dad didn't want to buy me any new shoes for camp."

Ricky raised his eyebrows. "Stay right there, son." He was back in a minute jangling his car keys. "C'mon."

The boy looked puzzled but obediently trotted after him. As they left the gym, Ricky hollered to his assistant. "J-Meeks! Cover for me. I'll be right back."

"Where we goin'?" the boy asked as Ricky unlocked his car door.

"To get you a pair of shoes. Put that seat belt on."

"Aw no, Coach. My dad wouldn't want you to do that."

"Why not, son? If you want to play ball, you gotta have good gym shoes—shoes that don't go outside playing in the mud."

The boy protested a few more times, but Ricky cheerfully ignored him. A half-hour later they walked out of a shoe store with a brand-new pair of athletic shoes.

Back in the car, the boy inspected the shoes. "My dad's gonna be mad. He'll make me bring them back."

Ricky just smiled. "Hey! Don't worry about it. Just part of the camp fee."

• • •

"Pastor! How come you're always calling people saints? I always thought saints were dead people."

Lyle Foster couldn't help but chuckle. A phone call from Coach *always* made him smile. "Because that's what God's people are called in the Bible."

"Where? Where, Pastor!"

"Tell you what. You keep reading your Bible regularly and coming to Wednesday-night Bible studies, and you'll discover a lot of stuff for yourself."

"You're right, Pastor. You're right. I'll see you there Wednesday night."

Pastor Lyle prodded. "Uh, Coach. You didn't call me up just to ask me why I call people saints, did you?"

Ricky's big laugh boomed on the other end. "How'd you like to travel with the team when we play New Jersey—as my guest. I'd like you to get to know the guys, and for the guys to get to know you. The team could use a chaplain."

Lyle Foster wasn't one to turn down an invitation like that. God was doing a new thing in Ricky Byrdsong—Sherialyn too, for that matter. Sherialyn had joined The Worship Center praise team soon after the Byrdsongs started coming to church. Anita Baker, a gifted musician who had been TWC's worship leader, saw the gift Sherialyn had for weaving the Word and praise songs together in worship and asked her to lead the praise team once a month or so. When Anita's husband settled down at another church, it was as if God had prepared her successor: Sherialyn Byrdsong. Lyle had to admit the lady was right: She *was* a worship leader.

According to Sherialyn, Ricky had never been this consistent about going to church. Once the strangeness of revival-style worship had worn off—or worn its way in—Ricky made a special effort to be in church on Sundays, even sometimes coming back from a road trip with the team late Saturday night so he could be there Sunday morning. He and Sherialyn had even started family devotions with the kids. "Although," he admitted, "trying to corral the Byrdsongs at the dinner table all at one time is harder than getting all my players to show up on time for practice."

"Coach," said Pastor Lyle, "you buy the ticket, you've got yourself a traveling pastor."

•　•　•

The sun was merciless, even for Chicago in June. And the concessions contract at Soldier Field wouldn't let anyone bring their own water into the stands. But Ricky, Pastor Lyle, his son Larnell, and several other men and their sons from The Worship Center were determined not to let a little sweat get them down. Promise Keepers, the Christian men's movement sweeping the country, had come to Chicago the summer of 1996, and men from TWC were going together as a group.

Ricky was curious. So far he liked what he'd heard about Promise Keepers—encouraging men to get right with God and fulfill their responsibilities to their wives and kids. Too many men were abandoning their families—fathering kids outside of marriage, leaving the home after divorce, or putting in mega-hours climbing the career ladder—and society had been reaping the results in neglected children. Promise Keepers was trying to stem the tide.

At the very least, it'd be a great day with the guys from TWC.

But Ricky wasn't prepared for the impact of seventy thousand men filling a football stadium with masculine cheers, all worshiping God together. The speakers and music group on the stage at the north end of the field were racially mixed—more so than the crowd—and the call to put an end to racism among Christian believers was strong. Bill McCartney, former head football coach for the University of Colorado, challenged the men: "Inside this nation there is a spirit of white racial superiority that has left a deep hurt in men and women of color. I have never met a man or woman of color who has not felt that oppression. It's not enough to say we feel their pain. We must move into that pain and die to ourselves."

Ricky had never heard a white person talk like that! He had a lot of white friends, people he loved and respected—but they didn't talk much about race.

But McCartney wasn't through. Even while faces, necks, knees, and arms fried in the sun, and men and boys drained two-dollar bottles of water one after the other, the former football coach told his captivated audience that if they had not already done so, they should develop a committed friendship with another man beyond their own culture.

"Hey, Pastor!" Ricky shook his head. "Look at all those white guys down there taking a stand against racism. Can you believe it?"

The lines for food and bathrooms were ridiculously long; the heat relentless. But another speaker who grabbed Ricky's attention was Wellington Boone, an African American minister working on college campuses. Ricky had recently read Boone's book *Breaking Through*. The book had had a big impact on Ricky's thinking. What would the man have to say?

He listened carefully as Boone challenged the men. If they wanted to be leaders in their homes and in their communities, it meant learning how to serve. "That's the biblical principle of leadership: If you want to be great, learn how to become a servant. If you want to be like Jesus, wash your brother's feet."

Ricky's heart skipped a beat. Something inside his spirit—something that had been searching for words to articulate it—seemed to mushroom, like an air bag inflating on impact. Something he'd never heard in his motivational tapes.

Tired, hot, hungry, and thirsty, The Worship Center guys walked what seemed like miles back to their parked cars, then crawled with the traffic north along Lake Shore Drive toward Evanston.

"So? How was it?" Sherialyn's expression was curious when, long after dark, Ricky finally dragged into the front door.

He sank into a chair. "Hot and miserable." Then he managed a grin and pulled her down into his lap, giving her a big squeeze. "One of the best days of my life."

• • •

Shawn Parrish, Paul Swanson, and Jamal Meeks sat glumly in Coach Byrd's office. The atmosphere was curious, given that the Wildcats had just pummeled Central Michigan, 70-49. But Geno Carlisle, the Wildcats star junior guard and by far Northwestern's best player, had just announced that he was transferring to a "higher-profile" program only a few months into the 1996–97 season.

It felt like a low blow. Too many injuries. Too many defections.

A lot was on the line. Last spring, three years into his five-year contract, Ricky had asked athletic director Rick Taylor for a contract extension, to provide team security for new recruits as he continued to try to build up the Wildcat team. But the team's third season had ended 7-20. Taylor had put him off. "We'll see what happens next season."

Now this. Ricky surveyed his gloomy staff. "Okay, I'm disappointed, too…but not surprised. We live in an impatient culture. But we can't let it get us down. Trust me. It's going to be all right."

After all, he pointed out, hadn't they just defeated Central Michigan? Center Evan Eschmeyer had led the Wildcats with thirteen points and guard Nate Pomeday followed close behind with eleven. Carlisle's departure would leave a big hole, but the team still had talent, still had a core of players committed to each other.

"But it's up to us to set the tone. Stay positive; no complaining."

The meeting broke up, but Shawn Parrish was still glum. Ricky called him back. "Hey, Coach P!"

"What?"

"Anchor deep."

That got a smile. Ricky had given him Max Lucado's book *Six Hours One Friday.* Shawn could hardly put it down. In the book, Lucado wrote that people who anchor to the cross of Christ have three solid truths they can count on: our lives are not futile, our failures are not fatal, and our deaths are not final. "We can survive tough times," Lucado had written, "but we have to anchor deep."

The hour was getting late. Ricky knew he'd missed seeing the kids before bedtime. He'd been trying to get home in time to eat with the family and spend time with the kids several nights a week. But…this wouldn't be one of them.

Lights were on but the house was quiet when he let himself in the front door. Sherialyn must be upstairs, too. Ricky passed pictures of the kids along the hallway and dumped his briefcase in a kitchen chair. That's when he saw the note.

Dear daddy, I won't be able to say Good night or, "I love you" so I'm saying it now. I love you. See you tommaroww and I hope we can go to the park to play some B-Ball.

Love, Kelley Skinny Binny

•   •   •

Ricky sat in his car on a narrow side street on the near north side of Chicago, taking in every detail of the infamous housing project known as Cabrini Green. What a contrast to the pleasant, tree-shaded neighborhood in Evanston where he was raising his children! The tall, unadorned buildings, their blunt, square windows arranged like a checkerboard, marched in a row as far as he could see. At the feet of the buildings, in grassless vacant lots strewn with litter and broken glass, young children played double-dutch or chased each other around in an ageless game of tag. Older teens leaned listlessly against walls, against cars, not doing anything. A few big boys, stripped to the waist in the warm October sun, tossed a basketball at a rusty, netless hoop.

Painful fingers seemed to tighten around Ricky's heart. These kids were losing the game of life. No one was teaching them the fundamentals. Fathers were probably absent. Mothers were overworked or untaught themselves. The future was bleak for these kids. Most of their role models were in gangs, selling drugs, or in prison.

If only these kids—even one!—had a coach, a mentor, a youth pastor—*somebody* to call them out as Coach Lester had called him out years ago: "Hey, son! Yes, you! You can do it! I'm going to help you!"

God, it's too big. I don't know where to start. But you've put me in a position of influence. You've blessed me in more ways than I can count. If you can use me, Lord, I'm ready. You know I love coaching basketball. But the real game is the game of life.

• • •

"So things have been changing at the Byrdsong household?"

Lona Foster and Sherialyn had gone shopping then stopped for lunch before Sherialyn had to head over to Sabrina's school to coach after-school basketball.

Sherialyn smiled wryly. "You could say that. Ricky decided 'no TV' during the week for the kids. They have to earn weekend TV privileges by finishing their homework and doing their chores."

Lona looked surprised. "You don't think that's good?"

"Well…sure. I probably wouldn't have made it cold turkey. I agree we need to moderate it. I figure if we keep them busy with sports and activities, TV won't be all that big a deal. But you know Ricky. He calls the shots."

Lona hid a smile. "Didn't you say you had something you wanted to show me?"

"Oh. Right." Sherialyn dug in her bag and pulled out a letter. She handed it to Lona. "Ricky wants to send this to Christian leaders all over the nation. What do you think?"

Lona skimmed through the letter written on Wildcat letterhead.

I am deeply grieved by the degenerate condition of our nation. I have always felt a calling on my life to help change things, but resisted. However, a recent visit to one of Chicago's ghettos made it clear to me that I cannot run from this calling any longer. As I prayed for what I was to do, the Spirit of God led me to this passage and I felt led to share my heart with you:

"If my people, who are called by my name, will humble themselves and pray and seek my face and turn from their wicked ways, then will I hear from heaven and will forgive their sin and will heal their land" (2 Chronicles 7:14)."

...the problem lies with those of us who call ourselves "Christian." We have failed in our responsibility to have our lives reflect the values that we say we believe in.

The letter continued, proposing that Christian pastors and ministries all over the nation encourage those under their influence to turn off the television for a week because "TV is a distraction, and God wants our attention."

Let's use the time to fast (as we are able) and pray concerning our own lives and the condition of our nation, focusing our prayers in three different areas: (1) rebuilding of broken and weak families; (2) a renewed compassion and responsibility for our brothers and sisters in our nation's ghettos; (3) raising the moral standards in television programming.

The letter was signed by Ricky. Lona looked up. "I think it's awesome. Don't you?"

Sherialyn nodded thoughtfully. "Yes. I think it's great. But he's really going out on a limb in a public way with his faith…as Ricky Byrdsong, head basketball coach, Northwestern Wildcats."

"But isn't that what you wanted, Sherialyn? You told me you prayed for years that Ricky would take his faith more seriously, to go really deep. Pastor and I see him taking big strides. Sometimes we get to the church and Ricky's already there in the parking lot. Been there for an hour, just reading his Bible."

Sherialyn nodded. "I know," she said quietly. "But he's going so deep so fast, it's scary."

A Hale of a Revival

Possibly anticipating that the COTC might have to go underground, Klassen had advised Rick McCarty to appoint a Guardians of the Faith Committee composed of twelve of the most tried, true, and tested ministers in the church. They were to be entrusted with renewing the ten-year reign of a Pontifex Maximus or naming a new one.

Without a Pontifex Maximus after McCarty's resignation, the organization split into factions and lost membership, but Klassen's ideas remained virulent.

In October 1995, COTC Reverend Brian Kachikis endorsed Matthew Hale, a twenty-four-year-old law student at Southern Illinois University, to become the new Pontifex Maximus. Kachikis wrote, "Matt has been a supporter of the COTC for many years, put out a monthly Creativity newsletter, and put many Creativity shows on cable access. Matt also has experience in political parties, has run for public office, has great speaking abilities, and has put out a national COTC hotline."[1]

Soon most Creativity branches expressed support for this suggestion, and the next summer during a convention at the Reverend Slim Deardorf's ranch near Superior, Montana, the Guardians of the Faith Committee unanimously confirmed Matt Hale as the new Pontifex Maximus. According to a local newspaper, only about thirty-five Creators were present,[2] and Hale himself won't say how many of those were Guardians, suggesting that he was endorsed by less than twelve.[3] But it was enough to secure his position.

One of his first acts as the group's leader was to christen a new name, the *World* Church of the Creator, possibly achieving a little legal insulation from the old organization but also extending its horizons.

While the wary-eyed, thin-faced young Hale looked nothing like the beefier Klassen, who had worn a Hitleresque mustache, they nevertheless had several things in common.

Hale had grown up in East Peoria, a small city in west central Illinois, most noted for being the home of Caterpillar, Inc., the world's largest manufacturer of earth-moving equipment. He and his parents and three older brothers lived in a small frame house that had been built by his German immigrant grandfather near the top of Pekin Hill. Matt doesn't have many positive family memories. They took a trip to West Virginia one time, a trip he enjoyed, but his parents didn't get along very well and divorced when he was only eight.

In that same year, Matt had his only extended acquaintance with a black person, a boy who lived in the neighborhood. "He wasn't a particularly bad fellow or anything. We played sports and things like that. On a personal level, I guess he was a friend," Matt recalls.

But then Matt went to live with his mother. After a year or two with her, he returned to live alone in the old family house with his father, an East Peoria cop, and there were no further friendships with black people.

As a boy, Matt accomplished somewhat more in baseball than had Ben Klassen. In fact, he considers one of the greatest days in his life the day he struck out sixteen batters and walked none in a Little League game at age eleven. "If my arm hadn't gone bad the next year, I might have made something of myself. I loved the game, and I had a heck of a fastball that most people couldn't hit."

But he had other, more solitary interests as well, such as history and politics. And he chose his own guides for exploring those fields. Before age twelve he purchased a secondhand copy of William L. Shirer's *The Rise and Fall of the Third Reich,* which was emblazoned with a swastika on the cover. Even though Shirer's book critiques the Nazis, Matt became enchanted by their objectives. Like Eve in the Garden of Eden hearing the serpent's question, "Did God really say…?" Matt listened and began to doubt the claim that "all men are created equal." His eyes were opened, and he saw the disparity in ability, appearance, privilege, and performance among people around him. Indeed, people weren't "equal." Possibly no one bothered to explain to him that the equality on which our democracy is based is the sacred value of every human life that is of immeasurable and equal worth because every person is made in God's image. But then that whole premise falls apart without God, and Matt was beginning to doubt his existence as well.

For hours at a time Matt sat in his room alone, consuming the twelve hundred pages of *The Rise and Fall of the Third Reich,* and growing envious of the Nazis' vision.

"Are you all right up there?" his father would call up the stairs to him.

"Oh yeah, I'm just reading."

"But you've been up there all afternoon. Don't you want to come down and watch some TV with me or something?"

"No. I'm satisfied."

There was silence, and Matt could tell his father was still standing at the bottom of the steps. "You're not reading any girlie magazines or anything, are you?"

"No, Dad. I'm just reading about history."

Finishing that tome in a month, young Hale went out and bought Hitler's *Mein Kampf* and read it as well. Though he admits that he couldn't grasp all of the content the first time, he kept on reading. In fact, he read Hitler's book so many times that it began to fall apart.

"Matt," his father said one day at supper, "I don't think your grandpa would like you to be reading that stuff by Hitler."

"But he was against communism, Dad, and you're against communism."

"Oh yes. I'm very much against communism. But Hitler... I don't know, it seems like he was just as bad. Your grandpa was from Germany, and—"

"But, Dad, he wasn't there when Hitler came to power. Everybody in this country has been propagandized. If you are told constantly that National Socialism is bad, you are going to believe it unless you are very unusual. I've been learning a lot, a lot more than they teach in school, and I don't think it was so bad. Hitler just wanted to preserve the white race. You want to preserve the white race too don't you, Dad?"

"Well, yeah, but..."

The meal ended in silence, and Matt returned upstairs, closed his bedroom door, and continued reading.

National Socialism and Hitler fascinated him to the point that he gathered a few eighth-grade friends and formed a group he called the "New Reich."[4]

Filled with Nazi propaganda, Matt one day noticed an interracial couple kissing in public. "It made me physically ill," he recalls, "and I decided then and there that my mission in life was to make sure no one had to see anything like that again."

Consequently Matt reduced his social activities such as baseball even further. "I became a very serious person," he recalls with pride, "and this marked me as different from my peers. When other kids were thinking about playing after school or what was on television, I was thinking about the world and ideas. I played classical music on my violin. I had no use for their foolish popular music. Another thing that marked me as different was that I was very skeptical. When someone told me something, I didn't just accept it. I examined the evidence to see whether it was true or false."

Matt Hale got to the point where he thought no one knew better than he did. One classmate from his sophomore year in high school recalls a time where Hale took over the class and led a discussion on Hitler. "I don't think the teacher knew what had happened until it was too late. Hale had a charisma that really sucked you in. Later you'd say to yourself, 'Hey, wait a minute. That's crazy.' But at the time, wow! It made me so upset that I asked him to not talk like that in class anymore. The discussion got heated, and the next day I asked the teacher to move me from sitting next to him, or we were likely to come to blows. The teacher said, 'Yeah, well, I've had several students ask me the same thing.' Fortunately, there weren't any people of color in class, or who knows what would have happened."[5]

"In a sense, I was never a teenager," Hale says. "I essentially went from age twelve to being an adult. My idea of having a good time on a Friday night was reading or playing Axis and Allies or Stratego or Risk—anything to exercise my intellect."[6]

Being more studious, rejecting popular music, and not wasting time on television or even in sports may have had some advantages, but to the degree that it caused young Hale to think that he was better than other kids, he paid a price. Many kids inevitably resented such narcissism and in turn rejected him, giving rise to a persecution complex for himself and those he could gather around him.

And gather them he did. He organized what he called the White Guard among several high school classmates and began creating and distributing crudely written white supremacist literature. When the administration discovered it, they searched the kids' lockers and confiscated the materials until the kids' parents could pick it up. The dean waited to call Hale into his office until last, knowing he was the ringleader. As far as the school was concerned, the White Guard was a gang, and any more activity would result in expulsion.

As a local policeman, Hale's father was upset by these developments, and Hale curtailed his overt political activities until his senior year when the school got a new and more permissive dean.

When he was fifteen, Hale read Friedrich Nietzsche. Nietzsche's assertions that people are *not* all created equal affirmed the Nazi philosophy Hale had already embraced, but Nietzsche was also severely anti-Christian and considered Christianity a curse on mankind. Prior to this, Hale had believed that there was a God somewhere, albeit a God who wanted to keep the races separate. Nietzsche got him thinking.

"I'd gone to a Sunday school one time when I was a kid," Hale recalls, "but all we did was paste some Jesus stickers in a book. I found it very boring, and I didn't understand what it was all about. My older brothers went to church, but by the time I came around, the churchgoing had pretty much stopped. We had a Bible in the house, but it was never read. God had never spoken to me or done anything for me, and I'd never seen God do anything for anyone else. Maybe Nietzsche was right, 'God is dead,' if he ever existed at all. I have since read the Christian Bible three times—far more than most Christians," he brags, "but I don't find much to agree with in it."[7]

The convergence of Hitler's ideas with those of Nietzsche fueled Hale's own racial opinions, giving him a sense that he had a better handle on the world than did most other people.

"In high school, I was perceived as being aloof in a lot of ways," Hale relates. "Now and then someone would call me a Nazi or something, but I just attributed that to their ignorance—they just didn't know what I knew. I basically took the view then as I do now, 'I forgive them for they know not what they do.' "[8] He says this seemingly oblivious to how ironic his appeal to the virtue of forgiveness sounds—even quoting Jesus.

Like a neglected child who decides that negative attention gained from a temper tantrum is better than no attention at all, Hale was learning to thrive on the ridicule and disdain of others. It got so bad that, as one classmate remembers it, "Matt got beat up repeatedly after school when he got off the bus and headed for home. Those ambushes ended only when he got his own car to drive to school."[9]

One fellow music student of Hale recalls, "Everyone avoided him like he was a leper. Once, an entire music class moved to the opposite side of the room when Matt came in and sat down."[10]

But those experiences bothered Hale less and less. Throughout his senior year of high school, he remained very serious minded. He didn't date and didn't go to the prom. In fact, there were no girls in the little club he came to call the American White Supremacist Party. (He had changed the name from the White Guard partially to avoid getting accused again of heading up a gang.) Some adults might have missed the dangerous potential he represented because he appeared so clean-cut. "I've never been drunk," he says. "The closest I got was being a bit tipsy once, but I didn't like it because I didn't feel fully in control of myself. So I've never been interested since. I've never done drugs. I've never smoked. I was just totally driven by my ideas."

When Hale went to Bradley University in Peoria, Illinois, to major in political science and music, he passed out fliers announcing a meeting of his American White Supremacist Party. The press got wind of it, and on February 5, 1990, Matt Hale made headlines: "Bradley Student Trying to Form White Supremacist Group." Before this he claimed to be so self-conscious that he was petrified at having to make a public speech, but after coming out at Bradley, he says with glee, "My life has been different. Once I was in the public eye, it didn't take long for any shyness to be drummed out of me."[11] Soon he was giving interviews to NBC, CNN, and AP.

Developing the ability to stomach a diet of negative attention—even thrive on it—groomed him for something bigger.

● ● ●

About this time Hale became aware of the existence of the Church of the Creator through a borrowed copy of *Nature's Eternal Religion*. Hale found that Creativity encompassed all of the ideas of National Socialism and Nietzsche that had so entranced him. And the idea of packaging it all as a religion—a militantly anti-Christian religion—what genius! He began distributing hundreds of copies of *Racial Loyalty* and maintained close contact with COTC headquarters in North Carolina.

But, as he describes it, "I was still caught in the rut of trying to find a political solution to the racial problem [through his American White Supremacist Party] and feared that promoting Creativity publicly would be detrimental to public opinion."[12] Even though his AWSP had only seven or eight members before the media caught wind of it, few of whom were really committed, Hale's dreams of grandeur were stoked by being invited to Denver, Colorado, to speak on the state capitol steps on Hitler's birthday at a rally attended by other pro-white activists, counterdemonstrators, and police. Parts of his speech were broadcast on CNN.

In May 1991 he was arrested on a charge of felony obstruction of justice for refusing to provide details of an episode in which his brother David, whom Hale says shares his racist views, drew a pistol on a black man. David was convicted of a misdemeanor, and in October of that year Hale was found guilty of obstruction, but the conviction was later overturned reportedly because the police failed to read him his rights.[13]

In August 1992 Hale formed the National Socialist White Americans Party with himself as leader. This organization staged numerous demonstrations and rallies. He appeared on *The Montel Williams Show*, the *Jane Whitney Show*, the *Jerry Springer Show*, and *The Geraldo Rivera Show*.

In April 1995 he surprised many East Peorians when, after a four-month campaign, he won 14 percent of the vote for a seat on the city council. While this was a big ego boost, Hale decided that politics was simply a symptom of a greater problem. Only a racial religion like Creativity would free the white race from Christianity that preached the "fatal" quality of care for people of other races.

After five years of public activism and going from organization to organization, he says, "I had finally found my home. I would dedicate my life to Creativity and become the great promoter for whom Ben Klassen had searched!"[14]

First, however, Hale dedicated his life to someone else. In May 1997, the twenty-six-year-old "great promoter" married sixteen-year-old Terra Herron. But when the couple divorced three months later, another wave of members left the WCOTC.[15]

Time-Out!

"Don't schedule your 'Turn Off the TV' campaign during December!"

Sheri Donaldson, Ricky Byrdsong's secretary at Northwestern, wasn't tiptoeing around the issue. "Kids are home from school and there are a lot of family-oriented programs on around the holidays. How about the first week of February, when Nielson's trying to get viewer ratings?"

"That's a great idea, Sheri." As usual, Ricky paid close attention to his secretary's advice. His letter went out in September to a mailing list of nearly two hundred national ministries, denominations, publishers, broadcasters, and individual pastors, targeting February 1–8, 1997 as the date for the National Time-Out.

Ricky was energized. This effort was a new way to make a difference in the spiritual lives of families. As a basketball coach, he tried to make a difference in the lives of his players, just as many coaches and pastors had made a difference in his. But if he could influence pastors, radio broadcasters, and ministry leaders across the nation, thousands of families might be inspired to take a "time-out" to get their homes in order.

As enthusiastic responses came back—from groups as disparate as the Salvation Army, Teen Challenge, Campus Crusade for Christ, World Relief, Latin American Mission, Christian Business Men's Committee, and National Religious Broadcasters—follow-up letters were sent. Ricky's excitement grew. What a great way to bring people together in a common cause. What if this wasn't just a one-time event? Could it be the beginning of a ministry that would bring Christians together across denominational lines and racial barriers to pray together and seek God?

• • •

As the date for the National Time-Out drew closer, however, sports reporters covering Big 10 basketball were speculating that Ricky Byrdsong might be facing a more permanent "time-out" from his career.

If you just looked at the numbers, the sports columns said, the 1996–97 Wildcats were delivering another disappointing basketball season, with seven straight conference losses. But after a hard-hitting, competitive game January 15 against Bobby Knight's Hoosiers, sportswriters were saying, "Wildcats finally playing Big 10 Ball!" and commending their "inspired, aggressive style of basketball," even though the Hoosiers won at the buzzer, 66-63.

The Wildcat players weren't discouraged by yet another loss. Junior guard Joe Branch, who sank two huge three-pointers in the second half, told a reporter, "It goes beyond just having a better attitude this year. The basketball family here is a lot closer, and every single one of us believes that we should win every game."

At the press conference after the game, the Hoosiers' hard-nosed coach, Bobby Knight, a man who doesn't easily pass out compliments, said, "I think Ricky Byrdsong is one helluva basketball coach. If I were looking for a basketball coach, I might just stop with him."

Ten days later, Northwestern ended its losing streak with a thirty-one-point win over Ohio, 78-47. Coach Byrd's grin would have lit up Broadway. "What's impressive," he told reporters, "is that they keep coming with all this energy. When you're losing games, and close games, it's easy for a team to split. You have to be thankful they keep believing in themselves."

Even though the team had been hurt by a few players defecting to other programs, assistant coach Paul Swanson gave Coach Byrdsong credit for holding the team together. "He's able to build a cause among the team that's bigger than just winning a game. Sure we want to win games; that's our goal. But our cause is to become the best players we can be and hang together even when things are tough."

But in spite of the hopeful turn of events, the question kept pushing itself into the sports columns: Would Northwestern keep Ricky Byrdsong? Rick Taylor, NU's athletic director, had let it be known that a decision regarding Byrdsong's future would be made at the end of the season.

But the uncertainty was creating a recruiting nightmare. High school prospects weren't eager to be recruited by a coach who might not be there when they set foot on campus. "Doubts about my future are hurting our performance and our prospects for next year," Ricky admitted to reporters "Personally, I hope to stay, but…I won't be surprised either way."

Taylor, annoyed that the issue was being played out in the media, decided to remove the uncertainty. On Monday, February 10, he called a press conference to announce that Ricky Byrdsong had been fired with one year left on his contract and seven games left in the season. "Ricky and his staff and his kids put forth a good effort," Taylor said. "They just didn't get it done. You guys have access to the records."

The normally talkative Byrdsong, known for his friendly banter with reporters, was absent from the Monday press conference, and issued a brief written statement that said he would coach the remaining seven games only if his players gave their consent, ending with a quote from the New Testament:

> Consider it pure joy, my brothers, whenever you face trials of many kinds, because you know that the testing of your faith develops perseverance. Perseverance must finish its work so that you may be mature and complete, not lacking anything. (James 1:2-4)

But the players, stunned and shaken by Coach Byrd's firing, staged an emotional display of support later that same afternoon, speaking to reporters in the Nicolet Center team room. Senior guard Jevon Johnson had a hard time controlling his anger and frustration. "Coach Byrd didn't get his chance. You've got to look at everything as a whole. You can't just look at these Xs and Os and say that Coach Byrdsong doesn't deserve to be here. Coach Byrdsong really cares for his players—that's what really matters. He really cares for all of us beyond basketball, beyond wins."

Evan Eschmeyer, the Wildcats' top scorer and rebounder, pointed a finger at the whole college sports system. "We all know and can name teams that get away with doing things that are highly illegal, but nothing happens to their coach, because they make money for the NCAA. But somebody like Coach Byrdsong—who next to my father has been as big an influence on me as anyone because of the things he really does believe in and has taught me to believe in—gets taken out."

A reporter spoke up. "Did you talk to Coach Byrdsong since Taylor's announcement?"

The question hung in the air for several tense moments. Players were having trouble keeping their feelings in check. But Jevon Johnson nodded. "Yes. He told us to stay together—that's one thing he taught us from Day One—and regardless of the situation or the circumstances, we will persevere." Then he added, "Coach Byrd will persevere to the end too, regardless of what Northwestern does to him, because that's the type of person he is. He's a Christian, he really does believe in his work, and he works hard. Wherever else he will go, he will teach that to his players, and he's going to be successful."

Freshman Carvell Ammons said Coach Byrdsong was "one hundred percent the reason I came here." Ammons, Jevon Johnson, and other black athletes said it was difficult for African American athletes to fit in at Northwestern. But they also stressed that the gap had been partly bridged by Ricky Byrdsong's family-style approach to coaching. "He knew the type of things I've been through to get here and what kind of support I needed to make my transition to NU a little bit easier." But the bottom line, said Ammons, was the respect Byrdsong had for his players. "It's remarkable how much you really want just respect—somebody who thinks you can get the job done."

Some of the players displayed "the Byrdsong spirit" in spite of the shock they'd just experienced. "I'm going to run for student body president for next year," said Joe Branch. "Being an athlete, you don't hear that a lot. But I talked about it with Coach Byrd, and he told me how important it was not to let my dream die."

Eschmeyer said Northwestern's new emphasis on win-at-all-costs didn't sit well with him. "I believe I'm going to win here because of what Coach Byrdsong has done. I came here to win, I believed all along that we were going to win, and I still believe we're going to win."

The question of whether the team wanted Ricky Byrdsong to coach the last seven games of the season was a no-brainer.

• • •

Ricky flopped on the family room couch and closed his eyes, letting the oasis of the Byrdsong home wrap around him. He could hear Ricky Jr. and Kelley, six and seven respectively, playing downstairs with the neighbor kids.

Heavy thoughts rattled in his head, like stones in a rock tumbler. He knew his getting fired would hit his family hard. A job change for him surely meant a move, leaving behind their home, their beautiful neighborhood, and their brothers and sisters at The Worship Center, and having to find new schools for the kids. But Sherialyn wasn't one to get bent out of shape. She might not know *what* God was doing, but she definitely believed God was going to work it out.

At least the one year left on his contract provided some financial cushion and gave him time to look for the right job. Maybe he ought to—

"Daddy?"

Ricky opened his eyes. Nine-year-old Sabrina stood at his elbow, her forehead puckered.

"Hey, Sabrina." Tall as she was, he hauled her into his lap.

"What does 'fired' mean?"

Ricky winced. How do you explain getting fired to your daughter, for whom it would mean leaving the only home she could really remember, not to mention all her friends? Leaving The Worship Center was going to be painful for the kids, too. Pastor Lyle and Pastor Lona were like uncle and aunt, and their teenage kids, Larnell and Leah, were the Byrdsong kids' favorite babysitters.

"It means Daddy needs to look for another job," he said carefully. He didn't need to give her too much too soon.

But Sabrina still held him with her sober gaze. "You going to keep trying to coach?"

"Yes, I am."

"You going to try to be a football coach?"

"Football coach! Why football coach?"

"Because they win. Their games are easier."

Ouch. The reputation of NU's head football coach, Gary Barnett, who had taken his team to the Rose Bowl the previous year, wasn't making this any easier. Sabrina wiggled out of his embrace and disappeared downstairs to the basement playroom.

"Hey, Ricky." Sherialyn's voice floated behind his ear as she leaned over the back of the family room couch and gave him a kiss. "Did you see the letter that came for you from my dad?" She handed him an envelope postmarked from Atlanta.

Ricky swallowed. Was this going to be another challenge? *How are you going to support my daughter, young man?* He cautiously slid a single typewritten sheet out of the envelope.

February 17, 1997

Dear Ricky,

Just writing this letter to let you know that I love you, respect and appreciate you. You have nothing to be ashamed of. You did the best you could with what you had to work with. As the head coach who had just been fired, the national news media talked about how you still continued to try to help the team to win. This says a lot about the kind of man you are, and to do that, I know that you had to be guided by the Holy Spirit. Only when you have God, can you do something like that with the humility you showed as I watched you on television.

I want you to remember what Romans 8:28 [KJV] says. "And we know that all things work together for good to them that love

God, to them who are called according to his purpose." It did not say some things, or most things, but all things. So a year from now we will think back and laugh, while we praise God for his goodness.

I am very proud that you are a Christian and that you do not do some of the things I have seen other coaches do. Continue to trust God and have faith, and always put him first in your life and he will continue to lead, guide, strengthen, and comfort you and your family....

When I saw you on TV that night, I saw a handsome, well dressed, good mannered Christian man who had no animosity, no fear; but a man filled with the Holy Spirit, full of power, love, understanding, and showing complete self-control. It made me proud to be your father-in-law. You have been like a son to me....

I never will forget the time you told me that you were getting paid to do something that you would do for free, if you had the time, because basketball means a lot to you. Every day, remember to continue to give God the glory, the honor, and the praise, and he will give you the victory.

With love,
Joe Kelley

Ricky's eyes blurred as he folded the letter back into the envelope. He looked up; Sherialyn had been reading over his shoulder. He reached up for her hand and pulled her around to sit beside him. "Thanks, Joe," he murmured. "Thanks for the gift."

Ricky Byrdsong was blessed, and he knew it.

● ● ●

Expectations for the Wildcats versus Michigan State at Northwestern's Welsh-Ryan Arena—the first home game since Coach Ricky Byrdsong had been fired ten days earlier—bordered on dismal. Michigan State was favored, and the reporters didn't relish watching a good man go down.

But even the reporters were out of their seats when the buzzer sounded:

Wildcats 70, Spartans 58! "Rout!" "Upset!" "Byrdsong's Swan Song!" the sports headlines would read the next day.

The players, still pumping adrenalin and sweat, were eager to comment to the press. "It makes the next three weeks that much easier and reminds people we're still in this to win games," said Evan Eschmeyer, who led the Wildcats with twenty-two points.

Guard Nate Pomeday had come alive during the game, nailing six of nine shots, including four three-pointers for a career high. "We felt really proud out there for Coach Byrd with what we did," said the six-foot-three sophomore. "It showed people that he is giving us what he needs to give us in order to win."

The reporters listened with half an ear, craning their necks for the person they really wanted to see. What would Ricky Byrdsong have to say on his way out the door?

The laughter started as he walked into the press conference cheerfully holding a clipboard with a sign that read: WILL WORK FOR FOOD.

As the reporters jumped in with questions about the night's game and what it meant for his future, Ricky laughed. "I think I've got it figured out. I'm going to reapply!" More seriously he added, "Prior to the decision to release me, my players at least had my job to play for." And now? "We just want to stress that it's personal pride at this point, and that's the greatest thing you can play for."

•　•　•

But personal pride doesn't help much in the wee hours of the morning when a man lies awake, wondering how to fill his time, where to turn, how to support his family. Even with the one-year financial cushion, Ricky was anxious. Sure, he'd told Pastor Lyle, he'd like to be offered a head coach position. "But how many athletic directors want to introduce their new coach as the guy who just got fired at Northwestern?" Nonetheless, he filled out applications for several college coaching positions that were open around the country and put the house up for sale.

Sympathetic coaching friends promised they'd keep his name in the hopper. But no real leads materialized. Ricky got on the phone. Ray McCallum, head coach at Ball State in Muncie, Indiana, said he had an opening for an assistant coach if Ricky wanted it. Want it? It would be a step backward at this stage of his career—but it was better than no job at all. Ricky and Sherialyn decided to drive down to Muncie the next Monday, look for housing, and sign the contract.

But on Sunday, Norma Cox, a member of the prayer team at church, spoke privately to Sherialyn. "God told me he has something better for you," she said. Sherialyn raised her eyebrows skeptically. Norma added, "I don't believe you'll be going anywhere."

Sherialyn didn't say anything to Ricky. How could she ask him to pass up an honest-to-goodness job offer just because somebody else said God had something better? If that were so, God would tell *them*, wouldn't he?

Sherialyn and Ricky were in bed when the phone rang shortly after midnight. Ricky fumbled for the phone, listened, said, "Uh-huh" a couple of times, then hung up. "That was Ray McCallum," he said glumly. "Another guy they were considering thought he had a firm offer. Ray just found out he's packed up his family and is already on his way."

"What?" Sherialyn said. She felt like laughing. Quickly she told Ricky what Norma had said to her that morning at church.

Ricky could hardly believe it. "God is up to something," he agreed. "Okay, we're going to pray, not panic."

But Ricky was not a man to just sit around while he waited. He kept Pastor Lyle's work number on the speed dial of his cell phone. "Pastor! Can I have some office space at the church?" The Worship Center had finally purchased their own building, a former warehouse on Dempster Street in Evanston, which they were slowly renovating. "I'm going to work on my book! Eight-to-five every day, just like a job."

Pastor Lyle laughed at the other end. "Which book? So far the titles I've heard you toss around are *What's the Problem?* and *Quit Complaining!* Or was it *Count It All Joy?*"

"Pastor! I'm serious! I'm serious!" Even when he was serious, Ricky's upbeat attitude managed to keep Lyle laughing. "People always said my coaching looks like parenting. And it's true! I'm on my players' case like a mother hen. What if I switched it around and encouraged parents to apply the things I've learned in coaching to parenting? I've already got a title!"

Pastor Lyle sounded intrigued. "I know you're going to tell me."

"I'm going to call it *Coaching Your Kids in the Game of Life—Because They Can't Afford to Lose.*"

Finding a Patsy

Becoming the great promoter for the World Church of the Creator required more than putting out regular issues of *The Struggle,* the publication with which Matt Hale replaced Klassen's *Racial Loyalty.* Coverage by the hated public media became the tool of choice for Matt Hale. Knowing that the public media would seldom do a sufficiently in-depth job of reporting to do their cause any real damage, Hale concluded that any publicity was good publicity.

Inflammatory talk shows became Hale's specialty. Between February 10 and March 30, 1999, he lined up appearances on more than sixteen national talk shows. As far as Hale was concerned, the more volatile the better. He appeared on the *Today* show, *TalkBack Live, Politically Incorrect, The Montel Williams Show,* and *The Leeza Gibbons Show,* among others. He debated Johnny Cochran on *Court TV.* By this means, Hale said he would "continue to fan the flames of media attention."[1]

"What's wrong with loyalty to your own kind?" Hale would often say on talk shows. "If you are black and wear a T-shirt that says *Black and Proud,* everyone accepts you. Why can't you wear one that says *White and Proud* and be just as accepted?

"It's true that ultimately we would like to see a white world in which the populations of the other races would decrease every year through famine and starvation until they cease to exist.... If they can't feed themselves, it would be better to let them wither on the vine."[2]

A second promotional strategy also utilized the media. "What we mean to do is to force the government to persecute us," boasted Hale. "By forcing the government to try and stop us or shut us up we can generate sympathy among the public. When Martin Luther King Jr. marched down the street, he knew his actions would be considered provocative, and people might throw things at him or yell at him or even worse. But then on the nightly news the whole country would see King and his followers being attacked by police dogs, and that was a powerful image for people. Their natural compassion came into play, and they tended to side with him. We're just doing the same thing."[3]

His third approach was to go after the nation's alienated youth on college and university campuses. Hale realized that there was a large and susceptible population of young people who were computer literate and could be easily reached by the Internet.

Hale continued attending law school at Southern Illinois University in Carbondale until his graduation on May 9, 1998. Then, following up on an e-mail he had received from a young man interested in the WCOTC, he arranged a meeting in Champaign, Illinois.

Hale turned into the parking lot of the Bob Evans restaurant and frowned at the insipid-looking kid sitting on the curb with his head shaved like a skinhead. "Are you Benjamin Smith?" he asked as he got out of his car and shut the door.

The kid stood up—all six feet on which hung only 135 pounds—and brushed off his faded camouflage pants. "Yeah." He looked at Hale for the first time from under slightly drooping eyelids. "Matt Hale?" He extended his hand.

They went inside. After ordering something to eat, Smith came alive with questions. "How are you different from other racial organizations?"

"Primarily," said Hale, "we are not only racial loyalists but we are anti-Christian."

"Oh yeah?" Smith's eyes lit up. "Well, I disagree with just about everything Christian."

"Here," said Hale, "this is one of our booklets that might interest you, *Facts that the Government and Media Don't Want You to Know.*"

Smith popped a fry into his mouth as he flipped through the pages.

After scanning several items about Jews, Smith grabbed his loose T-shirt with one hand. "Here, check this out," he said with a wry grin as he lifted his shirt.

Hale frowned and glanced embarrassed around the restaurant before focusing on Smith's pale chest, which was emblazoned with a tattoo: *Sabbath Breaker.* Then he grinned. Smith lowered his T-shirt and continued scanning the pamphlet.

Hale had patched this pamphlet together under his own name from material that had long been circulating among other racist groups. The charges against the Jews, presented as "shocking but exact quotes from the various books of the Talmud," were far from accurate. Some were complete fabrications. Some were distorted, embellished, or edited so as to barely resemble the original statements. Still others were quoted so out of context that they were entirely misleading.* In addition to attacking Jews, the pamphlet asserted that all ancient civilizations in Egypt, India, Asia, and North and South America were actually white, and it made a series of specious claims concerning the superior intelligence of whites based on brain size.

Smith grinned and looked up at Hale. "Is it true that the brain of the average white person is larger than a black person's?"

"Oh, yes." Hale leaned back and spoke in his most professorial tone. "That's why their test scores are always lower than ours. That's the main reason we're so opposed to mixing the races. It'll bring down our intelligence."

Of course, if IQ tests were valid and other races were truly of lower intelligence, why have IQ scores risen twenty-four points in the United States since 1918—a period in which we have had a dramatic influx of nonwhite immigrants and in which whites are approaching minority status?[4] But Hale was practicing the technique he had learned from Ben Klassen: "Talk as if you were an authority…even if you are not." Hale was not about to admit that the size-and-shape-of-head theories had long ago been debunked by the most reputable research.[5] A conclusion published in *Scientific Monthly* as far back as 1948 stated: "All recorded facts indicate

---

* See "Cracks in the 'Facts' " on the Web at http://www.daveneta.com/no-random-act/cracks.

that neither the size nor the form of the brain, the surface of the hemispheres or their wrinkled pattern in general or in detail furnishes a reliable clue to the amount and degree of general or specific mental qualities."[6] Nor was he about to mention that the cranial capacity of the Neanderthal Man was more than 24 percent larger than that of the average modern, showing that brain size has little relevance.[7]

Researchers believe environment plays the primary role in the disparity among test scores for groups of people. This can be demonstrated by the fact that discriminated minorities among white people show the same variables in IQ test scores as appears between other races where discrimination exists. Perhaps the most dramatic example is the Northern Irish, where the Catholics (the discriminated minority) score fifteen points lower on IQ tests than Protestants. A similar disparity shows up in Belgium where the dominant French people score much higher on IQ tests than the discriminated Flemish people. In South Africa, the English score notably higher than the Dutch Afrikaners.[8]

But even the very mention of test scores caused Smith to squirm. "Yeah, well, I hate tests, myself."

"Who doesn't?" Hale assured Smith. Actually, Hale had loved school, tests and all. He toyed with his ruby class ring from law school. "The point is, white people have simply accomplished more than the other races. I was giving a speech once and someone said, 'Well, what about all the black inventors?" And I said, 'Name five.' He couldn't do it. Most people can't do it. Most people say, peanut butter. So okay, peanut butter, but I don't think that compares to sending rockets to the moon, computers, automobiles, telephones, radios, cassette recorders, light bulbs, and what have you."[9]

Again he was pushing the bluff. Very few modern inventions are the product of individuals. Most patents are held by corporations and universities. Nevertheless, if Hale had desired to learn the truth, he would have found that African Americans hold hundreds and hundreds of patents for things like the hydraulic jack and the two-cycle gasoline engine and a nuclear reactor with self-orificing radial blanket.[10]

But Hale pressed on. "The main thing is, we have all the advantage right now. Everyone has questions about race, but they are afraid to talk about them."

Smith frowned. "What do you mean? I'm not afraid."

"Of course not. But the liberals have drummed it into everyone else's head that it is politically incorrect to talk about racial differences, so most people are afraid. But they still have questions. They can laugh that white boys can't jump, but no one will admit the obvious about why test scores are so much lower in black schools. We can tell 'em why: Blacks' brains just aren't as highly evolved as ours. It's as simple as that."

Ignorant of Hale's hyperbole or the legitimate reasons for test scores variations, Smith nodded his head. "Can I get some of these booklets to distribute?"

"Sure. How many do you want?"

Smith paid for five thousand copies with his own money, and Hale helped load them into his car. The next thing Hale knew, Smith was making news in Bloomington, Indiana, for throwing them on people's lawns and slapping them on windshields.

•   •   •

Benjamin Nathaniel Smith grew up in Chicago's affluent north suburbs. His mother, Beverly Smith, was an attorney working in high-end real estate and had served as a Wilmette village trustee. His father, Kenneth Smith, was a physician in internal medicine at Northwestern Memorial Hospital who left his nineteen-year practice in 1996 to sell real estate as well.

Neighbors in the country club world of Wilmette found Kenneth Smith a little hard to warm to, even withdrawn. But they described his wife as "a wonderful person—Soccer Mom 101."[11] Scott Dubin, who was Jewish, met Ben when they were thirteen and considered Ben his best friend at New Trier High School in Winnetka.[12] Jason Miller, who also knew Ben in high school, said, "He seemed like a normal guy. He was a quiet student who kept to himself and never showed any signs of bigotry toward Jews or Asians."[13]

But things began to change for Ben Smith. Neighbors rarely saw Kenneth Smith interact with him, and at school Ben confided in one of his teachers that he was not close to his family and felt alone.[14] Though the family had never been churchgoers, Ben launched his own search for God and briefly declared himself a Muslim.

By the time he graduated, he had tattooed his chest with *Sabbath Breaker.*[15]

Shortly before Christmas in 1995, the Skokie, Illinois, police were called to the Old Orchard Shopping Center. Police Sergeant Michael Ruth recalls, "We got a call about someone fighting with Santa Claus in Santa's workshop at the north end of the mall near Starbucks. When we got there, this kid—who turned out to be Benjamin Smith—was wrestling with Santa Claus. Things were flying everywhere.

"It appeared like the kid was on drugs, and witnesses said he had been jumping off the fountain. Then he went into the shop and punched some black guy. I guess that's when Santa stepped in.

"He fought with our officers, too, and by the time we got him to the station, he was pretty messed up. His arm was obviously hurt, so we called in the paramedics and also called his parents.

"When they arrived, his father told us that he was a physician and asked if he could see his son. We agreed, but as soon as he saw him, he said, 'You are not to touch him. You are not to treat him. I will take him.'

"He posted bond and took his son. A day or two later, the parents returned and told the chief, 'Your police officers brutalized my son, and you broke his arm. Unless you drop the charges, we are going to sue you.' The chief reviewed the incident and simply replied, 'Do what you've got to do.'

"We didn't hear anything more about it until it came up in court where Ben pleaded guilty. He received one year of supervision and was ordered to seek drug counseling."[16]

In the spring before graduation from New Trier High School, Smith signed his yearbook *Sic Semper Tyrannis*—or "Thus ever to tyrants," said to be the words of John Wilkes Booth after shooting Abraham Lincoln.

The phrase also appeared on a T-shirt worn by Timothy McVeigh on the day he bombed the Alfred P. Murrah Federal building in Oklahoma City.[17]

The following fall, Ben Smith enrolled in the University of Illinois at Champaign-Urbana. In September 1996, just a month after arriving on campus, police responded to a call that someone was peeking into the windows of a woman's residence hall. When the police spotted Smith running, they arrested him. Smith, however, produced a fake identification with the name Erwin Rommel—Hitler's field marshal known as the Desert Fox.

Later that night, two more women reported to police that a student who said his name was Rommel had rubbed his hand along their legs in the computer lab. When Smith didn't appear for his court date in October, the judge issued a warrant for the arrest of Erwin Rommel.

Smith had a girlfriend, Elizabeth Sahr, who recalls that he was becoming more offensive and violent during this period when he seemed to be searching for some identity. Among the students that he hung out with were Sandeep Gyawali, a student from Nepal; Luke Myzyka, his roommate; Sam Chen, a Korean student; and Jackson Potter, a Jewish friend. They talked leftist causes and joined the Student Environmental Action Coalition (SEAC) where, Jackson recalls, Smith was unusually suspicious of the government—not uncommon for leftist students—but Smith seemed to be most upset by incidents like the Ruby Ridge shooting and the Branch Davidian fiasco in Waco.[18]

Jackson says that Ben's interest in SEAC seemed to peak over the militant student mobilizations against incinerators, biotechnology, chemical companies, and genetically altered food. He later dropped out of SEAC and several other organizations he cycled through, always saying, "I couldn't trust those people." Ben also began accusing his roommate, Luke, of going through his stuff every time he was out of the room.[19]

Jackson recalls that one day Ben and his girlfriend Elizabeth were standing in a cafeteria line when a guy insulted Liz for being overweight. Ben grabbed a plate and confronted the guy: "That was really insulting. You should be more respectful to people." Then he smashed the plate over the guy's head.[20]

Smith began spending inordinate amounts of time on the computer looking up white supremacist Web sites. He avidly read *The Turner Diaries,* a grisly white-supremacist novel by William Pierce about the overthrow of the U.S. government that provided the blueprint for a series of terrorist acts in the 1980s by the Order, an offshoot of the National Alliance and the Aryan Nations. He also began reading Hitler's *Mein Kampf.* "Heck, man," he told his roommate, "this guy did some admirable things." Some time later he said, "You know, I think I could kill someone. I don't think it would bother me at all."[21]

30

Walking on Water

Ricky Byrdsong showed up at The Worship Center every morning at eight o'clock to work on ideas for his parenting book. The more ideas he put down on his yellow legal pad, the more parallels he saw between coaching and parenting. Who's the most valuable player on a basketball court? A good rebounder. Teaching our kids how to "rebound" from mistakes makes our kids MVPs in life. What do you do at halftime when the game isn't going as planned? You make adjustments in your game plan.

That's exactly what I'm having to do right now, Ricky mused. *Making adjustments in my personal game plan.* He had to consider not only his next career move but also how it would affect his growing family.

As head basketball coach at Northwestern, he had written a mission statement for his players. Why not a mission statement for his own family—something that set out the expectations and goals of what it meant to be a Byrdsong?

Working in a quiet corner of the warehouse-turned-sanctuary, Ricky wrote, crossed out, and wrote some more. Finally he came up with a family mission statement:

> The mission of the Byrdsong family is to make our world a better place
> by helping others to fulfill God's plan for their lives so that God will
> say to us when we see him, "Well done, good and faithful servants."

That was good for a start: an overarching purpose by which to evaluate their priorities. But he knew that for the kids, he'd have to break it down. Once again he got busy with his yellow tablet and purple pen on a "Mission Statement for the Byrdsong Children":

> Sabrina, Kelley, and Ricky are first of all grateful.... "Please" and "Thank You" are two of their frequent expressions.... They will respectfully, yet boldly, reject any philosophy that is contrary to the Word of God. They know that they are responsible for their actions and will not seek to blame others for the choices they make.

The purple pen kept filling the page:

> ...They will treat all people, even their enemies, the way they would like to be treated. They will obey their parents and seek their guidance regarding the issues of life.... They understand that their parents' discipline is proof of their deep love for them....

Sherialyn was impressed. Eventually the mission statement was typed up and framed. It would make a good "talking point" with the kids when they needed a course correction—just like the *Desiderata* that hung on the wall of Frederick Douglass High School back in Atlanta.

• • •

"Ricky, I'd like you to preach one of these Sundays."

"Preach! Me, Pastor?" Ricky looked down at Pastor Lyle to see if his friend was joshing him. "I'm a coach, not a preacher."

But Lyle Foster was serious. "Since God hasn't taken the Byrdsongs away from us yet, I think you have some things to offer this church. God has been stretching your faith in major ways. Talk about that."

So now Ricky's eight-to-five office hours at The Worship Center were devoted to sermon preparation. Giving a motivational talk to a basketball team or even to a group of businessmen was one thing. But preaching the Word was another! He'd never considered what a huge responsibility that was.

But Lyle Foster said, "Just talk about what God has been teaching you."

Ricky started to get excited. This faith walk he'd been on was a thousand times more thrilling than the biggest roller coaster at Great America.

By the time his scheduled Sunday rolled around on September 21, Ricky was ready. His sermon title: "Be Water Walkers, Not Just Faith Talkers!" No pulpit for Ricky. Following Pastor Lyle's style, he wore a lapel mike that freed him to walk around. He bantered with the congregation for the first few minutes, joking that "those that can't coach, preach!" But then he got down to business.

"Some people don't think their actions are important, but trust me! Actions are important. They express what we believe." Other people, said Ricky, say you don't have any control over your feelings. "But that's wrong too. We have a lot of control over our feelings. Some actions feed our feelings in one direction. Other actions move our feelings in another direction. Our belief system controls our actions, and our actions influence our feelings. It's as simple as that."

To illustrate, Ricky told the familiar story of Jesus' walking on the water. "The disciples were commuting back home after a day-long business trip where they'd been listening to Jesus teach and watching him perform miracles—healing people, feeding over five thousand with only five loaves and two fish—you know, a regular day on the job for those boys. Now, the shortest route home was across the lake in a leaky old boat, but they'd already put in some overtime, so it was late when they got started. Soon darkness engulfed them, and a big storm came up.

"Jesus' boys didn't think they were going to make it. They were afraid. When we feel fear, it's not because we've been talking with God. God does not give us the spirit of fear! So if there is fear in us, it can only come from one source. We have been communicating with the Enemy."

The congregation saw where Ricky was going. "That's right!" some encouraged. "You're preaching now!" But Ricky wasn't thinking about "preaching" now. He was just telling a story, a story that had a lot of personal relevance.

"To make matters worse," Ricky continued, "they saw the figure of a man walking toward them on the water. On the water! Talk about scared! If they weren't already terrified by the storm, that figure coming across the water had them white-knuckled and wide-eyed. The Bible says they cried out—not with joy, not with relief—but in fear. Great big tough guys wailing like babies."

The laughter of recognition rippled across the rows.

"Then they heard a voice say, 'It's all right. I'm here. Don't be afraid.' Everyone else screamed in terror, thinking it was a ghost. But in the middle of that confusion, Peter said, 'Wait a minute. I know that voice.' "

Ricky stopped his story and said, "If you haven't had a storm in your life, at some point you're going to. But when you have that storm, you better be able to recognize God's voice, because there will be a lot of other voices in your ear, and most of those voices are going to be whispering fear and confusion. 'Don't speak up, or you'll be out of a job. Do this; don't do that.' But when you hear all those voices, you need to be able to step up like Peter and say, 'I know that voice! Jesus, is that you? If that's really you, Lord, tell me to come to you on the water.'

"But how are we going to recognize God's voice? You can't wait until the storm comes, you've got to start when things are going all right. You've got to say, 'Good morning, Jesus.' And he'll tell you, 'Everything is going to be all right. You're going to have a blessed day. Check back with me at the noon hour, and I'll talk to you some more. Let's have some lunch together—long as you don't have those chitlins. I'll sit with you.' "

Laughter broke out again.

"Calm down, now! I'm serious. He'll sit with you." Ricky smiled but he went right on. "Did you ever wonder why Peter didn't say, 'If that's really you, Lord, calm this storm. Get rid of our problems, quick!'? Instead, Peter said, 'If that's you, don't take me out of my problems; walk me through them. Let me become a water walker!'

"How realistic was *that*? If you're going to walk on the water, you're going to need *unrealistic* faith. God gave us access to the same power that filled Jesus. He wants us to forget everything else and step out of the boat to become water walkers. He wants us to say, 'Nothing else matters anymore.' "

Ricky explained that one day he had bought a CD of Dr. Martin Luther King Jr.'s speeches so that his kids would know how much others have sacrificed for some of the privileges they take for granted. "In Dr. King's speech that he gave in Memphis on April 3, 1968, he noted that he had been coming under increasing threats. He was in a dangerous storm. But he said, 'It doesn't matter now. Because I've been to the mountain top.... And I've seen the promised land.' He recognized that he might lose his very life, but he said, 'It doesn't matter now.'"

Ricky felt passion now. "Don't you know that I had to come to that in my own life? Don't you know that they didn't want me talking about God to the basketball team? Don't you know that I had to say, 'But it doesn't matter now'? Don't you know that they didn't want me having Bible study in my own office with my own staff? But I said, 'It doesn't matter now.' Don't you know that they'd rather that I not quote any Scriptures to the newspaper? I was a coach of a major institution, and my words were going everywhere. They wanted me to keep that kind of talk in the church. But I had to get to the point where I said, 'It doesn't *matter* now.' Some of us are afraid to discipline our children, scared they're going to get mad and walk out on us, but we've got to say, 'It doesn't matter now. It doesn't matter now.'"

Half of the congregation were on their feet.

"Now I can just hear the other disciples in the boat saying to Peter, 'You better calm down now. You're talking nonsense now. You know you've been a fisherman a long time. You can't be walking on no water. You know better than that. You're getting ready to step out there and get yourself drowned. And then you're going to cause us to have to come out there and take care of some mess!'"

This was a Ricky Byrdsong many at The Worship Center had never seen before. They knew he didn't have a job. Some could identify. Being unemployed was *tough*. But Ricky was sharing his heart.

"You know, if you're going to walk on the water, if you're going to turn your family around from the way the rest of society is going, you're going to have to watch who you hang with. Because some folks don't want to see you walk on the water! Get away from people with a boat mentality.

They're not going to get out of the boat, and they don't want you to get out of the boat, because that rocks the boat. Get away from folks who say you *can't* if God says you *can!*"

Now the rest of the congregation were out of their seats. But Ricky wasn't through.

"As long as Peter kept his eyes on Jesus, as long as he kept his eyes on his goal, things went fine. That's all he had to do, just keep his eyes on Jesus. But whenever God calls us out of our boat, and we have the courage to respond with faith, we tend to do just what Peter did. We start looking around. We turn away from God and look back at the folks in the boat and start bragging. 'Uh-huh. You didn't think I could get out of the boat, did you? You talked about me. You thought I was crazy. But look at you sorry folks. Look where you're sittin', right there in that leaky old boat. And look at me out here on the water. Yeah, I'm on the water, y'all. Don't you wish you'd have come out here on the water with me?' " Everyone knew what happened next. "When Peter looked back and began talking all that junk, he went down! And so will we if we don't keep our eyes on Jesus."

Ricky had come right down to the buzzer. "Know this. Folk don't like water walkers. But just remember: *It doesn't matter now.* When you start to become a water walker, folks are going to tell lies on you, and they're going to backstab you, *but it doesn't matter now.* You need to say, 'I'd rather be walking on water with Jesus than sitting in that leaky boat with a bunch of backstabbing people.' "

Ricky closed his first-ever sermon with the question: "What I want to know is, are you ready for the walk?"

• • •

The sermon was over. Ricky was glad he'd had a chance to share what was on his heart. On Monday he was still unemployed, but he'd had a lot of time to think and write. It was time to get even more serious about his book. And he loved to talk to kids, parents, and businesspeople about succeeding in the game of life. Maybe the two things went together?

"Sherialyn! I'm going to call Pat Ryan, see if we can get together." Pat

Ryan was the CEO of Aon Corporation, the second-largest insurance company in the world. He was also chairman of the board of trustees at Northwestern University and a huge basketball fan. The Welsh-Ryan Arena where the Wildcats played carried his name. While he was at Northwestern, Ricky and Pat Ryan had always been on friendly terms. "With his connections, maybe he could help me get my book published."

A breakfast meeting was set up for Wednesday, September 24. When Ricky left the meeting, he could hardly get Sherialyn on the phone fast enough.

"Sherialyn! Are you sitting down? You're never going to believe this!"

"Try me."

"Pat Ryan just offered me a job as vice president of community affairs for the Aon Corporation!" He let it sink in a little.

"But you don't know anything about insurance."

"That's what I said! I would need to represent Aon at various community functions in the Chicago area." Ricky could hardly contain his excitement. "And my *primary* responsibilities would be speaking in schools and developing programs to help underprivileged youth reach their full potential. We talked about my idea for Not-Just-Basketball Camps to introduce kids to the corporate world and job opportunities outside of sports. He said that's exactly the kind of thing Aon wants to sponsor!"

Sherialyn had gotten past the shock and was catching the excitement. "What about the book?"

"He liked my idea for *Coaching Your Kids in the Game of Life.* Said I'd have time with this job to keep working on it."

As they talked, it began to sink in what this job meant. They wouldn't have to sell the house, they wouldn't have to move, they wouldn't have to uproot the kids, they wouldn't have to leave church family and friends. And Ricky would be doing what he loved doing most—coaching young people in the game of life.

His halftime was over. It was time to get back in the game.

31

The Setup

"If you think you can kill a man, and then escape, and go back to life as usual, you're kidding yourself," wrote Ben Smith in a spiral notebook while at the University of Illinois. "Once you take a man's life, you are until the end of your days, a wanted man. And as such, you must constantly live in fear.... If you know they're going to arrest you, are you going to go with them...to be interrogated, beaten, and raped, or are you going to defy them until your last breath, and take your own life?"[1]

That fall, Smith was assigned an African American roommate. Smith's drug and alcohol use and his violent outbursts became more common.

After dating Elizabeth Sahr for eleven months, he saw her with another man and, in a jealous rage, he beat her up on October 15, 1997. She reported it and he was arrested, but she didn't press charges at that point. However, by February 1998, when she had received several hang-up phone calls and other threatening messages from him, she changed her mind and pressed charges. She also told police that Ben Smith was the Erwin Rommel involved in the Peeping Tom incident.

By this time the university had received a number of other complaints about Smith—from his African American roommate, who'd moved into a different dorm—and also because of hate literature Smith had distributed and posted around campus. University authorities searched Smith's room and found a large knife and marijuana. When the police coordinated with the university authorities, they decided to throw the book at Smith. According to Captain Barry Silverberg of the Skokie police, Ben's father engaged an attorney who struck a deal to help him avoid prosecution. In exchange for Ben's leaving the university and promising never to return, charges against him were dropped.[2] Ben immediately withdrew from school and went home where he did billing for a Chicago north shore construction company. However, from time to time he apparently returned to Champaign and harassed Elizabeth.[3]

Two months later, in April 1998, Elizabeth obtained her order of protection preventing Smith from having any further contact with her for two years. Shortly thereafter, Smith moved to Bloomington, Indiana, where he enrolled as an English major at Indiana University. He rented an apartment in a predominantly African American housing complex across from Hoosier Stadium.

It was shortly after his move to Bloomington that Smith drove to meet Matthew Hale, Pontifex Maximus of the World Church of the Creator, at the Bob Evans restaurant.

● ● ●

Once Ben Smith had returned to Bloomington with his carload of literature, it wasn't long before Matt Hale began to hear about his escapades. Smith switched his major to criminal justice, hoping to follow in Hale's footsteps and become a lawyer to fight for the white supremacist cause in court.[4] But there were other things he could do in the meantime. He began distributing literature and writing letters to the editor of the *Indiana Daily Student*, the campus newspaper, and the local paper, the *Bloomington Independent*. He signed his letters August Smith, in honor of Augustus Caesar and because the name August sounded more Roman and less Jewish.

When dean of students Richard McKaig called Smith in and told him he couldn't just stick his literature on people's windshields, Smith insisted that he had a right to distribute any pamphlets he wanted. But he did switch his efforts off campus, placing two thousand pamphlets on area car windows.[5]

His efforts gained him a large article and picture in the *Bloomington Independent* on August 28, in which he declared his intentions to start an official WCOTC chapter on campus. If the university resisted, he warned,

Hale would provide seven thousand protesters. "It's freedom of religion," Smith asserted. He also said, "We're not big fans of democracy. We believe in totalitarianism.... We believe we can legally come to power through nonviolence. But Hale says if they try to restrict our legal means, then we have no recourse but to resort to terrorism and violence."[6]

By November 10 more than five hundred residents of Bloomington became so incensed with Smith's hate literature that they staged a rally and marched down main street declaring their intentions to fight hate crimes and hate literature. On one corner the irate citizens faced a lone protester holding a large placard that read, *No Hate Speech Means No Free Speech*. It was Benjamin "August" Smith.

Since Smith listed his phone number on some of his literature, he also began receiving threatening phone calls, and the windows of his apartment were broken as often as once a week.[7]

In December, Smith publicly debated John Fernandez, the mayor of Bloomington. During the debate the mayor called the WCOTC a violent and criminal organization and revealed that he had been seeking help from the FBI.

At the same time, Ben's relationship with his parents became severely strained, though he claimed they still talked. As for his former Chicago north shore friends, he dismissed them as "race traitors and nonbelievers."[8] With few sympathizers in Bloomington, he had become more and more isolated.

He called Matt Hale. "Pontifex, it's not going so well over here. They've been coming down pretty hard on me. I've been wondering whether there isn't some better way I can serve the cause."

"I know it can get rough, Brother August. I don't know if you've heard, but in February the Illinois State Bar denied me my law license."

"Really? How can they do that?"

"Well, in my opinion, it's illegal. America can only be headed for violence. England tried to pull this stunt on us in the 1770s and got a revolution for their arrogance."[9]

"You think it's time to start the RAHOWA? I'm ready!"

"We're already in RAHOWA, but no, no violence, not now. I want the world to see how they are denying us our rights. I'm going to make this a national spectacle. You just keep up your good work. We'll figure out something for you later."

"Yeah, but I have lost friends I thought cared about me. Family members have stopped talking to me. I have had people threaten me with baseball bats, fists, and knives. I have received innumerable death threats. The Skinheads Against Racial Prejudice smashed in my front windows at three in the morning, have threatened in the papers to send twenty people to my door and confront me, and have made fliers detailing my beliefs, actions, and home address."[10]

"But you've survived," Hale said.

After these revelations, Hale decided to encourage Smith by honoring him as "Creator of the Year" in the January edition of *The Struggle*. Hale wrote that August Smith "brought more media attention to the Church than any other Creator resulting from his massive distribution of the Facts." In March, Hale featured him again, this time with a multipage interview in *The Struggle*.

On April 10, 1999, Hale appeared before the five-member hearing board of the Illinois State Bar to appeal the denial of his law license. He invited August Smith and the Reverend Chris Peterson to testify on his behalf. The hearing lasted more than five hours, and when the board asked Smith about violence, he responded by saying, "I considered violence one time, but Reverend Hale talked me out of it." Afterward, Hale made a point of saying, "That was a fine job, August. You have helped show that we stand united in solidarity, and will let *no one* attack our existence and beauty of our ideal with impunity."[11]

At the end of the month, Smith took a trip in his light blue 1994 Ford Taurus to his old hometown, Wilmette, Illinois. He was letting his hair grow out slightly. His parents had moved to neighboring Northfield. Whether it was on this trip or at some other time, a further rift occurred between him and his parents when he discovered that his father, who had been an agnostic, had converted to Christianity.[12] But Smith's purpose in returning to the north shore was not family reconciliation.

Patrick Langballe, an old acquaintance from New Trier High School who had been accused in 1997 of spray-painting swastikas on a Northfield synagogue, had introduced Ben to Christine Weiss, a blond-haired girl who had similar racial feelings. Twenty-year-old Christine had recently left her husband in central Illinois and returned to her home in Glencoe, the second suburb north of Wilmette.

Smith picked her up and they drove back to Wilmette, where they distributed racist literature to people's doors and yards in a town Smith characterized as having a "significant Jew infestation."[13] The pair were promptly arrested and charged with littering. Smith was also charged with driving under the influence of alcohol. Placed in separate holding cells in the Wilmette police station, Christine and Ben carried on a yelling conversation with one another.[14] The hate in what they said as well as their literature caused their arresting officer to intuitively go beyond normal procedure. He took several photographs of Christine, Ben, and Ben's blue Ford Taurus. Maybe the photos would be useful at some point.

When Ben and Christine were released, they drove to East Peoria to report to the Pontifex Maximus.

Earlier, in the March issue of *The Struggle,* Ben Smith had said, "Whether people love me or hate me, I will be a Creator regardless."[15] He had given Hale more than five thousand dollars of his own money to finance the printing of WCOTC literature, but more significantly, by returning to his own backyard to distribute it and by getting arrested, he had proven his total commitment to the cause.

• • •

"You have a lot of dedication and courage," Hale said. "As you know, things are heating up around my law license dispute. I could use someone like you. What if you came to work for me?"

Smith lost no time dropping out of school. About May 1 he and Christine Weiss moved into a small apartment in Morton, Illinois, just south of East Peoria. Day after day, Smith—and sometimes Christine—walked through bachelor-cluttered living quarters that Hale still shared with his retired police officer father. They climbed the narrow stairs to Hale's attic headquarters, a small gabled room painted bright red. Blinds or curtains darkened all the windows in the house, but the one window in the red headquarters room was draped with a red curtain overhung with the red, black, and white WCOTC flag.

Both men stepped casually on the Israeli flag that Hale used as a door-mat, then sat down to work—Hale on the computer or the phone and Smith stuffing envelopes or sending out books from the various waist-high stacks around the room.

Records from the Harris Bank in Wilmette show that prior to Smith's literature blitz in the same city, he withdrew $6,795, a large portion of which probably went to pay for the literature. On May 17 he withdrew another $10,275.[16] Other than living expenses, there is no evidence of any other major expenditures. Matt Hale did not receive a salary but said, "Our church members take care of me." Perhaps Smith was his source at this time.

Hale later reported that one day while they worked he had the follow-ing conversation with Smith. "You said your family doesn't talk to you any-more. Is that because of your beliefs?"

"Yeah, my mom's pretty upset, but I don't know why my father objects to me being an activist since he was the one who said I should read *The Turner Diaries,* and he is very anti-Communist."[17]

"He actually turned you on to *The Turner Diaries?*"

"Yeah. Said if I was interested in this kind of stuff, I should read it."

"Well, how about that. Nevertheless, older people get set in their ways and don't want to rock the boat. Maybe you ought to sit down with them and explain that you are young and full of energy and want to change the world. Hey, show them the *Facts* booklet. It might disturb them, but then you can say, 'Look, I'm just trying to stop all this stuff.' Tell them that if they were still young, they'd probably be doing the same."

Smith frowned. "We don't seem to be doing much good, your being denied your law license, and all."

"Now, it's not time to give up yet."

The two worked silently for a while. Then Smith said, "You know in

The Turner Diaries how they bombed the FBI headquarters in Washington and then mortared the Capitol building? You think we could win if all the militias joined in with us?"

"August, that was a novel. Besides, the 'liberation' happened only after atomic bombs were dropped on several East Coast cities."

"But what about terrorism? Ben Klassen said, 'When persuasion and reason fail, the only recourse is violence.' And he said, 'Terrorism and violence work and have been used repeatedly since the beginning of history.' Even if we did it just to publicize our cause, the world would hear about Creativity. What if we—"

"August, I know what *The White Man's Bible* says. But simple terrorism in the streets won't win the masses. Besides, we have not yet exhausted our legal options." Hale paused for a moment. "Let's wait for the decision from the hearing board."

"But what are we going to do if they deny you again?"

"Let's talk about that later. By the way, brother, I notice in the records here that your dues are due."

"Okay. Thanks for telling me."

Technically, Hale could have declared Smith's membership lapsed. Instead, he said, "Well, obviously, you are doing a lot of work here and everything, so I guess we can keep it at that."[18]

32

Going Deeper

Some Aon employees were a little mystified at their new vice president of community affairs. What in the world was an insurance holding company going to do with a *basketball coach?*

But to philanthropist Pat Ryan, Aon's CEO, Ricky Byrdsong was exactly the right man for the job.

"Take your basketball camps to the inner city, to kids who normally don't have that kind of opportunity," he encouraged Ricky. "We'll underwrite it."

Ricky could hardly believe it. As much as he loved basketball, he had always been concerned about kids in the inner city who only had one ambition—to be NBA basketball stars. But who could blame them? Even the poorest home had a television, so those were the black role models they saw. But the vast majority never made it to college, much less the NBA. Too many young people were falling under the spell of gangs and drug dealers promising an alternative route to a fancy ride and respect.

A fire began to burn in Ricky's belly—to give inner-city kids a vision for who God created them to be and the opportunities available to a young person willing to set goals, work hard, and make positive choices.

With a group of kids from one of Chicago's public schools in tow, Ricky herded them into an elevator in the Aon Building on Wacker Drive. He hustled them out again on one of the upper floors and stopped at a secretary's desk. "We're here to see Pat Ryan."

The secretary's grin matched Ricky's own as she ushered the wide-eyed group into Ryan's office. After introducing Ryan to his charges, Ricky said,

"Okay, team, if you want this man's job some day, now's the time to ask him some questions."

Hands shot up. "What did you do to get this job?" "How much money do you make?" "Do you have to go to college to work here?" "What do you sell?" "How do you make money if you don't have something to sell?"

Ricky finally took pity on Pat and called a halt to the questions. He beamed on the way out. "That was good for starters, Mr. Ryan. I'll be back with some more future presidents!"

• • •

James Saunders maneuvered his wheelchair into "his spot" on the corner of Wacker Drive and Monroe in Chicago and locked the wheels. The wind off Lake Michigan bit through his winter jacket, but he figured he could stand it for a while—at least through the lunch hour when corporate executives and managers walked past this corner on their way to the slew of upscale eateries in the area. Unlike some of the other panhandlers in downtown Chicago, James knew he wouldn't get snide remarks like, "Get a job, buddy." Not many people could pass by the wheelchair of a double amputee without throwing *something* into his hat.

A tall, handsome black man walked briskly up Wacker Drive: suit and tie, smart London Fog coat, looked like a good mark. "Got a dollar or two, mister?"

The man stopped. "Sure," he said, digging out his wallet and pulling out a five. "Say, losing your legs must be tough. What happened?"

James was surprised. Most people just dropped in the money and scurried off, like they might catch something. Not many stayed to talk.

It wasn't a pretty story. James had been stabbed in the back at age twenty-two and was paralyzed from the waist down. Infection had set in, taking first one leg, then the other. For the past twenty-five years he had been in and out of hospitals, had married three times, and had held occasional jobs.

"Yeah, being out of a job is the pits," said the man. "By the way, my name's Ricky Byrdsong. I used to be the head basketball coach up at Northwestern University—until I got fired a year ago." He rubbed his chin thoughtfully. "Never thought about panhandling, though. You make good money on this corner?"

James threw back his head and laughed. Byrdsong was obviously doing all right now, he noted aloud.

"Oh, yeah. I've got the greatest job in the world." The tall man pointed at the Aon building across the street. "Can you believe it? They're actually *paying* me to run basketball camps for inner city kids, teach them computer skills, and help them understand there's dignity in education and hard work."

Ricky Byrdsong stopped to chat with James regularly after that, and he never failed to put something in the hat. But there was something about Ricky that made James Saunders want to get off that street corner and do something with his life.

"Ricky," he said suddenly one morning, "could you help me get a job?"

Ricky threw his hands wide. "Sure. Can't promise anything, but I'll look into it."

A few days later he came back. "Put on your best suit and tie tomorrow, James. There's somebody I want you to meet."

James felt funny dressing up to sit on his street corner. But instead of bringing someone for James to meet, Ricky Byrdsong cheerfully pushed the chair into Aon's front door and into the elevator, then to a door whose sign read *John Azzarello, Human Resources.*

"This is the man to meet!" said Ricky, introducing James.

Aon had a job in the mail room, said Azzarello. Did James think he could handle the hours?

James couldn't believe what was happening. The Aon Corporation was actually offering him a job? "I'll be the most dependable employee you've got! I'll show up on time, even stay overtime if I need to."

"Oh man, he's got *that* right." Ricky jerked an appreciative thumb in James's direction. "If this guy can show up on a street corner, rain or shine, summer or winter, without fail, you *know* he's going to show up for an inside job."

The laughter of the three men carried all the way down the hall.

• • •

The men's discipleship group at The Worship Center had agreed to meet regularly on Monday nights during 1998. Pastor Lyle encouraged each man to set a personal spiritual goal he wanted to reach during the year.

Setting personal goals. That was right up Ricky's alley. As a head coach, he had constantly urged his staff to do the same thing. Now he was being challenged by the pastor to do that on a spiritual level.

"I'm going to read the Bible all the way through this year, Pastor. Even Lamentations and Habakkuk." And he laughed. But he was serious.

Funny thing was, once Ricky got started, he couldn't stop. He found himself waking up at 4:30 in the morning, wide awake, eager to read for a couple of hours before he had to help round up the kids' homework, shoes, and backpacks and get them out the door to school. He loved coming across scriptures he had heard in gospel or praise music that he had never read before in context. "No weapon formed against you shall prosper" had become one of his favorite songs, and even though he wasn't a regular member of the worship team, they had pulled him in to sing the lead on this one. And as he was reading the book of Isaiah, there it was in chapter 54, verse 17.

Ricky read through the Old Testament then the New Testament. And then he started over again.

This time last year, who would have thought life could be this great! Sabrina was eleven, shooting up like a future WNBA star and looking forward to middle school. Nine-year-old Kelley and seven-year-old Ricky Jr. were thriving. Sherialyn was doing some volunteer coaching for the kids's basketball teams as well as taking The Worship Center's praise and worship team to conferences and introducing new music to the church.

And with his new job, Ricky was able to keep a more regular schedule with the family—a big plus when it came to working together with Sherialyn on parenting challenges. He still kept his yellow legal pad handy, jotting down things he and Sherialyn were learning "on the job" as the kids got older. Might make good illustrations for the book he was writing.

Now Ricky began to understand what people meant when they said their "cup of blessing was overflowing." His was so full, he just wanted all that goodness to overflow and bless everybody the Byrdsongs came in contact with.

He tried to tell Lyle Foster how he felt. "Pastor, God has been so good to me, I've told the Lord that no matter what happens to me in the future—even if I have to live the rest of my life in a wheelchair like James Saunders—I won't complain. I'd still count it all joy."

This was a good place to be spiritually in April 1998 when Ricky heard the news that Kenneth Dion Lee, one of his players that fateful second season at Northwestern in 1994–95, and several other NU athletes had just been charged by federal prosecutors in a point-shaving gambling scandal. At first, Ricky couldn't believe it. Didn't want to believe it. On top of losing five graduating seniors that year, on top of all the injuries the team had sustained, his own players had conspired to *fix the games?*

It was a betrayal of the worst kind. A basketball team is like family. You depend on each other through good times and bad. To betray your own team... Ricky couldn't fathom it.

He couldn't help but think, *If the players hadn't fixed the games, would I still be coaching?* But he couldn't go there. Couldn't drag up the "what-ifs." Count it *all* joy!

Plans for the first Ricky Byrdsong Not-Just-Basketball Camp sponsored by Aon Corporation helped Ricky take his mind off the gambling scandal. He reported to the other brothers in the Monday night discipleship group how Aon employees volunteered to set up computers at the gym and teach some computer basics to the kids after basketball practice. Visits to "the projects" were frequent as he encouraged parents to bring their kids to the one-week camp.

Visiting the housing projects dug deep into Ricky's soul. "Pastor, it's rough down there. I can't imagine trying to raise a family at Cabrini Green. But I just want to make a difference. I've told the Lord, even if it costs me my life, I want to make a difference."

• • •

As Ricky started his second year at Aon in the fall of 1998, it was Lyle Foster chasing Ricky down on his cell phone. "Coach! We have a new couple at church I think you ought to talk to. They're professional writers, and they've helped other people get their book ideas into print."

"Really? Really?" Ricky could hardly believe it. He had the ideas—pages and pages of ideas for his parenting book. But he didn't have a clue how to go about getting them published.

Ricky met with the couple and reported back to Pastor Foster, "They got really excited about *Coaching Your Kids in the Game of Life*! We worked on a chapter-by-chapter synopsis of the book, and they're putting together a proposal to send out to publishers. But I know they can't work for free."

"Why don't you talk to Pat Ryan? See if he could fund the actual writing. You told me more than once that he's willing to help get your book published."

Proposal in hand, Ricky made an appointment to see his boss. The meeting was short and to the point. Yes, Pat Ryan would underwrite the cost of hiring cowriters to work with Ricky.

Now Ricky had another ball to juggle. But with a couple of writers doing the actual writing, Ricky swung into high gear. Following the synopsis, he used a tape recorder to talk about the fundamentals of family life using basketball metaphors ("Skills and Drills"—chapter 4) and dealing with television, music, and peers ("The Game Plan"—chapter 6). When a couple of chapters had been put in manuscript form, the book proposal went out to prospective publishers while Ricky kept working at the tape recorder, sometimes driving his Chevy Blazer down Lake Shore Drive with one hand and talking into his minicassette recorder with the other.

As he fed raw material on tapes to the writers, manuscript chapters began to pile up. Every time Ricky and his writers met to work on the book, they joined hands and committed the whole project to God in prayer. Ricky's excitement mounted. Now all he needed was a publisher!

• • •

Sherialyn had never seen Ricky so excited—not even when he took the Northwestern Wildcats to the NIT. He'd been talking about his book for so many years, but was it possible that it would actually happen?

God had definitely been doing something new in Ricky's life. Where was it all going to lead? What plans did God have for Ricky? For her?

Sherialyn only knew one way to prepare for the future: Soak herself in the Scriptures and discover the promises of God. If she'd learned anything in her walk as a Christian, it was that the circumstances of the moment—both good and bad—were not the whole picture. Only God knew the whole picture. As Ricky had said in his sermon at The Worship Center, their job was to keep their eyes on Jesus and obey God's commandments. If they looked at circumstances, they'd make the mistake of thinking all these blessings were their own doing—or sink when the storms raged.

As she prepared for each Sunday morning's praise and worship time, Sherialyn decided to memorize Isaiah 54, the chapter that was the basis of the song Ricky often sang.

But as she read and reread the chapter and repeated it day after day, the words seemed to be speaking directly to her. "Do not fear.... [You] will not remember the reproach of your widowhood anymore. For your Maker is your husband, the LORD of hosts is His name" (Isaiah 54:4-5, NKJV).

Your Maker is your husband. What did this mean? Why did she choose this chapter? What was God saying to her?

Other phrases leaped out: "For the LORD has called you like a woman forsaken and grieved in spirit.... For a mere moment I have forsaken you, but with great mercies I will gather you.... With everlasting kindness I will have mercy on you,' says the LORD, your Redeemer" (verses 6-8).

The words from Isaiah burned in her heart. God was preparing her for something, but what?

Finally the last verse: " 'No weapon formed against you shall prosper, and every tongue which rises against you in judgment you shall condemn. This is the heritage of the servants of the LORD, and their righteousness is from Me,' says the LORD" (verse 17).

You will not remember the reproach of your widowhood.... Your Maker is your husband.... No weapon formed against you shall prosper.... I will have mercy on you.... Deep in her spirit, where words did not even form, Sherialyn knew. She was going to lose Ricky. A car accident? A heart attack? She didn't know. But one day she would have to face being a widow.

This wasn't the kind of thing you told people. What should she do with this strange knowledge? Nothing. God was in control. Ricky, herself, the kids—their lives were all in God's hands. The promise was right there in Isaiah 54: "Great shall be the peace of your children. In righteousness you shall be established; you shall be far from oppression, for you shall not fear.... Whoever assembles against you shall fall for your sake" (verses 13-15, NKJV).

Whatever happened in the future, God would not abandon her.

33

RAHOWA!

Ricky Byrdsong leaned back in his swivel chair and scratched his head. Where in the world were those shoes? Ricky was sure he had two, maybe three pairs in his office somewhere.

The fourth-floor office of the Aon Corporation looked like a storage locker. Stacked against one wall were boxes of T-shirts for the second Not-Just-Basketball Camp coming up in August plus a couple of basketballs, clipboards, books he was reading, and assorted file folders stacked on boxes and windowsills. He kept a couple different suits, shirts, and ties in the office too—as well as several sets of sweats and casual clothes—for the various events he might have to attend during any given week.

But what good were they if he couldn't find his shoes!

Ricky folded up his long body and peered under the desk just as the phone rang. No shoes—and he nearly cracked his head as he came up, reaching for the receiver.

"Ricky Byrdsong here." He listened to the excited voice on the other end, his own emotions mounting. "Really? *Really?*" he shouted. "I can't believe it!…Yes, yes, we definitely have to go out to celebrate. Sherialyn's out of town this week. Soon as she gets back we'll set up a date."

He dropped the receiver in its cradle and didn't know what to do first. Open the door to his office and shout the news to everyone within earshot? Call Sherialyn down in Pensacola? Call Pastor Lyle? Drop to his knees in thanksgiving?

Impulsively he grabbed his desk calendar and wrote on that day's date, June 17, 1999: *Publisher wants my book!!!*

• • •

Christine Weiss moved out of the apartment she shared with Benjamin Smith at the end of May, but on June 18 she joined him in the Cook County Circuit Courthouse in Skokie, Illinois, to face littering charges stemming from their literature distribution in Wilmette. Claiming that the First Amendment protected their activities, Smith gained a continuance to prepare their defense.

At some point—possibly on this trip—Smith also looked up Patrick Langballe, his old acquaintance who had introduced him to Christine. In the course of their conversation about racial issues, Smith revealed to Langballe that "the shooting [would] begin in Rogers Park."[1] Apparently, some kind of plan was taking shape.

Smith also applied for an Illinois state firearm owner's ID card, using A—perhaps for *August*—as his middle initial. His application came back stamped *Approved*.[2]

• • •

Sherialyn Byrdsong's trip to Pensacola to attend the Brownsville revival had injected her with a continued sense of God at work. For years she had prayed for Ricky, thanking God for a husband who was so full of life and who loved being a father. She prayed for his career, for all the coaches and players and kids in his sphere of influence, and for his growth as a person and as a Christian. And Sherialyn wasn't beyond telling God a thing or two she wanted God to fix. But on this trip to Pensacola, God seemed to be telling her, "Stop praying to me about Ricky. I will take care of Ricky."

Summer was starting off in high gear. Her half sister, Jocelyn Kelley, still a teenager, had just arrived to spend the summer. The kids were happy; Aunt Jocelyn was more like a big sister than an aunt to them. Jocelyn was already making herself useful, cooking up a soul-food feast of Southern fried chicken, green beans, and corn for Ricky's forty-third birthday on June 24. Pastor Haman Cross from Detroit had a golf date with Ricky that day and would be there to celebrate. Better tell Jocelyn to make *lots* of chicken.

And the following evening, she and Ricky and his cowriters were going out for Cajun food—Ricky loved nothing better than a plate full of hot wings—to celebrate landing a publisher for *Coaching Your Kids.*

She'd never seen Ricky so excited. They had a lot to celebrate. God was so good!

• • •

In addition to working in the East Peoria headquarters with Matt Hale, Ben Smith kept in regular contact with him by phone. In fact, they spent more than thirteen hours on the phone during these weeks.[3]

On June 23 Smith walked into the Peoria Heights Gun and Hunter Supply. "Can I help you?" asked Tony Schneider, the store's co-owner. His square face, set off by thinning dark hair and a mustache and small beard, didn't move much when he talked. He planted both beefy hands on the counter and surveyed his new customer through wide-set, expressionless eyes and let his black POW/MIA T-shirt say the rest.

"Yeah," said Smith. "I'm looking for some weapons."

"Weapons?"

Smith glanced at the sign on the wall above the long rack of hunting rifles and shotguns. *We reserve the right to refuse service to anyone!* the sign read. He tipped his head back and smiled pleasantly. "Yeah, weapons. You know…for hunting."

Schneider gestured over his shoulder with his thumb toward the hunting rifles and shotguns.

"No," said Smith. "I'm interested in these." He bent low over the glass showcase between the two men that contained dozens of handguns. After a while, Smith selected two Smith & Wesson 9-mm handguns and a 12-gauge shotgun.

"What you going to hunt with these?" asked Schneider.

Smith laughed through a sideways grin. "Varmints."

"How you plan to pay for 'em?"

"Cash. Got it right here." Smith patted his left rear pocket.

Schneider shook his head and tossed a form on the counter. "Here," he said. "Fill out this background check. If it goes through, you can pick 'em up tomorrow."

"But I already got a state firearm owner's ID card," Smith said, pulling his wallet from his pocket. "Just got it last week."

Schneider took the card and looked it over. "Don't make no difference. You still gotta pass the background check."

Smith shrugged. "Good enough." He filled out the form, handed it to Schneider, and waved as he walked out the door. "See you tomorrow."

But when Smith returned the next day, Schneider said, "Sorry," as he shuffled through some papers until he found the one he wanted. "Says your girlfriend took out an order for protection against you for domestic violence."

"What?" Oh yeah. That would be Elizabeth Sahr. "*Former* girlfriend," he corrected. "But that shouldn't show up. That was a long time ago."

Schneider shrugged. "Well, as long as it's in the computer, it disqualifies you from buying firearms. Nothin' I can do about it."

Smith steadied himself. "Well, I'm gonna check that out," he said evenly and left the store.[4]

So much frustration, but he had to stay cool. His ID card had gone through because he had used "A" for his middle initial, but somehow he had been caught on the background search. He would have to try something else.

Two days later, on Saturday, June 26 Ben Smith found what he needed. Donald R. Fiessinger, a sixty-four-year-old former elementary school janitor, did a little side business from his trailer house in Pekin, Illinois, just south of Peoria. And he didn't subject *his* customers to foolish background checks. He didn't need to; he wasn't a licensed dealer. If his customers had the cash and he had the merchandise, why ask questions? On June 26, he had the merchandise. In fact, ATF agents were investigating him for purchasing sixty-five handguns, but they weren't yet ready to move on him.[5]

Smith studied his choices and finally bought a Bryco Arms .380-caliber semiautomatic handgun.

The next day, Sunday, Smith drove down to Cerro Gordo, near Decatur, and talked with forty-nine-year-old John McLaughlin. McLaughlin knew all about guns. He had been convicted five years earlier of amassing weapons for an impending race war.[6] The .380 Smith had purchased was a rather cheap gun. In a tight spot, a guy might need something more accurate—and with more shots.

• • •

On Tuesday evening, June 29, Ricky Byrdsong dropped in at the prayer meeting at The Worship Center. He didn't usually make it to Tuesday night. The men's discipleship group last year and the regular Wednesday-night Bible study had been about all the evening church meetings he could make—if he wanted to have time with his family. So his presence this particular Tuesday night was noted.

At first he joined the prayer warriors in their small room, but after a while he went alone into the adjoining warehouse and paced around in the dimly lit cavern. On Sunday he had given a challenge to the congregation —even the kids—to dig deep, to sacrifice, to put the capital campaign for building out their sanctuary over the top.

Had he done the right thing? He didn't want to run ahead of God. She-rialyn thought he had put people on the spot, that they needed time to make such big financial commitments. But he couldn't shake the feeling that God was on the verge of something big. He had to think big for The Worship Center's capital campaign. He had to think big in order to finish his book now that he had a publisher and a deadline. He had to think big if he wanted God to use him to make a difference with the kids down in the projects and in the schools.

Ricky returned to the prayer room and, doing something he'd never done before, prostrated himself on the floor. *God, use me. I want to make a difference.* It was not an unheard-of posture for Worship Center members, but it was unusual enough that Sister Carrie Roach went over, stooped down, and placed her hand on Ricky's shoulder. "O Lord," she prayed fervently, "bless Coach right now. Whatever's on his heart, Lord. Just minister your grace. Uphold him by your mighty hand, Father, and use him however you please."

"Yes…yes…yes," affirmed Ricky. Nothing else mattered.

After the prayer meeting, he drifted into the office to talk to Brenda Shorter, the church secretary-treasurer, who was also on the capital campaign committee. But his mind seemed to wander. "You know," he blurted suddenly, "I can't imagine living in a community where you had to worry about gangs or your kids getting shot when they're out playing."

Brenda looked up from some filing she was doing. "But, Coach, you already live in a safe neighborhood. Nothing around here quieter and safer than Skokie."

"Yeah, I know. But every week I'm working with kids in the projects. Sometimes I just drive through Cabrini Green and stop and pray for those kids. There's shootings all the time. It's not safe for anybody out there."

Brenda Shorter was perplexed. Coach was usually so upbeat—why was he so preoccupied with death and dying? Suddenly she remembered a vision she'd had a few weeks earlier while the praise team was praying for one of their members who was ill. In her mind she had seen a casket sitting at the front of the church. She hadn't told anyone—what does a person do with a vision like that? Was Coach having some kind of premonition? The thought scared her so much that she jumped up and blurted, "Hey, I gotta go!"

•   •   •

On Monday, June 28, Smith spent part of an afternoon with Hale at the local Bob Evans restaurant just down the hill from the headquarters. Hale jokingly referred to it as "the official World Church of the Creator restaurant." That evening, they went together to the storage locker rented by the church. A second batch of one hundred thousand copies of the *Facts* had just been printed and was stored there on a pallet. Ben Smith had personally distributed much of the first batch. Again he loaded three thousand copies of the *Facts* into his Ford Taurus and paid Hale $150, half price because he was picking them up himself.

"Well, good luck, brother," Hale said, shaking Smith's hand. "And be careful with the police up there in the Chicago area. You don't want to get picked up again like you did in April."[7]

They both laughed nervously.

"When do you think you might hear about your law license?" Smith asked.

"Any day now. By law they are required to answer by July 6,[8] but with the holidays and all, I expect it will be before the weekend. Just keep your radio on; I'll send out a news release one way or the other."

"I'll be listening."

Hale claims this was the last time he saw Smith and says he presumed his young disciple went to Chicago the next day.

But Smith had decided that one gun wasn't enough. On Tuesday, June 29, he returned to Donald Fiessinger's Peoria trailer and bought a .22-caliber Ruger handgun with a nine-round magazine. He also stopped by the local Wal-Mart and purchased plenty of ammunition. He had learned that even though legal gun purchases required a background check, ammunition purchases required only a valid ID card.[9]

Phone records show that on Wednesday, June 30, Smith spent thirty minutes talking to Hale,[10] even though Hale claims ignorance of Smith's whereabouts at this point.

In his Morton apartment, Smith packed up his personal computer and other belongings. On Thursday, July 1, neighbors saw him loading a large box, a suitcase, and a laundry basket into his car outside his apartment.[11] Later, Smith's computer was found in Hale's WCOTC storage locker.[12] But Smith could not have put it there by himself on July 1 because he did not have a key. Matt Hale held the key.

The very next day, with a gun for each hand, Benjamin Nathaniel "August" Smith would make RAHOWA!

34

No! No, No, No!

Dr. Michael, a physician at a Chicago hospital, was walking home from synagogue with his sixteen-year-old son. Dressed in dark suits with yarmulkes on their heads, they welcomed the evening breeze that blew the heat out of shady Estes Avenue in Rogers Park on Chicago's north side. As they turned up the walk to their attractive brick home, a car stopped at the curb behind them and a young man stepped out.

Michael paid little attention until, over his shoulder, he saw the man raise his arm. He looked back. Gun! Was this a plain-clothes police officer? A robbery? A joke?

"Father, look out!" he heard his son cry out.

Blam!

The man was shooting. Seeing his son dive for the front door of the house, Michael grabbed his yarmulke and fled up the drive along the side of the house.

Blam! Blam!

The shooting continued as he dashed around the back of the house, panting from fright more than exertion. "You okay?" he yelled to his son inside the house.

"Yes! You?"

"I'm okay!" Michael continued cautiously around the house until he could see the front of the bluish car pull slowly away from the curb. He ducked behind shrubs so the young man behind the wheel wouldn't see him. Then he ran out to his front yard. The license plate! He had to get the license plate.

Down at the corner, he saw his neighbor Hillel walking along in his distinctive Hasidic garb. The car slowed and a gun protruded from the window.

"Hillel, Hillel, look out! He's got a gun! He's—"

The shooting began again. Hillel went down.

"No! No! No!" Michael ran to his neighbor's aid as the war wagon turned south on Francisco Avenue.

Within fifteen minutes, six of Michael's neighbors, all Jewish, had been gunned down and wounded. Several others, like Michael and his son, were terrorized though without injury.

•　•　•

Ricky Byrdsong swung his Blazer into the driveway, glad to be home. Fighting Friday-night traffic on Lake Shore Drive was always a drag, but on a holiday weekend it had been twice as bad.

Not that he'd wasted the time. He had called Pastor Lyle on his cell phone and bent his ear once more about the capital campaign at the church. "We're going to do it, Pastor! We're going to do it!" And CDs—he had CDs. T. D. Jakes. Mighty Clouds of Joy, Men of Standard, the Winans.

As usual, the Byrdsong house was filled with kids running in and out—his own three plus assorted friends. But by the time food was on the table the crowd had narrowed to the Byrdsong five and Sherialyn's sister, Jocelyn.

And as usual, the kids kept jumping up like firecrackers, full of energy. Ricky felt charged up himself. These past two weeks had put him in the zone, and he had energy to spare. But...he looked at Sherialyn. They still had some talking to do about last Sunday. "You want to go for a walk?"

Their eyes met. "Okay," she said. "But I promised Jocelyn I'd give her a driving lesson right after supper. Maybe when I get back." She grabbed her car keys from the kitchen counter. "Won't be long. Twenty minutes or so."

"Okay." Ricky changed into jogging shoes and shorts and hollered, "Sabrina! Kelley! Ricky-J! Come on, let's go shoot some hoops!"

The familiar *thump, thump, thump* of the basketball on their neighbor's driveway was punctuated with the rattle of the backboard and the occasional swish of the net. Sherialyn wasn't back yet. After a little two-on-two, Ricky suggested to the kids that they all go for a walk before dark.

Sabrina hesitated.

"Sabrina?"

"I don't want to go." She ran into the house.

Ricky shrugged and turned. Kelley and Ricky Jr. were already on their bikes, his eight-year-old son doing figure eights in the street as Ricky started a gentle jog with Kelley just ahead of him.

"Ricky-J, come on, let's go. And get over to the side."

The boy wheeled in behind his dad. "Why? There aren't any cars." There were no sidewalks in this upscale neighborhood. Everyone just walked in the street.

"Still, you don't need to take up the whole street."

They turned the corner and headed west. This was one of Ricky's favorite times of the day—just hanging out with his kids.

A car approached from behind. Ricky glanced over his shoulder to be sure his son was out of the middle of the street. Fine. The car slowed. Ricky wondered for a moment if the driver was about to ask directions.

But when he heard the explosions—*blam-blam-blam!*—he knew immediately they weren't backfires or holiday fireworks. He reached his long arms toward his children. Safety! He had to get them to safety!

Blam! Blam! The shots were coming from the blue car.

Something hit him in his lower back like a baseball bat. He hopped around a couple times as though he could escape the blow. Then his legs buckled. He staggered, stumbled over the low curb, and sprawled on the green lawn under a huge elm tree—soft, cool grass. "Uhhhh—"

Blam! Blam!

The guy was still shooting. *The kids...*

• • •

Sitting in the front passenger seat as the red minivan traveled west in the quiet Skokie neighborhood, Sherialyn said, "Okay, turn here." At the wheel, Jocelyn cautiously made a left turn onto the Byrdsongs' street. Sherialyn nodded. "Good. That's good."

But as they were turning the corner, Sherialyn saw someone running toward them from the next block. Sabrina screaming. "Daddy's been shot! Daddy's been shot!"

Time momentarily slowed to half-second frames. *Click:* What's this child screaming about? *Click:* Don't mess with me like this. *Click:* Ricky? Shot?

Adrenalin pumped. Sherialyn threw open the car door and ran, Jocelyn and Sabrina at her heels. She cut across the lawn of the corner house, past…Kelley—thank God—talking to a police officer. But where was Ricky Jr.?

And then she saw. A police car, pulled to the curb at a rakish angle. Her husband on the ground, writhing and moaning. A policewoman kneeling beside him. A youth bike on the ground nearby. And—thank God!— Ricky Jr. standing with a neighbor, his eyes and mouth wide in shock.

Sirens wailed in the distance, coming closer. Sherialyn ran to Ricky's side. Where was he shot? Was it bad?

The policewoman looked up. "Are you Mrs. Byrdsong?" Sherialyn nodded. "He's been shot in the lower back. There's not that much blood. Don't worry. He's going to be okay."

A fire department ambulance pulled up and paramedics jumped out. While the medical team worked on Ricky, put him on a gurney, and rolled him into the ambulance, Sherialyn gathered her frightened children. "I'm going to go with Daddy. Don't worry. They say he's going to be okay." The Byrdsongs' next-door neighbor offered to take the children to her house. Sherialyn nodded gratefully. "Jocelyn, you stay there with the kids until someone from The Worship Center comes. I'll call you."

Sherialyn climbed into the ambulance. Ricky was obviously in a lot of pain. She laid her hand on him, praying, willing him to know that she was there with him. *He's going to be all right. The policewoman said he's just been shot in the back. We'll get through this.*

There was no time to ask, "Who shot him? Why?" That would come later. Right now, Sherialyn just focused on Ricky and prayed. She paused only to jerk out her cell phone and call the Fosters. "Meet me at Evanston Hospital. Ricky's been shot."

At the hospital, a crew of nurses and doctors whisked Ricky away. Pastor Lyle and Lona Foster showed up with their daughter Leah. "He was shot near your *house?*" Pastor Lyle could hardly believe it. Maybe down in Cabrini Green, but not here!

Other members of the church, people close to Ricky, started to come in one by one. Sherialyn told them what she knew. They told her that other church members were gathering at The Worship Center to pray.

●   ●   ●

At 9:10 that evening an Asian-American couple honked their horn as they passed a slowly moving blue Ford Taurus traveling down Willow Road in the northwest Chicago suburb of Northbrook. The young driver stuck a gun out his window and fired three shots at them. Was the guy crazy? Terrified, the couple stepped on the gas and escaped.

●   ●   ●

A doctor emerged from the Evanston Hospital ER. "Mrs. Byrdsong, your husband is hurt pretty bad. He's losing a lot of blood, but we're doing the best we can."

Sherialyn nodded. But the policewoman had said he would be all right. Okay, so it might be tough for a while. She couldn't imagine energetic Ricky being a very good patient. She'd have to be on his case to keep him in the bed and give himself time to recover.

She prayed. Waited. Talked to her Worship Center friends. Prayed some more.

The doctor came out again. "Mrs. Byrdsong..." He paused. "The situation is very grave." Startled, Sherialyn looked him in the face. His face matched his words.

Suddenly, fear knotted Sherialyn's stomach. Was he saying...Ricky might not make it? *No!* She started to weep and pray—loudly. She walked back and forth. She couldn't stop the tears. She called on heaven. God, save his life!

Minutes ticked by, moving the hands on the hospital clock past midnight.

Another doctor came out to speak to her. "We've done all we can do." She tried to focus on his words. They sounded strange. "The bullet did a lot of internal damage. He lost a lot of blood. We've sewn him up. But…"

Done all they can do? What did that mean? "Can we see him?" she whispered.

The doctor nodded. Lyle and Lona Foster went with her as she followed the doctor through the corridors and into a small room. Ricky lay so still—her big, giant of a husband—his legs and chest covered with a sheet. She moved to his right side, her lips moving, just praying. She could hear Pastor Lyle praying too.

After a few minutes, Sherialyn turned to the Fosters. "Let me be alone with him." Lona stepped away from the left side of the gurney, her face stricken. In a moment Sherialyn was by herself with Ricky.

She bent over him and put her mouth to his ear. "Live! *Live!* Come from the four winds, O breath of life, and breathe into this body slain!" Over and over she repeated, *"Live! Live!"*

Aware of another person in the room, she looked up. A nurse gazed at her compassionately. "You realize he's dead, don't you?"

Sherialyn looked at her, disbelief running like ice water in her veins. Surely she was wrong. The doctor hadn't said…."He's dead?" she repeated.

"Yes."

"He's *dead?*"

"Yes."

"Dead?"

"Yes."

Only one word welled up from Sherialyn's soul. "No! No, no, *no!*"

35

Shock Waves

Working with Chicago police, NORTAF (North Regional Major Crimes Task Force, a consortium of north suburban communities) began putting together a profile of the shooter. Upon hearing the description, the Wilmette police officer, who had intuitively taken those photographs back on April 30 after arresting Ben and Christine for littering, got out his pictures. They matched both the driver and the car! By 2 A.M. Saturday morning, the police knew they were looking for Benjamin Nathaniel Smith, associated with a white supremacist group based in East Peoria, driving a blue Ford Taurus with an Indiana license plate—and they had the number.[1]

•   •   •

Rollie Lewis sighted down his cue stick and gave a quick thrust. *Crack!* The white ball sent the colored balls flying. Rollie studied the playing field, choosing his next move carefully. If he gave that solid blue a good tap on the right side, he could probably sink the red…

He leaned his long, lean body over the edge and lined up his cue. Slowly he drew it back and—

"Hey, Rollie!"

Rollie glanced over his shoulder. One of the regulars had poked his head into the poolroom. *What* was so all-fired important that—

"Byrdsong's dead! It's on the TV!"

Rollie dropped his cue stick and ran upstairs to the bar, taking the steps two at a time. *Not Byrd!* The television hung at an angle in the corner, every eye at the counter turned toward the talking head on the flickering screen.

"…wounding several Jews as they walked home from synagogue. Then the shooter turned north, driving into a suburb just north of Chicago, where he shot former Northwestern University basketball coach Ricky Byrdsong. Byrdsong died early this morning…"

Rollie lost all sense of what happened after hearing the report. He couldn't remember going home. Did he eat? Did he sleep? He was probably drunk. Drunk for days. But finally someone pounded on the door of his house, a small, square box tucked between cars in various stages of repair just off a side street in south Atlanta.

He opened the door and squinted at the figure standing in the too-bright sunshine. "Man!" said a familiar voice. "You look terrible, Rollie."

Sylvester. What did Sylvester want? What day was it anyway?

"They're bringing Byrdsong back to Atlanta to bury him, Rollie. Gonna have a funeral over at Cathedral of Faith. You gotta go."

Rollie closed the door. Yeah, that's right. He had to go. *Wherever you saw Rollie, you saw Ricky. Wherever you saw Ricky, you saw Rollie.*

• • •

Saturday afternoon a thirty-one-year-old African American man was crossing East Matheny Street in Springfield, two hundred miles southwest of Chicago, when a white driver of a blue Ford Taurus leaned out the window and shot him in the right buttock.

Six minutes later two black men were shot at but uninjured only eight blocks away by the driver of a similar vehicle.

• • •

Valerie Lockett turned off the television and sat silently for a long time, surrounded by the framed pictures and mementos of a lifetime. Ricky Byrdsong—that sweet, gentle, broomstick of a high school senior in one of her early College Prep 101 classes—killed by a white supremacist on a shooting rampage?

Dear God, that hurt.

So many of the young people who had completed her classes weren't doing anything. Just making babies, living from check to check, tinkering with life. But Ricky had been doing so much!

He'd surprised her. Oh, yes, she was surprised that he'd gone so far. Not that he didn't have the potential. All her students had potential. But she'd worried about him, like she worried about all of her students. Would they get the opportunity? And if they got the opportunity, would they have the heart to pick it up and run? But Ricky had heart. He was never afraid to ask questions. He always believed he could learn something new. He listened to people. He respected their knowledge, their experience, their wisdom. He built on what he learned and made it his own.

And gave it back. All those young men he'd coached over the years, turning them into not only better players, but also better people. All the educational programs he'd started for disadvantaged kids in his new career...

Now he was dead. Shot. Killed. So senseless. Such a terrible waste.

Dear God, it hurt. Hurt so badly.

• • •

At 2:50 Saturday afternoon, the Reverend Stephen Anderson, pastor of Greater Faith Temple Church, parked his car across the street from his home in Decatur, Illinois, forty miles east of Springfield. He had just taken some clothes from the backseat when he turned to see a light blue Ford Taurus coming slowly down the street toward him. He paused for it to pass, but the driver leaned out and shot at him three times. He was hit in the forearm and the buttock. His cell phone, clipped to his belt, deflected one of the rounds, saving him from worse injury.

• • •

The summer was heating up in Kansas, but it promised to be nice for the Fourth. On Saturday, July 3, Jerry McCalla picked up the ringing kitchen phone at their country house in Lake Kahola. Jerry recognized his oldest son's voice. "Hey, Randy!"

The McCalla kids were all grown up and out on their own now. The

"Three Rs"—Randy, Ryan, and Rodney—had chosen to "go professional" as an attorney, podiatrist, and surgeon respectively. Daughter Andrea had her own beauty shop. Frankly, being empty nesters was great. After selling the house in Pratt and spending several years in Wichita, Jerry and Kathy had moved to the country ten miles outside Emporia, Kansas, where Jerry had his own body shop business. Since three of the four kids lived in-state, he and Kathy got to see their six grandchildren on a regular basis. Maybe Randy was calling to say they were coming down for the Fourth.

Except…Randy—thirty-four, a successful lawyer and a fill-in-judge—was crying.

"Randy! What's wrong?"

"Dad…Dad…"

One of the grandkids? Randy's wife? *What?*

"Dad, it's Byrd. They're saying he's been shot. Killed."

"Who's saying? Shot? What are you talking about?"

"CNN. Turn on the TV, Dad. It's all over the news."

Jerry ran. "Kathy!" he yelled. But he hardly noticed when his wife came rushing into the room and sank down beside him on the couch. It couldn't be true. Surely, Randy had it wrong. Not Byrd…

But Randy had it right. A shooting rampage in Chicago…many wounded…but former Northwestern coach Ricky Byrdsong was dead.

The phone rang. Kathy answered then handed it to Jerry. "Charles Taylor," she said simply. Slowly Jerry took the phone. Taylor—another former member of the Beavers booster club. Knew Ricky back in the 1970s at Pratt Community College. Jerry knew why Charles was calling. He didn't want to hear what Charles had to say. He didn't want to hear the question Charles would ask.

He couldn't say the words. They wouldn't come.

• • •

Shortly before midnight on Saturday on the University of Illinois campus at Urbana, about fifty miles northeast of Decatur, six Asian students were heading home when a blue Ford Taurus pulled up. The driver fired at least four times. One round hit one of the boys in the leg, severing his femoral artery. Another was deflected by a purse, possibly saving one of the girls from injury.

● ● ●

Carlton Evans grinned as he watched his son talking to some of the Christian athletes. He was glad he and DeWayne had been able to make it this year to the Fellowship of Christian Athletes annual camp. They'd been on the campus of Northern Arizona University in Flagstaff since Wednesday, playing some basketball, hearing top-notch speakers, seeing how dynamic young men integrated their faith with sports. They'd planned this Fourth of July weekend for a long time.

Of course, they hadn't counted on Karen's getting sick with Valley Fever. The virus had really taken the starch out of his wife. She and the other three kids had flown to spend some time with Karen's parents, get some TLC, recuperate a little. God bless his in-laws—otherwise he and DeWayne wouldn't have been able to have this father-son weekend together.

"Okay, Dad, what's next?" DeWayne clapped Carlton on the back.

"*Next* we gotta call your mother. I promised I'd give her a call tonight." It was Saturday, time for a check-in.

They found a pay phone and punched in the numbers. Karen Evans answered.

"Carlton! Thank God you called. Have you heard?"

"Heard what?"

"Are you sitting down?"

Carlton's heart began to beat faster. "No. Just tell me, Karen."

He heard his wife suck in her breath. "Ricky was killed last night. Shot by…they don't know. A drive-by shooting."

He heard the words, but they didn't compute in his brain. Not in the same sentence. Ricky…shot…killed…drive-by shooting…

He felt a tap on his shoulder. "Dad? What's wrong?" Carlton looked at his son. Ricky's godson. A thousand images of Ricky's face—laughing, singing, smiling—rose before him. No! No, no, no!

"Carlton." Karen's voice was pleading. "If you come home, promise me you won't leave till the morning."

"All right." He returned to their dorm room and started packing. Then, on an impulse—a deep, hungry *need*—Carlton found a phone and dialed Ricky's work number at Aon Corporation in Chicago

Ring. Ring. Ring. "Hi! This is Ricky Byrdsong, vice president of community affairs. I'm not here right now but your call is important to me. Leave your name and number, and I'll get back to you right away. God bless!"

• • •

Lynn Nance heard his wife Sally pick up the phone in the next room. He wasn't used to all this inactivity! He might have meningitis, but he wasn't dead yet. The doctors, however, said it was still very contagious and he had to stay put. No riding the horses. No attending games over at Southern Baptist University. No visitors.

Other than getting sick, though, he'd have to say that, overall, early retirement had been good. They had room for the horses. He got to do some coaching over at Southern Baptist U and mentor some kids.

Not that he'd had much of a choice. Once the University of Washington had let his contract run out, no other university would touch him. Not after that "racism" flap. Once accused, it didn't matter that he'd been exonerated. All the major college programs were afraid the media would keep it alive. "Coach Lynn Nance, once accused of racism when he was head coach at…" And that would be a recruiting nightmare.

"Lynn?" Sally's voice cut into his thoughts. "It's for you. Carlton Evans. I think you want to take it."

The middle-aged former FBI agent and basketball coach broke into a grin. Carlton! Great kid. Always made it a point to stay in touch. In fact, it was people like Carlton Evans and Ricky Byrdsong, African American men who had played for him or coached with him, who had risked their own reputations to stand alongside him when he was accused of racism, that had made the whole mess easier to bear. He still had their friendship, and that's what counted the most as far as he was concerned.

"Coach Nance?" Carlton's voice sounded tight, heavy. "I've got bad news. It's about Ricky."

Nance listened in deepening shock while Carlton spoke. There were going to be two funerals, Carlton said. One in Chicago, and one in Atlanta where Ricky was going to be buried. "Thought you'd want to know, Coach. I know Sherialyn would want to see you. You meant a great deal to Ricky."

The retired basketball coach sat a long time in his chair after Carlton said good-bye. Frustration and anger mingled in his throat. Ricky Byrd-song shot by a white supremacist? The utter irony of it tasted bitter in his mouth. The last person in the world you'd want to hurt was Ricky Byrd-song. The man didn't have a prejudiced bone in his body. When you were with Ricky, you forgot black and white. You saw a *man*. A man of integrity. And so *full* of the joy of life!

Dead? At the hand of some knee-jerk racist who had *no idea* who he'd shot?

The frustration and anger mounted. Worst of all, he couldn't go. Ricky had been there for him in Seattle, helped bail him out of the hotseat. But he couldn't be there for Ricky. For Sherialyn. For Ricky's mother, Mary. He knew his doctor—not to mention Sally—wouldn't let him go.

Coach Nance didn't move for a very long time.

• • •

Shawn Parrish was in a deep sleep when the phone rang. He opened one eye and tried to focus on the digital alarm clock. Five o'clock! It'd been after midnight when he and Aimee crawled into bed. The concert up in Mil-waukee had been great, but that two-hour drive back to Northbrook…he'd planned to sleep at least until ten.

Riiiing! Riiiing! Reluctantly, Shawn reached out a big hand and picked up the receiver. "Yeah?"

"Shawn! It's me, Jamal."

"J Meeks? What are you doing calling me at five in—"

"Turn on the TV, man. Coach Byrd has been shot!"

"Shot!" Shawn bolted upright and swung his feet over the edge of the bed. "Is he—"

"No, no, I think they said he's going to be okay. But it's all over the news. Some crazy guy shooting at people all over Chicago."

"Thanks, J."

Shawn walked into the next room and flipped on the television. The birds were already chirping outside his Northbrook home and the sky was getting brighter. Channel 5—nothing. Channel 2? Channel 7? Nothing.

By now Shawn was wide awake. He had to know. He had to find out if Coach Byrd was okay. He called information and got a number for Channel 7, the local Chicago station. The phone rang and rang. Finally a man's voice answered.

"What's the latest news about"—Shawn's tongue tripped over the words—"the shooting of Coach Ricky Byrdsong?"

"Just a minute," the man said, and put Shawn on hold. Shawn chewed on his lip. Jamal said he thought Coach was going to be okay. Must mean he was just wounded. But how bad was it? What hospital was he in? He'd go see him today, give Byrd a ribbing about trying to make headlines—

The voice came back on the phone. "Coach Byrdsong died about one o'clock this morning."

Shawn didn't remember hanging up the phone. For a full minute, he just walked—back and forth, back and forth, trying to keep the news from sinking in.

Coach Byrd…*dead?*

He couldn't think. He didn't know what to do. He had to do something.

He awoke Aimee and told her Coach Byrd was dead. "I'm going to Sherialyn's house. I don't know what to do. That's the only thing I can think to do."

"Then that's what you should do," his wife urged. "Go on. It's okay."

Shawn drove through the quiet streets of Chicago's northwest suburbs. July Fourth weekend. Pretty soon people would be swarming to parks and forests and the lakefront for picnics and barbecues. Like nothing had happened.

But to Shawn it felt as if the whole world had changed.

Are you anchored deep? He could hear Ricky's voice in his head. It had become a watchword between them during tough times after they had both read that book by Max Lucado.

Our lives are not futile.

Our failures are not fatal.

Our deaths are not final.

The words taunted him now. Still he heard Coach Byrd's voice: "Anchor deep, P!"

He drove up the quiet streets of Skokie to the Byrdsong home, the home where he and the rest of Northwestern's basketball staff and players had been so free to come and go. A light was on; someone was moving around inside.

He parked the car along the grassy curb, walked up the driveway, and stood with his finger poised over the doorbell. What was he *doing?* It wasn't even six in the morning yet!

Shawn pushed the bell, heard *ding-dong* in the distance.

• • •

Scott Perry drove the six hours from Richmond, Kentucky, to the north side of Chicago in a daze. Surely it was all a bad dream. The feeling of unreality clung to him when he arrived at the Byrdsong house in Skokie and saw Sherialyn and the three kids.

Sherialyn. The woman who had mentored his wife, Kim, in being a coach's wife and a mother and a Christian. Kimberly had been visiting her parents in Michigan when they got the news; she had flown immediately to Sherialyn's side. Scott had rattled around the house, gone to the store, gone to his office at Eastern Kentucky University where he'd been head coach for two years, worked out in the gym—anything to keep busy until it was time to drive north for the funeral.

Now, amid the revolving door of people going in and out of the Byrd-song house, Sherialyn stood calmly in the center, talking to visitors, taking phone calls, making arrangements. Kimberly was at the computer typing up the program for the funeral. At the top of the screen she had typed, *A Celebration of Life.*

Scott watched Ricky Jr., his godson, playing with a couple of neighborhood kids in the driveway next door. Ricky Jr., who had been with his dad when he'd been shot, had seen him fall and bleed, had run terrified to the neighbor's house, yelling for them to call 911. What did it mean to be godfather to an eight-year-old who had seen his own father murdered?

Unsure what to do with himself, Scott walked to the site of the crime. He could have sprinted the distance in ten seconds. Yellow police tape blocked off half the street. Bouquets of flowers had been placed where Coach had fallen.

The only traffic sounds came from a distance. Sunlight filtered through leafy treetops. Birds chirped in the branches. The street was peaceful... quiet...eerie beyond belief. Scott had been raised in Detroit, where he knew how to keep his guard up. But here he stood, a black man in a mostly white neighborhood.

Suddenly he felt vulnerable.

• • •

Steve Burgason drove steadily, covering the miles between Ames, Iowa, and Chicago. The Fourth of July traffic was heavy as usual, but he barely noticed. He was still in shock—had been ever since his father had called to tell him the news.

How could God let this happen? Yes, *you,* God!

Steve glanced over at his son sitting beside him. He was glad Andrew had wanted to come along. Andrew was only thirteen. Would he know— *could* he know?—how much Ricky Byrdsong had meant to his dad? Steve wanted his son to understand. He *needed* his son to understand.

Salt and Pepper. That's what people had called them back at Iowa State when they had co-captained the Cyclones. Ricky had been Steve's first close African American friend, someone he could be honest with and not feel threatened. Their friendship had started like the handclasp in the middle of a team huddle—and stayed clasped even when they disagreed. Even when they argued about racial stuff.

Steve had been just a kid when Dr. Martin Luther King Jr. had been murdered. It was a terrible thing, sure. But as a white person, he'd never really understood *why* black people revered King so much. What his life and death really meant to African Americans. After all, Dr. King hadn't been a perfect man. Why make him into such a hero?

But he could talk with Ricky. Ricky let him ask questions. Ricky had helped him see that God uses imperfect people. "I grew up in a segregated world that basically sheltered me from a lot of blatant discrimination," Ricky had admitted. "But I can't let myself forget that the opportunities and things I enjoy are because of people like Dr. King who were willing to rock the boat, willing to stand up against racism, even die preaching respect for one another." Ricky had helped Steve see from the heart.

Steve glanced over again at Andrew. He wanted his son to *see*. He wanted him to meet Ricky's wife, Sherialyn, and Ricky's three kids. He wanted him to go to the funeral, to hear what people said about Coach Ricky Byrdsong, to catch a glimpse of a man so full of love and acceptance for other people, it boggled the mind to think that someone full of hate had killed him.

But he knew what Ricky would say. "Trust me! It's going to be all right."

Yes, it *was* going to be all right. Ricky knew Jesus! The last few times Steve had talked to Ricky, it was obvious that God had really gotten his attention.

He broke the silence in the car. "We live in evil times, Andrew. I won't deny it. When we go to this funeral, you're going to see people full of sorrow. Full of sorrow, but *not without hope*."

•　•　•

Steve Laube, senior editor of nonfiction at Bethany House Publishers, walked over to the desk in his Texas hotel room and clicked on his laptop computer. He'd check his e-mail then get some work done before his next appointment.

He was eager to get home. Traveling was a major part of his job—meeting with authors, speaking at writers conferences. He got to meet a lot of great people, but he hated being away from home so much. At least Bethany let him work out of his home office in Phoenix so he was home when he *wasn't* traveling. And work was piling up at home. For one thing, he needed to get out the contract for the Byrdsong book ASAP. They had an agreement by phone, but nothing had been signed yet.

"Rebounding Makes MVPs." What a great concept to teach kids about how to deal with setbacks and failures! That chapter title by itself had sold him on Ricky's book.

The CNN home page booted up, and the headlines for July 3 rolled across the small screen. Steve stared. *Ricky Byrdsong, shot yesterday evening in a drive-by shooting, died early this morning...*

No. It couldn't be. Was there someone else named Ricky Byrdsong?

Steve called up his phone numbers on the computer than snatched up his cell phone and dialed Ricky's writers, the ones who had sent him the manuscript in the first place. "Tell me it isn't true," he said into the phone.

But it was true. Everyone was in shock. They'd tell Steve more when they knew more.

Before he hung up, Steve went out on a limb. "I just want you to know, from our end of things, we're still committed to publishing Ricky's book."

• • •

The news splashed all over the Chicago headlines: *Manhunt follows trail of bullets...Byrdsong slain, 6 Jews shot in spree tinged with hate.*

Jewish households talked of nothing else that weekend. It touched painful memories that went back generations. Who was hunting them down? Did they dare go outside? When would the shooter be caught? How could he elude capture so long?

In one such household, a teenage Jewish boy listened to the talk, the disbelief, the anguish, the sorrow. But one headline kept ringing in his ears: *Byrdsong slain.*

Coach Ricky Byrdsong. The Ricky Byrdsong Basketball Camp. A pair of hidden shoes...

The boy dug into his closet and found the athletic shoes, too small now but almost brand new. He had not wanted his father to find out, so he'd hidden the shoes Coach Byrd had bought him and had smuggled them to basketball camp each day. At the end of camp, they'd stayed hidden in the closet.

Now holding the shoes as evidence of two lives that had once touched, of a coach who had cared about a young Jewish boy he thought couldn't afford shoes, he approached his father—owner and CEO of a large Chicago company, a man able to buy his young son hundreds of pairs of shoes.

Gulping back tears, the teenager spoke. "Dad, I have something to tell you."

36

Stronger than Hate

Sherialyn Byrdsong closed the basement door behind her, shutting out the houseful of relatives, friends, and neighbors coming in and out of the front door with food and sympathy and staying to wash dishes or run errands. The phone had been ringing constantly: friends, the media, the mayor, even the president of the United States. She had been making funeral arrangements all day. Flowers were piling up on the tranquil lawn where Ricky had fallen, a spontaneous memorial from friends and neighbors who came to see the spot, unbelieving that such violence could touch them...here.

She needed time alone with her three children.

O God, my children need their daddy! Did he have to go?

The rec room in the basement was amazingly quiet, given the nonstop activity above their heads. The shock was still great; she could see it in the eyes of her children, in the heartrending sobs in the night, in the armored tank of blank protection each one wore on their faces as they maneuvered through all the commotion on the first floor.

She needed to give them a perspective—a foundation—on which to build their lives from this point forward. As they slumped silently against her on the well-worn couch cushions, she opened her Bible to Ecclesiastes 3:1-2 and read the familiar words:

There is a time for everything,
and a season for every activity under heaven:
a time to be born and a time to die...

"We all have our time," she said quietly. "This was Daddy's time. He fulfilled his purpose. Even though we don't understand it. Even though it hurts. Even though an evil act has taken him away from us."

She knew the kids had heard the frequent news updates about a gunman on a rampage throughout Chicagoland, shooting Jews and Asians and African Americans. How senseless! How outrageous! But they wouldn't find solace in anger or rage. Only in trust.

Trust me! It's going to be all right!

How many times had Ricky used those very words to get someone over a big bump in the road of life? He had come to trust God implicitly and wanted to share that absolute confidence with others.

"Daddy's in heaven with Jesus. He's all right now. We're going to miss him terribly…but one day we're going to see him again."

Sabrina blurted, "I felt something bad was going to happen. That's why I didn't go with them!"

Sherialyn caught her breath. Had God been protecting Sabrina that night? Now, more than ever, she had a rock-bottom confidence that God was still in control. One day she'd be able to say, like the biblical Joseph, the boy with the coat of many colors, whose own brothers sold him into slavery, who rose to become prime minister and rescuer of Egypt, "You intended to harm me, but God intended it for good" (Genesis 50:20).

Sherialyn was worried about Ricky Jr. the most. He had seen his father fall. She didn't want that to be his last memory of Ricky. When the girls wandered off to write "letters" to their dad, she held Ricky-J close.

"Your daddy was a great man, Ricky. He loved you kids so much. And people loved your daddy—a lot of people. He was a good man, an honest man, a man of integrity. A man who loved God and wanted to serve God with his whole heart. People will remember him as a truly great man, and you're going to grow up to be a great man, just like your daddy."

Ricky listened to her words, pondered them, then fixed his eyes on his mother. "Does that mean I'm going to get shot too?"

• • •

By Sunday morning, July 4, the blue Ford Taurus had made its way to Bloomington, Indiana, the university town where only months before a lone white student had defied five hundred citizens with his placard reading *No Hate Speech Means No Free Speech.* The blue car cruised past the United Methodist Church on East Third, where a small group of worshipers had just arrived. The driver stuck his .380 semiautomatic pistol out the window and fired at least four shots, two of which struck Won Joon Yoon in the back. A doctoral student from South Korea, Yoon had attended the Bloomington church faithfully. But on this day, his attendance was fatal.

One of the witnesses jumped into his car and followed the Taurus for several miles, confirming that it bore Ben Smith's Indiana license plate.[1]

Back at the church, other members frantically administered CPR until an ambulance arrived, but it was to no avail. Won Joon Yoon had died.

•   •   •

Network television crews set up their lights and cameras in the all-purpose room at the front of the warehouse sanctuary known as The Worship Center. Putting off the media for thirty-six hours, Sherialyn Byrdsong had agreed to a six o'clock press conference Sunday evening.

Earlier that morning, as an emotional and heartbroken congregation gathered in the same building for worship, Pastor Lyle had said, "We're all asking, 'Why Coach?' I'll tell you why. Because Coach was *ready.*" Quoting Romans 12:21, he charged his flock to respond to this tragedy the same way Ricky had lived his life: "Do not be overcome by evil, but overcome evil with good."

Now the family filed in and sat at a table at one end of the room. The three Byrdsong children, dressed in their Sunday best, their impassive faces only hinting at the tension they felt in front of all those lights; Sherialyn, Pastor Lyle Foster, and Sherialyn's father, Joe Kelley. Sherialyn looked steadily at the bank of cameras that stretched wall to wall and said she had a statement she would like to read. Her voice was steady, articulate, and clear.

"My beloved husband and the father of our three children was a great man, because he gave his life doing God's will and to making this world a better place for all people. His deepest desire was to see America return to and embrace with a new zeal the biblical principles of living upon which this country was founded. He was committed to building strong families. He gave his life to teaching others to love one another and to treat others the way they would want to be treated."

The journalists listened quietly, aware that this was an unusual woman, a woman standing strong in the face of unimaginable tragedy.

"There were three Scriptures that Ricky centered his life's work around," she continued. And she read:

"Love the Lord your God with all your heart and with all your soul and with all your mind." This is the first and greatest commandment. And the second is like it: "Love your neighbor as yourself." All the Law and the Prophets hang on these two commandments. (Matthew 22:37-40)

I have set before you life and death, blessings and curses. Now choose life, so that you and your children may live. (Deuteronomy 30:19)

If my people, who are called by my name, will humble themselves and pray and seek my face and turn from their wicked ways, then will I hear from heaven and will forgive their sin and will heal their land. (2 Chronicles 7:14)

"I honor my husband for his faithfulness to me throughout our nineteen years of marriage," she continued. "For consistently operating in the utmost integrity in a profession where compromise and dishonesty are not only rampant but tolerated and sometimes encouraged; for providing exceedingly and abundantly for his family; for being a father who constantly challenged and encouraged his children, always believing that their destiny was greatness; for setting an example to our son on how to be a godly father; and for loving and caring for us dearly."

Her words thus far were personal. But Sherialyn Byrdsong had a message. "The violent act that took my husband's life is yet another clarion call to our nation. It's time to wake up, America! God is crying out to us the words of Ephesians 5:14: 'Wake up, O sleeper, rise from the dead, and Christ will shine on you.' It's time to put prayer and the Bible back into our schools and daily family living. This is not a gun problem, it's a heart problem, and only God and reading his Word can change hearts."

At her side, Joe Kelley spoke on behalf of Ricky's and Sherialyn's family. "I have no hate in my heart for the person who did this horrible crime. If the law does not catch him, the Lord surely will. We are hurt but do not hate."

Not hate? Yes, hate for the sin but not for the sinner. It was an improbable reality that confounded newsmakers and lawmakers and noisemakers, who could not understand.

Soon Sherialyn's press statement was being cut into sound bites for the ten o'clock news: "The violent act that took my husband's life is yet another clarion call to our nation." "Wake up, America! It's time to turn back to God." "This is not a gun problem, it's a heart problem."

• • •

The next morning the *Chicago Sun-Times* headline screamed in two-inch-high letters: *Spree Ends: Alleged Gunman Kills Self Near Salem, Ill.*

Getting feeds from the Associated Press and police reports, staff reporters wrote: "A former Wilmette resident and disciple of a white supremacist group wanted in connection with a two-state hate crime shooting rampage apparently shot himself late Sunday.

"A man fitting the description of Benjamin Nathaniel Smith, 21, allegedly carjacked a van in downstate Ina [Illinois] on Route 37. A chase with police ensued, and Marion County sheriff's police caught up with the man near Salem."[2]

According to the Associated Press: "It was 9:28 P.M. [July 4] when the van veered left across the highway, slammed over a culvert and skidded another 30 feet before colliding with a metal gate post and coming to a stop.

"Authorities would later learn that Smith lost control of the vehicle after he put a pistol under his chin and pulled the trigger."[3]

He was following the example and advice of Ben Klassen, the founder of the WCOTC: "There are certain conditions under which we Creators would prefer being dead."[4]

Ben Smith had to pull the trigger two more times before police could break into the stolen van and wrest the gun from him. He later died in the hospital of self-inflicted wounds.

• • •

On that day Matthew Hale was first questioned about his connections to Ben Smith. He claimed that he didn't know Smith very well and had met him only once about eight months before the shootings.[5]

Later, as the investigation intensified, Hale admitted that he knew Smith a little better—quite well, in fact—and had seen him about one or two weeks before the shooting spree.[6]

By Wednesday afternoon, Hale had finally received that certified post-card Smith had mailed from Wilmette before he began shooting. "I always felt I should have received something from him," he told reporters that evening.[7] Perhaps believing Smith's written resignation from the WCOTC gave him enough legal distance that he could be more forthright about their dealings, Hale acknowledged, "We met about ten days ago at the Bob Evans down the hill to discuss my efforts to get a license to practice law."[8]

Counting back "about" ten days (actually nine) put their meeting on June 28—only four days before the shooting.

Eight months, then two weeks, then four days—and that's as close as Hale would admit to. He would leave it to the FBI and police to try to prove that the two had interacted as little as one day before the shootings. "I'm an attorney," he later assured his followers. "I know the law, I know how to fight back with the tricks of the trade."[9]

Fight...and accept no responsibility that either he or the WCOTC might have inspired Smith's shooting spree. "I lay the blame on the individuals who denied me a law license. Instead of Ben Smith having hope for the future, looking to me as an example to follow participating [with]in the system…, their denial of my license crashed his dream and his image of how we can win. We should know that if somebody is mistreated in society, they might decide to commit some kind of a violent act. And that's what happened: July 2, I told the press my license had been denied. July 2, he started shooting."[10]

• • •

On July 7, family, friends, former players, fellow coaches, sportswriters, dignitaries, and church leaders from coast to coast filed past the casket at the front of the First Presbyterian Church in Evanston, Illinois, which had graciously offered to host the funeral. Even Kenneth Dion Lee, still on probation after pleading guilty to charges of point shaving while playing for Coach Byrdsong, came to pay his respects. As Lee stopped by the casket, he suddenly broke down and wept. Immediately Shawn Parrish rose from his seat nearby and locked Lee in an embrace. "It was as though Byrdsong had whispered in Parrish's ear and told his assistant to tell Lee that all was forgiven," wrote sportswriter Neil Milbert later, "and that he could overcome this."[11]

Many others who did not personally know Coach Ricky Byrdsong came to pay their respects "to a flat-out good man," as Northwestern athletic director Rick Taylor put it. But there was a deeper reason. One after another, the mourners insisted that the murder of Ricky Byrdsong would not go down as a victory for racial hatred.

"Being able to bring a community like this together at such a sad event is one way to say to the whole world, 'This will not be tolerated,'" said the Reverend David Handley, the pastor of First Presbyterian.

Outside, Michael, the Jewish doctor who had been shot at in Rogers Park, along with more than a hundred other Orthodox Jews, sat on folding chairs during the Christian service. Their number included one of the Jewish men who had been wounded during the weekend shooting spree. Even though their religious convictions prevented them from entering a Christian church, they came to show their respect for one who had died during Smith's rampage of hate in which Jews had been the first targets.

Inside, all eyes were drawn to the woman in the front row, dressed in a white suit, standing on her feet, head thrown back, arms lifted, praising God with her whole being along with the gospel choir made up of praise team members from both The Worship Center and Rosedale Park Baptist. Could this be Sherialyn Byrdsong, who had just lost her husband in a tragic drive-by shooting, suddenly made a widow, left to raise three children alone?

Yes! Yes! she seemed to be saying. God is still in control! *Nothing*—not even death—can separate us from the love of God.

When the exuberant singing had finally quieted, several speakers shared brief memories of an unforgettable man. After recounting Ricky's efforts at Aon to develop Project Y.E.S.!—Youth, Education, Service—for disadvantaged kids, putting Aon employees to work refurbishing local parks, and mounting a fund-raiser for juvenile diabetes, Ricky's former boss Pat Ryan turned to the casket as if he were speaking to Ricky. "Forget the court; forget the playing field. You were an impact player in *life!*"

Pastor Tom Nesbitt from Ames, Iowa, recalled the challenge he had given Ricky during their wedding ceremony to "let Jesus lead you in order for you to lead her and keep that sparkle in her eye." Tom looked at Sherialyn, sitting with her children in the front row, and declared, "The woman who sits before me right now, who stood and worshiped and praised the Lord a while ago, is more beautiful than she was nineteen years ago when he married her."

The white pastor also noted that, in the footsteps of his Savior, Jesus Christ, Ricky had died because of someone else's sin. "The secret of Ricky Byrdsong's life, the difference that enabled him to love everybody, is that Jesus Christ was Lord of his life."

Pastor Haman Cross, from Rosedale Baptist in Detroit, spoke more directly to the tragedy that had snuffed out the life of his friend. "It looks *bad*. The Enemy got in a good punch. But evil will not win! Ungodliness will not win! The devil will not win! Racism will not win! Bigotry will not win! The score looks bad, but we're going to win!"

The last speaker, Pastor Lyle Foster, gave the eulogy, referring to Ricky as a "gentle giant." "Coach was the kind of man who was willing to offer himself as a living sacrifice, so that even in his death, we would learn how to come together and get to the point where the things we think are so important don't matter anymore, and the things that are *really* important would begin to matter."

At this point in the eulogy, Pastor Lyle played part of Ricky's "Walking on Water" sermon.

• • •

Sitting in the front row, flanked by her children, Sherialyn listened to Ricky's voice boom from his taped sermon. "It doesn't matter now! It doesn't matter now!" She closed her eyes, letting his words wash over her. It seemed that Ricky was talking directly to her. "Sherialyn, it doesn't matter now if we didn't always see eye to eye on everything… It doesn't matter now that we didn't get to go for a walk and talk that last night… It doesn't matter now! It doesn't matter now!" Deep down, she felt the touch of the Holy Spirit, healing all that was unfinished, uniting her and the kids and their friends around what was really important—their love, their faith, their family, their trust in God. *Thank you, Lord! Thank you!*

• • •

The congregation sat in a hush after listening to Ricky Byrdsong's familiar voice challenging their priorities. Noting that members of the Jewish community, the Korean American community, the black community, and the white community were all represented among the congregation, Pastor Lyle thundered, "[Coach's death] isn't defeat! The Enemy wanted to drive us apart, but we're going to come together!"

Preacher that he was, Pastor Lyle took it to the point of decision. "If you want to say to the Enemy, to our city, to our nation: We are not going to let tragedy stop us from loving…we are not going to let what the Enemy has done keep us from serving our God…we are not going to be embroiled in bitterness, misery, and shame…I'd like you to stand to your feet!"

All over the building—in the balcony, in the aisles, in the pews—people rose to their feet. Young and old, black and white, men and women, responded to the call: "Make a difference! Make a difference!"

• • •

The service was over. Steve Burgason—"Salt" of "Salt and Pepper"—watched with deep emotion as Sean Elliott and Steve Kerr (whom Ricky had coached at the University of Arizona; Kerr had gone on to star with the Chicago Bulls and was now playing for the San Antonio Spurs) and former coaching colleagues Scott Perry, Paul Swanson, Shawn Parrish, and Jamal Meeks wheeled the casket down the center aisle.

As close to two thousand people spilled from the church, Steve couldn't help thinking about Tom Hunter (not his real name), the talented player for the Iowa State Cyclones back when Ricky was graduate assistant coach, who had built up his own ego by tearing down the black players with racial slurs. He'd heard from a mutual friend that Tom had died not long ago of a heart attack while betting on the horses at a racetrack in Kentucky.

Only seven people had attended Tom's funeral.

O God, I want to make a difference!

• • •

Sportswriter Neil Milbert of the *Chicago Tribune* left the funeral service and went back to his computer to write his column for the next day. "Ricky Byrdsong wouldn't have believed his eyes Wednesday night," he wrote. "Not even the outpouring of emotion that greeted his greatest victory—Northwestern's monumental 1994 upset of Michigan that sent the Wild-cats to the National Invitation Tournament—could hold a candle to this.

"That was a celebration of the biggest day in the coaching career of Ricky Byrdsong.

"This was a celebration of the life of Ricky Byrdsong."[12]

37

Is God Really Good?

Ricky's second funeral took place in Atlanta the following Saturday, July 10, at the Cathedral of Faith Church of God in Christ. Again a parade of people—this time high-school teachers and coaches and principals and childhood friends—gave witness to a life well lived. Again the mourners were challenged not to let evil score a victory by responding in turn with violence and hate.

"God did not keep back his own Son," said Valerie Lockett, Ricky's high-school English teacher. "Nothing"—not even death—"can separate us from the love of God."

Dr. Lester Butts, former principal of Frederick Douglass High School, challenged mourners to follow Ricky's example of goodwill and acts of love toward all people. "He refused to lower himself by allowing someone else to make him hate."

This time the hundreds of mourners, many still in shock that Ricky Byrdsong had been killed by the purveyors of hate, proceeded from the church to the rolling hills of Lincoln Cemetery, where Ricky's body was laid to rest.

●　●　●

Sherialyn Byrdsong's life had changed overnight.

She had lost her husband of nineteen years abruptly, tragically. She was suddenly a widow at the age of forty-two. She now faced raising three children by herself as a single mom.

Because of the nature of Ricky's death and his prominence as a former Big 10 basketball coach, Sherialyn was suddenly thrust into the national media. *Dateline, Good Morning America, Oprah, The Leeza Gibbons Show* all wanted interviews. Requests for speaking engagements were pouring in. Ricky's book needed to be finished. (She and the writers together had vowed: It *will* get finished!) And an idea was tumbling in her brain for forming a foundation in Ricky's name to continue the work he had started to inspire and encourage young people.

She needed time—time to sort it all out.

Sherialyn and the three kids stayed in Atlanta for the rest of July to recover from the media glare and to work through their grief among family. While the kids were soaking up the love and security of a mighty army of grandparents, aunts, uncles, and cousins, Sherialyn took time to be quiet, to read her Bible, and to pray.

"How are you doing?" everyone wanted to know. She just said, "Ever since I became a Christian twenty years ago, every worship song I've ever sung, every Scripture verse I've ever memorized, were like bank deposits made into my heart—and now I'm making withdrawals big-time."

"How could a loving God let this happen?" Stated or not, *that* was the real question in people's minds. Sherialyn read and reread familiar Scriptures with that question in mind, and as she read her excitement began to grow.

God is sovereign. It's not about *us!* It's about *God!*

It's not what happens to us in life, but our attitude about what happens, that determines our destiny. (She remembered Joyce Meyer had once said, "You can be pitiful or powerful, but not both!")

If she wanted to experience the fullness of God in her life, she would have to let go of the "if onlys."

The bottom line was, did she trust God? Did she truly believe God's grace was sufficient for *everything?*

Sherialyn read and reread the story of Joseph in Genesis 37. Even though he had been betrayed by his own brothers and taken to Egypt as a slave, the Lord was with Joseph. He could have wallowed in the "if onlys."

He could have been bitter. But he kept his trust in God, and God used him in a mighty way!

The seeds of a Bible study titled "Is God *Really* Good?" grew in her mind and she began to jot down the Scriptures God showed her. These were important insights to share with others who experienced tragedy!

While still in Atlanta, Sherialyn took a few days to attend a praise and worship conference—always a time when God planted new songs and new words into her spirit. During one of the sessions, one of the praise and worship leaders began to sing extemporaneously. The woman had only sung a few words when Sherialyn recognized them: Isaiah 54. Like a slash of lightning revealing what had been only shadows before, the familiar words had her name stamped all over them.

> *Do not fear....*
> *For your Maker is your husband,*
> *The LORD of hosts is His name....*
> *For the LORD has called you*
> *Like a woman forsaken and grieved in spirit....*
> *For a mere moment I have forsaken you,*
> *But with great mercies I will gather you....*
> *All your children shall be taught by the LORD,*
> *And great shall be the peace of your children.*
> *In righteousness you shall be established....*
> *Whoever assembles against you shall fall for your sake....*
> *No weapon formed against you shall prosper.*
> *(verses 4-7, 13-15, 17, NKJV)*

So *this* is what God had meant: Ricky would die suddenly, tragically. When she had been memorizing Isaiah 54, she had had that strange "knowing" in her heart, but the shock of Ricky's death had not allowed her to put it together until now. God had been preparing her.

Yes, the Enemy had struck a deathblow, taking out a man who was not only her husband and the father of her children, but a man coming into his destiny, who was starting to make a difference. Everyone, including the newspapers, were using the words, "Tragic…senseless…so ironic that a man so filled with love would be killed by a man consumed with hate…"

But as the woman sang, the message of Isaiah 54 rang triumphantly in Sherialyn's spirit: God would not forsake her! The Enemy *would not win.* Not only would the Enemy not win, but the seed of Ricky's death would blossom and flourish and multiply.

Enlarge the place of your tent,
And let them stretch out the curtains of your dwellings;
Do not spare;
Lengthen your cords,
And strengthen your stakes.
For you shall expand to the right and to the left,
And your descendants will inherit the nations,
And make the desolate cities inhabited. (verses 2-3, NKJV)

Strength poured into Sherialyn—body, mind, and spirit. Ricky had completed his mission, had run his race, and received his prize—the Master's "Well done, good and faithful servant."

But this was not the end. It was a beginning!

It was time to return home—home to Chicago, home to her church family, home to the multitude of opportunities awaiting her to proclaim the faithfulness of God. The torch had briefly fallen and flickered; now God was urging her, "Pick it up."

God had prepared her. God would go with her. God had already won!

Afterword

Not an End, but a Beginning...

THE WALK

Shortly after Ricky was shot and killed, some of the Byrdsongs' neighbors organized nightly "walks" through the neighborhood—their way of saying, "We are here in support of the Byrdsongs. We will not be intimidated by these tragic shootings. We will not let it drive us into our homes, away from our neighbors. Instead, we commit ourselves to getting to know our neighbors better." Every evening at eight o'clock, neighbors gathered at the spot where Ricky had been shot. Sometimes thirty or forty people came, from two doors away and from two towns away, and they walked—white, black, Jew, Christian, young, old. The Skokie police usually sent a car to watch over the gathering.

"The Walk," as it came to be known, continued night after night, week after week, throughout the rest of the summer and into the fall of 1999. Two years later, as this is being written, the Walk still continues on an occasional basis.

RICKY'S BOOK

Using his tapes and notes, Ricky's cowriters were determined to finish his parenting book. Sherialyn worked closely with them to make sure the manuscript reflected Ricky's heart. A contract was signed and *Coaching Your Kids in the Game of Life* was released by Bethany House Publishers in time for Father's Day 2000.

When the mail carrier dropped a package at her door late that spring,

Sherialyn didn't think too much about it. It was hard keeping up with her mail as it was. But when she opened it, there lay an advance copy of the book. Ricky's book. She took it out and held it tight against her chest. Ricky would be so excited. She could just see his delighted grin and hear him say, *Can you believe it, Sherialyn? They published my book!*

She went upstairs to their bedroom, lay down on the bed, and wept.

THE RICKY BYRDSONG FOUNDATION

In the wake of Ricky's tragic death, Sherialyn had a vision: to establish a foundation in Ricky's name to continue his work with youth. What better way to arrest the growing epidemic of hate and violence in our society than to provide opportunities for youth that broaden their perspective, build character, and instill a sense of purpose in their lives!

By September 1999 the Ricky Byrdsong Foundation had been established with Sherialyn as president of the board. Among its initial efforts were Corporate Camp (introducing inner-city kids to job and career possibilities), which Ricky had started as part of Project Y.E.S.! (Youth, Education, Service), and The Ricky Byrdsong Not-Just-Basketball Camp, which runs for a week each August.

Meanwhile, back in Arizona, Carlton Evans—Ricky's college roommate and teammate—was asking God some big questions. Why had God brought Ricky into his life? How did God want him to respond to Ricky's death? Phone calls and visits flew back and forth between the foundation and the Evans family. A lot of people prayed. And in August 2001, Carlton packed up his family and moved to Evanston-Skokie, Illinois, to become executive director of youth development—the first full-time employee—of the Ricky Byrdsong Foundation. Their arrival was cause for great celebration for the foundation, The Worship Center, and the Byrdsong family!

For further information and current events, check out the Ricky Byrdsong Foundation Web site: http://www.byrdsongfoundation.org. Or write the Ricky Byrdsong Foundation, 2101 Dempster Street, Evanston, IL 60201; or call toll-free 877-273-7664.

MEMORIALS, HONORS, AND AWARDS

Crack! "They're off!" The anniversary of Ricky Byrdsong's death has been marked by an annual "Memorial 5K Race Against Hate," presented by Aon Corporation, to raise awareness of the problem of hate crimes and help to raise money for the foundation. More than eighteen hundred runners and walkers ran along Northwestern University's beautiful campus and the Lake Michigan shore on the first anniversary; twenty-two hundred participated in the second memorial race.

The anniversary of the July 4 tragedy has also been marked by a memorial celebration bringing together various churches and people of faith in the Chicago area around the theme From Tragedy to Victory! At the second celebration, the Ricky Byrdsong Victory Award was presented for the first time to STAND, a group of middle-school students from northwest Indiana, to honor their efforts to promote respect for different cultures and races and to stand against hate and violence portrayed by popular music posters.

Marcia Byrdsong, Ricky's sister and the family historian, has recently relocated to Evanston, Illinois, to support Sherialyn in raising her brother's three kids, and is a board member of the foundation. She has also been present with Sherialyn for the many honors awarded to her slain brother—such as when he was inducted posthumously into the Chicago Sports Hall of Fame; when he was awarded an honorary doctorate in public service by National-Lewis University; and when Pratt Community College retired Ricky's jersey number thirty-three and established an athletic scholarship in his name.

Sherialyn herself was chosen as one of seven Chicagoans of the Year in January 2000.

For a complete list of honors and awards, go to http://www.byrdsong-foundation.org.

A NEW CALLING

Sherialyn realized that the many requests for media interviews and speaking engagements were an opportunity to bring her faith to the marketplace.

She has been a guest on *Oprah, The Leeza Gibbons Show, Today, Dateline, Good Day Atlanta, Peachtree Morning,* and *The 700 Club,* was featured as the cover story in *Today's Christian Woman* (July/August 2001), and was awarded *Family Circle* magazine's Halo Award as a "Crusader Against Hate" (January 15, 2002 issue).

Speaking engagements have included invitations from the White House, the Crystal Cathedral, Harvard University Foundation, and the National-Lewis University commencement (where she spoke on "How to Leave a Legacy") as well as teaching opportunities at churches and women's conferences.

By circumstance, she has become a spokesperson on the problem of hate crimes. But whether the audience is secular or sacred, Sherialyn makes sure everyone knows that it is her faith in God that helps her turn hate from tragedy to victory.

At the New Year's Eve service heading into 2001, Sherialyn said to The Worship Center family, "God has given me several promises in recent times that sustain me from day to day. Psalm 92:12,14 says, 'The righteous will flourish.... They will still bear fruit in old age.' Also Job 42:12: 'The LORD blessed the latter part of Job's life more than the first.' That's awesome! These promises help me look to the future. And I *know* God is faithful. It's true, just like Joshua said, *If* you follow the Lord in obedience, 'You know with all your heart and soul that not one of all the good promises the LORD your God gave you has failed' (Joshua 23:14)."

A Personal Note from the Authors

Although Benjamin Smith shot a black man he did not know, it was the spiritual stance of Ricky Byrdsong that made Ricky a Christian martyr. As Pastor Lyle Foster told mourners concerning why Ricky was the target: "Because Coach was *ready.*"

The more we worked on this story, the more momentous the choices of the characters became, from Ben Klassen's decision to reject God and later to create an anti-Christian religion based on hate, to Ricky Byrdsong's decision to serve God regardless of the cost. "Don't you know, it doesn't matter anymore!"

There is one thing we withheld in telling Ricky Byrdsong's story. He was murdered less than a week after our pastor, Lyle Foster, completed a very powerful sermon series on racial reconciliation. Coincidence? We don't think so. We have seen it happen before in other Christian bodies. When believers choose to deal seriously with racial reconciliation, quite literally, all hell breaks loose. That should tell us something about its strategic importance to both God and Satan, and about the courage we need to confront racial and religious hatred seriously.

Therefore, we didn't expect the devil to welcome our exposing his schemes. Before we began writing, we tested the idea with several wise counselors. We engaged a team of twelve prayer warriors who prayed for our work daily. We used blind and secure e-mail for all communications with Matt Hale. We checked in with the police before and after each interview with the WCOTC.

Nevertheless, from the day we submitted the book proposal to our agent, we encountered a surprising sequence of obstacles: a major health crisis, the deaths of two elderly parents, crises in the families of our adult children, a sudden plunge in our income. Even as we prepared to send the first draft of this book to our editor, the files suddenly froze. Not the computer—*just the files for this book.* By God's grace through a nervous all-nighter, we were able to salvage the files, piece them back together, and make our deadline.

The weekend of our deadline, Sherialyn and her kids emerged from the second Ricky Byrdsong Memorial Celebration to find that the back window of their van had been smashed. The next day, one of our church elders had a gun pulled on him by a man who looked like a skinhead. Moments before Pastor Lyle came out of an office building, a man had been shot and lay crumpled in the doorway near his parked car. The following Sunday we arrived at The Worship Center to find that someone had dumped more than fifty old tires and other assorted junk in front of our church.

Of course, many people experience tough times, but all these threatening experiences seemed to come in a rush. Was Satan trying to keep us from doing what God had asked us to do? Could we still believe God is in control?

Near the end, the obstacles had become confirmations that this book had a purpose larger than its story. We were working toward three goals:

- To expose the evil of hate groups that prey on the fears of whites as Caucasians become a minority in our changing society.
- To chart an incident of spiritual warfare for a world that loves to talk about angels or even "the dark side," but hesitates to acknowledge the reality of Satan.
- To portray the spiritual forces behind good and evil so powerfully that readers are compelled to choose whom they will serve—the devil or the Lord.

To the degree we achieve those goals, we will have accomplished our purpose. Personally, we have been profoundly blessed by the privilege of sharing this story, of meeting some of God's exceptional servants, and of experiencing God's victory in the teeth of the Enemy.

Besides, "Don't you know, it doesn't matter anymore!"

Choose for yourselves this day
whom you will serve....
But as for me and my household,
we will serve the LORD.

—JOSHUA 24:15

Acknowledgments

As Ricky Byrdsong would say, "Dave and Neta are first of all *grateful...*"

Without Sherialyn Byrdsong's blessing, we never would have embarked on this book. It is not only Ricky's story but *her* story, and she made herself available to us in the midst of an incredibly demanding schedule. Our respect and love for this amazing woman of faith has deepened with each passing day.

Pastors Lyle and Lona Foster pondered and prayed about the vision we shared with them for this book and gave us their unwavering support and input.

Mary Byrdsong Jasper and her husband, Bob, graciously took us into their home in Atlanta and made us fat on butter-and-cheese-drenched grits while we conducted numerous interviews with Ricky and Sherialyn's family and friends.

Marcia Byrdsong, Ricky's "kid sister," took days off from work to chauffeur us around Atlanta and introduce us to key people in Ricky's early life, helped with research, and answered endless questions.

June Fohesta, Sherialyn Byrdsong's cousin, lined up many interviews with family and friends who knew Sherialyn as a girl.

We feel humbled by the way other members of the Byrdsong and Kelley clans opened their hearts and family stories to us: Jannie Byrdsong Green, Ina Byrdsong Wise, Blanche Hollis, Elizabeth Fouch, Gwen Kelley, Kim Kelley, Joe and Loretta Kelley, Lucille Danley, and Derry Bradley. Special thanks to Curtis Byrdsong, for allowing us to use material from his personal writings about his mother, Jannie Byrdsong; also Eric Wise, for his professional and moving video interview of his grandmother Jannie.

Ricky and Sherialyn's childhood and high school friends, teachers, and coaches kept us laughing and shaking our heads: Waymon and Joseph Strickland, Rollie Lewis, Valerie Lockett, Coach William Lester, Coach

Donald Dollar, Dr. Samuel Hill, Jan Chandler Hilliard, Galetha Clemons Thompson, and Coach Anna Wade.

Ricky's years at Pratt Community College came alive in phone interviews with Coach Jim Lewis, Jerry and Kathy McCalla, and Carlton Evans.

We owe a *huge* debt of gratitude to the hours—yes, hours!—we spent on the phone with Coach Lynn Nance, Carlton Evans, and Steve Burgason regarding Ricky's years at Iowa State. These brothers have truly enriched our lives.

Other basketball colleagues who graciously granted us interviews: Steve Fisher (head coach, San Diego State); Rick Samuels (head coach, Eastern Illinois University); Lute Olson (head coach, University of Arizona); Kevin O'Neill (assistant coach, New York Knicks); Steve Kerr (San Antonio Spurs); Scott Perry (scout, Detroit Pistons); Shawn Parrish (former assistant coach, Northwestern University); and Paul Swanson (head coach, Pensacola Junior College).

Pastor Haman Cross (Rosedale Park Baptist, Detroit); Brenda Shorter and Carrie Roach (The Worship Center); Sheri Donaldson (Ricky's former secretary at NWU); and John Roskopf and Les Coney (Aon Corporation)—you all played an important part in this book.

The following persons also provided essential information:

- Jake Wiens, first cousin to Ben Klassen
- Earl Lafayette, black schoolmate of Ben Klassen
- Kim Klassen, daughter of Ben Klassen
- Kristin Hallahan-Svec, classmate of Matt Hale
- Matt Hale, Pontifex Maximus of the World Church of the Creator
- The Skokie police, especially Capt. Barry Silverberg and Sgt. Michael Ruth
- Jackson Potter, classmate of Ben Smith
- Neil Milbert, sports reporter for the *Chicago Tribune*
- Dave Ostendorf and Devin Burghart at the Center for New Community
- The ADL (Anti-Defamation League), especially Elana Stern

- Dr. Michael, representative for the Jewish people of Rogers Park who were wounded
- Peter Dyck, for his assistance in tracking down Mennonites of Russian origin

We are deeply grateful to our prayer team, who prayed regularly for us throughout the writing process: Rachel Jackson Berg, Marcia Byrdsong, Pastor Haman Cross, Norma Cox, Athol Dickson, Pastors Lyle and Lona Foster, Julian and Kristin Jackson, Drs. Brenda and Derek McNeil, Julia Pferdehirt, Pam Sullivan, and Pastor Virgil Vogt.

Chip MacGregor, our agent at Alive Communications, was quick to encourage this book, for which we are tremendously grateful. And it didn't take him long to find a home for it with WaterBrook Press where our patient and gracious editor, Dan Benson, and others have been most helpful.

Last but not least, special thanks to Sabrina, Kelley, and Ricky Jr., three courageous kids, who were willing to talk about "what happened that day."

Notes

PROLOGUE

1. Matt Hale, "The Desperation of Our Enemies," *The Struggle,* July 1999.
2. Lisa Sorg, "Dead Man Talking," *Illinois Times,* 8 July 1999, 3, reprinted from the 27 August 1998 issue of the *Bloomington Independent.*
3. Kirsten Scharnberg, "FBI Agents Quiz Church Leader over Rampage," *Chicago Tribune,* 8 July 1999, photo of note from Smith, 20.
4. Matt Hale, "Frequently Asked Questions About Creativity," World Church of the Creator, East Peoria, Illinois, question #43.

CHAPTER 3

1. Earl Lafayette, in a phone interview, 20 March 2001.
2. Ben Klassen, *Against the Evil Tide* (Otto, N.C.: The Church of the Creator, 1991), 93.
3. Klassen, *Evil Tide,* 67.
4. Klassen, *Evil Tide,* 90.
5. Jake Wiens, first cousin to Ben Klassen, in a phone interview, 19 March 2001.
6. Klassen, *Evil Tide,* 133.
7. Klassen, *Evil Tide,* 95.

CHAPTER 5

1. David Riazanov, *Karl Marx and Frederick Engels* (New York: Monthly Review Press, 1937, 1973), chapter 2. Found at http://www.marxists.org/archive /riazanov/works/1927-ma/ch02.htm.
2. Hugo Valentin, *Antisemitism, Historically and Critically Examined* (Upsala, Sweden: Upsala University), 257.
3. Joseph N. Moody, *Why Are Jews Persecuted?* Issued under the imprimatur of John J. Glennon, Archbishop of St. Louis, 26.
4. Moody, *Persecuted,* 26.

5. Valentin, *Antisemitism*, 257.

6. Valentin, *Antisemitism*, 257.

7. Ben Klassen, *Against the Evil Tide* (Otto, N.C.: The Church of the Creator, 1991), 104.

8. Klassen, *Evil Tide*, 105.

9. Ben Klassen, *The White Man's Bible* (Milwaukee, Wis.: The Milwaukee Church of the Creator, 1981), 109.

10. Klassen, *Evil Tide*, 121.

11. Klassen, *Evil Tide*, 125.

12. Klassen, *Evil Tide*, 150.

13. Klassen, *White Man's Bible*, 386-7.

CHAPTER 7

1. Ben Klassen, *The White Man's Bible* (Milwaukee, Wis.: The Milwaukee Church of the Creator, 1981), 222-3.

2. Ben Klassen, *Against the Evil Tide* (Otto, N.C.: The Church of the Creator, 1991), 156.

3. Ben Klassen, *Nature's Eternal Religion* (Milwaukee, Wis.: The Milwaukee Church of the Creator, 1973), 318.

4. Klassen, *White Man's Bible*, 461.

5. Klassen, *White Man's Bible*, 253.

6. Klassen, *White Man's Bible*, 255-6.

7. Harry Schneiderman, et al, eds. *American Jewish Year Book*, vol. 49, 1947–1948 (Philadelphia: The Jewish Publication Society of America, 1948), 733-4.

8. Klassen, *Evil Tide*, 168.

9. Ben Klassen, *The Little White Book* (Otto, N.C.: The Church of the Creator, 1991), 34.

10. Klassen, *Evil Tide*, 174.

11. Jake Wiens, first cousin to Ben Klassen, in a phone interview, 19 March 2001.

CHAPTER 9

1. Ben Klassen, *Against the Evil Tide* (Otto, N.C.: The Church of the Creator, 1991), 194.

2. Klassen, *Evil Tide*, 245.

3. Klassen, *Evil Tide*, 247.

CHAPTER 11

1. Stephane Courtois et al., *The Black Book of Communism* (Cambridge, Mass.: Harvard University Press, 1999), x. This 850-page systematic and scholarly work estimates between eighty-five and one hundred million victims of communism worldwide from the Russian Revolution in 1917 to the war in Afghanistan in 1989. It was first published by Robert Laffont in France in 1997 as *Le Livre Noir du Communisme: Crimes, Terreur, Repression*.

2. Ben Klassen, *Against the Evil Tide* (Otto, N.C.: The Church of the Creator, 1991), 293.

3. Klassen, *Evil Tide*, 376.

4. Klassen, *Evil Tide*, 293.

5. Richard H. Rovere, *Senator Joe McCarthy* (New York: Harcourt Brace, 1959), 241-50.

6. Ben Klassen, *Nature's Eternal Religion* (Milwaukee, Wis.: The Milwaukee Church of the Creator, 1973), 194.

7. Sigmund Livingston, *Must Men Hate?* (Cleveland, Ohio: Crane Press, 1944), 39-42.

8. Livingston, *Must Men Hate*, 46-7.

9. Ben Klassen, *The White Man's Bible* (Milwaukee, Wis.: The Milwaukee Church of the Creator, 1981), 301-2.

10. Livingston, *Must Men Hate*, notes on page 44, "In August, 1943, in Port Elizabeth, South Africa, a court decision rendered by Sir Thomas Graham and Justice Jutsche of the Supreme Court stated: 'The Protocols are an impudent forgery, obviously for the purpose of anti-Jewish propaganda.' In May, 1935, a Swiss court in Berne, in a proceeding where the defendant was charged with distributing seditious literature, said: 'I deem the "Protocols" to be a forgery, a plagiarism, and silly nonsense.' "

11. Klassen, *Evil Tide*, 302.

12. Klassen, *Evil Tide*, 334.

13. Kim Klassen, daughter of Ben Klassen, in a phone interview, 30 April 2001.

14. Klassen, *Evil Tide,* 301.

15. Klassen, *Evil Tide,* 307.

16. Klassen, *White Man's Bible,* 192.

17. Klassen, *White Man's Bible,* 307-8.

18. Klassen, *White Man's Bible,* 367-8.

19. Klassen, *White Man's Bible,* 373.

CHAPTER 13

1. Ben Klassen, *Against the Evil Tide* (Otto, N.C.: The Church of the Creator, 1991), 393.

2. Klassen, *Evil Tide,* 394-5.

3. Marcus Eli Ravage, "A Real Case Against the Jews," *Century Magazine,* January 1928.

4. Ben Klassen, *The White Man's Bible* (Milwaukee, Wis.: The Milwaukee Church of the Creator, 1981), 310.

5. Klassen, *Evil Tide,* 395

6. Klassen, *Evil Tide,* 396.

7. Klassen, *White Man's Bible,* 413.

8. Ben Klassen, *Nature's Eternal Religion* (Milwaukee, Wis.: The Milwaukee Church of the Creator, 1973), 42-53.

CHAPTER 15

1. Lisa Turner, "Our Stand on Abortion," an essay found at http://www.creator.org, 2001.

2. Lisa Turner, "Women's Frontier to the ADL: We Reject Your Feminist Smear!" *Women's Frontier Newsletter,* January 1999.

3. Turner, "Feminist Smear."

4. Turner, "Feminist Smear."

5. Turner, "Feminist Smear."

6. Turner, "Feminist Smear."

7. Turner, "Feminist Smear."

8. Jake Wiens, first cousin to Ben Klassen, in a phone interview, 19 March 2001.

9. Peter Klassen, nephew of Ben Klassen in a phone interview, 24 April, 2001.

10. George Wiens, e-mail to Dave Jackson, 22 March 2001.

CHAPTER 17

1. Ben Klassen, *Nature's Eternal Religion* (Milwaukee, Wis.: The Church of the Creator, 1973), 171.

2. Justin Martyr, *The Second Apology of Justin for the Christians; Addressed to the Roman Senate* (under Marcus Aurelius, circa 161 A.D.), chap. 10—"Christ Compared with Socrates." (Found at http://www.ccel.org/fathers2/ANF-01 /anf01-47.htm#P4012_776807.)

3. Kenneth L. Woodward, "The Changing Face of the Church," *Newsweek*, 16 April 2001, 50-1.

4. Ben Klassen, "Let Them Wither on the Vine," *Racial Loyalty*, no. 60, June 1990.

5. Ben Klassen, *Against the Evil Tide* (Otto, N.C.: The Church of the Creator, 1991), 410.

6. Klassen, *Evil Tide*, 448, 450.

7. Ben Klassen, *Trials, Tribulations, and Triumphs* (Niceville, Fla.: The Church of the Creator, 1993), 62.

CHAPTER 19

1. Ben Klassen, *Trials, Tribulations, and Triumphs* (Niceville, Fla.: The Church of the Creator, 1993), 163.

2. Klassen, *Trials, Tribulations, and Triumphs*, 138.

CHAPTER 21

1. Ben Klassen, *Trials, Tribulations, and Triumphs* (Niceville, Fla.: The Church of the Creator, 1993), 195-6.

2. Klassen, *Trials, Tribulations, and Triumphs*, 201.

3. Klassen, *Trials, Tribulations, and Triumphs*, 241-3.

4. Klassen, *Trials, Tribulations, and Triumphs*, 249-54.

5. Klassen, *Trials, Tribulations, and Triumphs*, 255-9.

6. Ben Klassen, *Racial Loyalty,* no. 55 (Otto, N.C.: The Church of the Creator, October 1989).

7. Klassen, *Racial Loyalty,* no. 55.

8. Klassen, *Trials, Tribulations, and Triumphs,* 238.

9. Crocker Stephenson, "Missionaries of Hate," *Milwaukee Journal Sentinel,* 19 March 2000.

10. Ben Klassen, *The White Man's Bible* (Milwaukee, Wis.: The Milwaukee Church of the Creator, 1981), 430.

11. Klassen, *Trials, Tribulations, and Triumphs,* 238.

CHAPTER 23

1. Ben Klassen, *The White Man's Bible* (Milwaukee, Wis.: The Milwaukee Church of the Creator, 1981), 68-72.

2. Klassen, *White Man's Bible,* 433.

3. This fact is obvious from the diarylike entries throughout his autobiographies of what he ate.

4. Septimus Winner (alias Alice Hawthorne), "Whispering Hope" (Boston: Oliver Ditson, 1868).

5. Ben Klassen, *Trials, Tribulations, and Triumphs* (Niceville, Fla.: The Church of the Creator, 1993), 261.

6. Rudy Stanko, *Racial Loyalty,* February 1990.

7. Klassen, *Trials, Tribulations, and Triumphs,* 262.

8. "Stanko and the Montana Supreme Court: From Women Prisoners to Salubrious Living," *Montana Human Rights Network News,* November 1999.

9. Klassen, *Trials, Tribulations, and Triumphs,* 287.

10. "The Search for a New High Priest" (Anti-Defamation League, 1993), found at http://ftp.nizkor.org/ftp.cgi/orgs/american/adl/cotc/cotc-1993.

11. Klassen, *Trials, Tribulations, and Triumphs,* 292.

12. Klassen, *Trials, Tribulations, and Triumphs,* 294.

13. Klassen, *Trials, Tribulations, and Triumphs,* 308. See also http://www.nizkor.org/hweb/orgs/american/adl/cotc/steve-thomas.html.

14. Klassen, *Trials, Tribulations, and Triumphs,* 311.

15. "New High Priest."

16. Klassen, *Trials, Tribulations, and Triumphs,* 288.

17. Kim Klassen, daughter of Ben Klassen, in a phone interview, 30 April 2001.

CHAPTER 25

1. "The Search for a New High Priest" (Anti-Defamation League, 1993), found at http://ftp.nizkor.org/ftp.cgi/orgs/american/adl/cotc/cotc-1993.

2. The following incidents are primarily documented in "New High Priest."

3. Mark Silva, "Leader of Separatist Sect Denies Ties to L.A. Hate Plot," *Miami Herald,* 17 July 1993, 1A.

4. "New High Priest."

5. Kim Klassen, daughter of Ben Klassen, in a phone interview, 30 April 2001.

6. Ben Klassen, *The White Man's Bible* (Milwaukee, Wis.: The Milwaukee Church of the Creator, 1981), 424.

7. World Church of the Creator Web site: http://www.creator.org.

CHAPTER 27

1. Matt Hale, "The Creator Membership Manual," 2d ed., found at http://www.creator.org, 1999.

2. "Recurring Hate, Matt Hale and the World Church of the Creator," ADL, found at http://www.adl.org/special_reports/wcotc/wcotc-new-lease.html.

3. Matt Hale, in a taped interview in East Peoria, Illinois, 5 April 2001, declined to say how many of the twelve Guardians of the Faith were there, suggesting that not all twelve were present.

4. Hale, "Membership Manual."

5. E-mail to Dave Jackson, 26 March 2001.

6. Matt Hale, taped interview, East Peoria, Illinois, 5 April 2001.

7. Hale, taped interview, 5 February 2001.

8. Hale, taped interview, 5 February 2001.

9. E-mail to Dave Jackson, 26 March 2001.

10. E-mail to Dave Jackson, 3 April 2001. This happened at Bradley University, where the e-mail author and Matt Hale were music majors.

11. Hale, taped interview, 5 February 2001.

12. Hale, "Membership Manual."

13. "Recurring Hate."

14. "Recurring Hate."

15. Southern Poverty Law Center, "Church of the Creator: a History." Found at http://www.splcenter.org/intelligenceproject/ip-4k4.html.

CHAPTER 29

1. Matt Hale, "Next Hearing for PM Hale's Law License Set for April 10," *The Struggle*, April 1999.

2. Hale, taped interview, 5 February 2001.

3. Hale, taped interview, 5 February 2001.

4. Sharon Begley, "Are We Getting Smarter?" *Newsweek*, 23 April 2001, 50-1. The authors suggest that there is a plasticity in IQ scores unaccounted for by genetic factors. That is to say, IQ (as measured) is flexible and is able to be shaped by factors other than genetics. Genetics is often thought to be rigid and determinative, but how could IQs rise so quickly if capacity is limited by the parents' genetic pool? Even evolution would not explain the increase in scores in this short amount of time.

5. Robert Gregory, *Psychological Testing: History, Principles, and Applications*, 3d ed. (Boston: Allyn and Bacon, 2000). Gregory outlines three lines of evidence that he believes weakens the genetic hypothesis of race/IQ differences.

   He argues that it is a questionable assumption, assumed by Jensen, for instance, that evidence of IQ "heritability" within groups can be used to infer heritability between groups. This particular argument pertains to the scientific methods and a weak causal explanation.

   "A second problem is that the genetic hypothesis does not hold up to additional logical examination. If, in fact, IQ differences are genetically based, then the degree of African ancestry should help predict average IQs within African American subgroups. In other words African Americans with a fully African ancestry should, on average, score lower on IQ test than African Americans with mixed African and white ancestry. However, researchers (Scarr, Paktis, Katz, and Barker, 1977) have not found a relationship between the degree of white ancestry and intellectual skills among African American population."

His final argument is that there is a weak analysis of environmental factors. Brooks-Gunn, Klebanov, and Duncan (1996) argue that the genetic hypothesis is unnecessary when environment factors are considered. They looked at poverty factors and other environmental factors, and suggested that the previous research underestimated the pervasive effects of poverty and its cofactors.

6. Franz Weidenreich, "The Human Brain in the Light of Its Phylogenetic Development," *Scientific Monthly,* August 1948, 107.

7. Arthur C. Custance, *Genesis and Early Man* (Grand Rapids, Mich.: Zondervan, 1975), part 3, chap. 4, 3. Found at http://www.custance.org/Library/Volume2/Part_III/Chapter4.html.

8. Steve Kangas, "Myth: Some Ethnic Groups Have Genetically Inferior IQ's," found at http://home.att.net/~Resurgence/L-inferiorIQ.htm. Another example appears in Japan between Japanese and Koreans. In the United States, both Korean and Japanese students score above average in IQ tests; many scholars agree that, genetically, they are about as close as two ethnic groups can get. But in Japan the Korean minority scores much lower on IQ tests than the Japanese. Why? The Japanese are extremely racist towards Koreans; they view them as stupid and violent, and employ them only in the most menial jobs. Also see, Randolph T. Holhut, "Challenging the Racist Science of 'The Bell Curve,' " 1996, found at http://www.mdle.com/WrittenWord/rholhut/holhut27.htm.

9. Hale, taped interview, 5 February 2001.

10. "African-American Inventors Database Search Results," fifty-five pages of listings found at http://www.detroit.lib.mi.us/glptc/aaid/index.asp.

11. *Daily Southtown Economist,* 6 July 1999, 3, 10.

12. Amanda Beeler and Evan Osnos, "Puzzling Path Down Road to Racism," *Chicago Tribune,* 6 July 1999, 1.

13. Mark Skertic and Carlos Sadovi, "Ex-Wilmette Resident's Past Familiar to Police," *Chicago Sun-Times,* 5 July 1999, 1, 3.

14. Kirsten Scharnberg et al, "The Making of a Racist," *Chicago Tribune,* 25 July 1999, 10.

15. Scharnberg, "Making of a Racist," 10.

16. Sgt. Michael Ruth, Skokie Illinois police, phone interview, 7 June 2000.

17. Evan Osnos and Diane Struzzi, "Suspect Known As Outspoken Racist," *Chicago Tribune,* 5 July 1999, 1, 14.

18. Jackson Potter, taped interview, 9 May 2001.

19. Scharnberg, "Making of a Racist," 10.

20. Potter, taped interview, 9 May 2001.

21. Scharnberg, "Making of a Racist," 10.

CHAPTER 31

1. Kirsten Scharnberg et al., "The Making of a Racist," *Chicago Tribune,* 25 July 1999, 10.

2. Capt. Berry Silverberg, Skokie Illinois police, taped interview, 17 July 2000.

3. Mark Skertic and Carlos Sadovi, "Ex-Wilmette Resident's Past Familiar to Police," *Chicago Sun-Times,* 5 July 1999, 3.

4. Matt Hale, taped interview, East Peoria, Illinois, 5 April 2001.

5. Steve Hinnefeld, "Despite Extreme Views, Killer Gave Few Hints of Turn to Violence," found at http://www.hoosiertimes.com, 6 July 1999.

6. Lisa Sorg, "Dead Man Talking," *Illinois Times,* 8 July 1999, 3, reprinted from the 27 August 1998 issue of the *Bloomington Independent.*

7. Bill Dedman, "Midwest Gunman Who Shot 11 Had Engaged in Acts of Racism at 2 Universities," *New York Times,* 5 July 1999.

8. Sorg, "Dead Man Talking," 3.

9. Matt Hale, "Illinois Bar Forbids Freedom of Speech and Religion," *WCOTC News Release,* 2 July 1999.

10. Matt Hayhow, "A Creator Profile: Brother Ben 'August' Smith," *The Struggle,* March 1999, 3.

11. Matt Hale, "Thoughts from PM Matt Hale Concerning the Law License Hearing," *The Struggle,* June 1999, 2.

12. August Smith to "David," on World Church of the Creator stationery, sometime in 1998 or early 1999.

13. Hayhow, "Creator Profile," 2.

14. Christine Weiss, "My Tribute to Ben," *The Struggle*, August 1999, 4.

15. Hayhow, "Creator Profile," 2.

16. "Cops Probe Hate Writing Found in Smith's Car," *Chicago Tribune*, 10 July 1999.

17. Hale, taped interview, 5 April 2001.

18. Hale, taped interview, 5 February 2001.

CHAPTER 33

1. Andy Kravetz, "Hale Changing His Story on Smith," *Peoria Journal Star*, 15 July 1999.

2. Todd Lighty, "Killer's Guns Are Linked to Illegal Dealer," *Chicago Tribune*, 7 July 1999, 10.

3. Kravetz, "Changing His Story."

4. Lighty, "Killer's Guns," 10.

5. Bob Merrifield, "Dealer Says He Sold Guns in Hate Spree," *Chicago Tribune*, 8 July 1999.

6. Kravetz, "Changing His Story."

7. Matt Hale, taped interview, East Peoria, Illinois, 5 April 2001.

8. Matt Hale, "Another Rule Delays Law License Decision," *The Struggle*, June 1999.

9. Capt. Berry Silverberg, Skokie, Illinois police, taped interview, 17 July 2000.

10. Kravetz, "Changing His Story."

11. Silverberg, taped interview, 17 July 2000.

12. Silverberg, taped interview, 17 July 2000.

CHAPTER 35

1. Sgt. Michael Ruth, Skokie, Illinois Police, phone interview, 7 June 2000.

CHAPTER 36

1. Capt. Berry Silverberg, Skokie, Illinois police, taped interview, 17 July 2000.

2. Mark Skertic and Abdon M. Pallasch, *Chicago Sun-Times*, Monday, 6 July 1999, sec. 1, p. 1.

3. Ray Long et al., *Chicago Tribune,* Tuesday, 6 July 1999, sec. 1, p. 1.

4. Ben Klassen, *The White Man's Bible* (Milwaukee, Wis.: The Milwaukee Church of the Creator, 1981), 385.

5. Kirsten Scharnberg, "FBI Agents Quiz Church Leader over Rampage," *Chicago Tribune,* 8 July 1999, 1, 20.

6. Scharnberg, "Rampage," 1, 20.

7. Scharnberg, "Rampage," 1, 20.

8. Scharnberg, "Rampage," 1, 20.

9. Matt Hale, "WCOTC World Headquarters 24-Hour Hotline," 21 July 1999.

10. Matt Hale, taped interview, East Peoria, Illinois, 5 April 2001.

11. Neil Milbert, *Chicago Tribune,* Thursday, 8 July 1999, sec. 4, p. 1.

12. Milbert, *Chicago Tribune,* sec. 4, p. 1.